WHAT ARE WE?

PHILOSOPHY OF MIND

Series Editor
David J. Chalmers, Australian National University

The Conscious Mind
In Search of a Fundamental Theory
David J. Chalmers

The Human Animal
Personal Identity without Psychology
Eric T. Olson

What's Within?
Nativism Reconsidered
Fiona Cowie

Dreaming Souls
Sleep, Dreams, and the Evolution of the Conscious Mind
Owen Flanagan

Purple Haze
The Puzzle of Consciousness
Joseph Levine

Consciousness and Cognition
A Unified Account
Michael Thau

Thinking without Words
José Luis Bermúdez

Identifying the Mind
Selected Papers of U. T. Place
Edited by George Graham
and Elizabeth R. Valentine

A Place for Consciousness
Probing the Deep Structure of the Natural World
Gregg Rosenberg

Three Faces of Desire
Timothy Schroder

Gut Reactions
A Perceptual Theory of Emotion
Jesse J. Prinz

Ignorance and Imagination
On the Epistemic Origin of the Problem of Consciousness
Daniel Stoljar

Simulating Minds
The Philosophy, Psychology, and Neuroscience of Mindreading
Alvin I. Goldman

Phenomenal Concepts and Phenomenal Knowledge
New Essays on Consciousness and Physicalism
Edited by Torin Alter and Sven Walter

Beyond Reduction
Philosophy of Mind and Post-Reductionist Philosophy of Science
Steven Horst

What Are We?
A Study in Personal Ontology
Eric T. Olson

What Are We?

A Study in Personal Ontology

Eric T. Olson

2007

OXFORD
UNIVERSITY PRESS

Oxford University Press, Inc., publishes works that further
Oxford University's objective of excellence
in research, scholarship, and education.

Oxford New York
Auckland Cape Town Dar es Salaam Hong Kong Karachi
Kuala Lumpur Madrid Melbourne Mexico City Nairobi
New Delhi Shanghai Taipei Toronto

With offices in
Argentina Austria Brazil Chile Czech Republic France Greece
Guatemala Hungary Italy Japan Poland Portugal Singapore
South Korea Switzerland Thailand Turkey Ukraine Vietnam

Published by Oxford University Press, Inc.
198 Madison Avenue, New York, New York 10016

www.oup.com

Library of Congress Cataloging-in-Publication Data
Olson, Eric T. (Eric Todd), 1963–
What are we? : a study in personal ontology / Eric T. Olson.
p. cm. — (Philosophy of mind)
Includes bibliographical references and index.
ISBN 978-0-19-517642-1
1. Philosophical anthropology. 2. Self (Philosophy). 3. Ontology.
I. Title.
BD450.O465 2007
126—dc22 2007060008

9 8 7 6 5 4 3 2 1

Printed in the United States of America
on acid-free paper

Preface

Judith Jarvis Thomson once distinguished the popular topic of personal *identity* from the neglected matter of personal *ontology*. This book is about personal ontology: about our basic metaphysical nature. Like Thomson, I believe that neglect of this topic, more than anything else, is responsible for the unserious air of many discussions of personal identity. The much-derided reliance on fanciful thought experiments is merely a symptom of this neglect.

The book falls into three parts. The first chapter is about what I take the question of what we are to mean, how it differs from traditional questions of personal identity, and why it is important. Chapters 2 to 8 examine in some detail what I take to be the main possible answers to the question. Each of these chapters is fairly self-contained and can be read in isolation, or skipped, without too much confusion. The final chapter argues that what we are depends on general considerations about the ontology of material objects.

It is not my aim in this book to promote any particular view of what we are. I am more concerned to show how hard the problem is, and above all to move it up the philosophical agenda where it belongs. In my earlier book, *The Human Animal*, I defended the view that we are biological organisms. The main argument I gave for it is found here in chapter 2 in what I hope is a clearer form. (Readers of the earlier book will also find parts of chapters 1 and 3 familiar, but most of the current work is new.) Although I still find the view that we are organisms at least as good as any other, I argue in the final chapter that it faces grave metaphysical objections that both its advocates and its critics have mostly ignored. One of my principal contentions is that the alternatives are at least as bad.

This book has been hard to write. It has taken several times longer to finish than I imagined when I began work on it in the summer of 2000. (I suppose I ought to have known better.) I am grateful to a number of people and organizations for their help with the struggle. My biggest debt is to David Hershenov, Jonathan Lowe, and Dean Zimmerman, whose generous and perceptive comments have resulted in many improvements and saved me from more blunders than I care to think of. I also had helpful advice from Arif Ahmed, Randy Carter, John Divers, Katherine Hawley, Rosanna Keefe, Jimmy Lenman, David Liggins, Trenton Merricks, Andy Taylor, and Richard Woodward. Finally, I thank the Arts and Humanities Research Board (as it was then) for funding an extra term's leave in 2001, which enabled me to complete the first draft of the book. Whether its money was well spent, the reader must judge.

Contents

WHAT ARE WE?

1

The Question

1.1 What Are We?

This book is about a question: What are we? That is, what are we, metaphysically speaking? What are our most general and fundamental features? What is our most basic metaphysical nature?

My first task is to explain what this question means. Rather than attempting to define the daunting phrases 'general and fundamental feature' or 'basic metaphysical nature,' I will try to give their meaning by example. We can break the large question of what we are into smaller ones that are easier to grapple with.

One such smaller question is what we are made of. I don't mean our chemical composition—what sort of physical matter makes us up. I want to know whether we are made of matter at all. Or are we made of something other than matter? Or partly of matter and partly of something else? Come to that, are we made of anything at all? Is there any sort of stuff, material or otherwise, that makes us up?

It may seem obvious that we are made of matter. When you look in a mirror, you see something material. You don't see anything immaterial. And don't you see yourself in the mirror? It follows that you are a material thing: something made of matter. But that would be too quick. You might have an immaterial ingredient that doesn't show in the mirror; so casual observation suggests at most that you are made partly of matter. Even if you were entirely immaterial, so that you didn't strictly see yourself in the mirror at all, you could still see your body there—that physical organism by means of which you perceive and act in the world. So our appearance of being material proves nothing. In fact the view that we are made entirely of matter—*materialism*—has not been popular throughout most of the history of philosophy. In any case, whether we are made of matter is an important question about what we are.

If we are indeed made of matter, or of anything else, we can ask *what* matter or other stuff we are made of. Most materialists say that we are made of all and only the matter that makes up our animal bodies: we extend all the way out to the surface of our skin (which is presumably where our bodies end) and no further. But a few take us to be considerably smaller: the size of brains, for instance. Someone might even suppose that we are material things larger than our bodies—that we are made of the matter that makes up our bodies and other matter besides.

A third question is what parts we have. This is not the same as what we are made of. Philosophers who agree about what we are made of—not only about what sort of stuff, but also about what particular stuff—may still disagree about our parts. They may disagree about whether we have *temporal* parts—such things as earlier halves—in addition to any spatial parts we may have, such as hands. They can even disagree about our ordinary spatial parts. Some materialists say that every part of the region of space you now occupy contains a material thing of its own that is a part of you. On their view, your current parts include not only your head and your left hand (supposing that you are made of your body's matter), but also your northern half, "all of you but your left ear," and many further arbitrary and gerrymandered objects too tedious to describe. Other materialists deny that we have arbitrary spatial parts. They may accept that your parts include elementary particles, but they deny that there is such a thing as all of you but your left ear. Some even say that we extend all the way out to our skin, yet have no parts at all. So knowing what we are made of does not by itself tell us what parts we have.

These considerations raise a more general question: What *makes* something a part of one? What determines where our boundaries lie? If your kidneys are parts of you but not your shoes, or *my* kidneys, why is this so? What is it about the way those things relate to you that makes some of them parts of you but not others? If you extend all the way out to the surface of your skin and no further, what accounts for this? Why say that your boundary is *there*?

Here is a different sort of question about what we are: Are we abstract or concrete? Though these terms are hard to define, it will suffice for present purposes to say that something is concrete if it can be causally active—if it can literally *do* something—and it is capable of change. Whatever is not concrete is abstract. So the number seven is abstract, and donkeys are concrete—as are gods and Cartesian souls, if such there be. Hard though it may be to imagine how we could be abstract, that is what a few people seem to think. They say that we are not so much like the number seven as like the novel *Moby-Dick*. That novel is not the same as any of the paper tomes sitting on bookshelves, or even the original manuscript in the author's hand. Nor is it something made up of all of these concrete objects. (The novel doesn't grow in size when more copies are printed.) It is, rather, an abstract object that all of those particular things exemplify. It is a *universal*: something that can have many instances. So it seems, anyway. A mountain, by contrast, is not an abstract universal but a concrete particular. Even if the people of Minnesota were to build an exact replica of Mt. Rainier on the outskirts of St. Paul, their creation would be a reproduction and not the real thing. Mt. Rainier is not something of which the original and the reproduction would both be instances in the way that different copies of *Moby-Dick* are instances of the novel.

We can ask, then, whether we ourselves are concrete particulars like Mt. Rainier or abstract universals like *Moby-Dick*. Could there be more than one of *you*? Suppose the people of Minnesota managed to make an exact replica of you: a concrete being both physically and mentally just like the original, right down to the last atom and quirk of personality. That being would be convinced (at first, anyway) that she was you. Would she be right? Would she be you in the same sense as the original is you, just as every copy of *Moby-Dick* is *Moby-Dick*? Or would only the original be you and the other a mere reproduction, as with Mt. Rainier? For that matter, might we be abstract objects other than universals?

If we are concrete beings, we can ask whether we are *substances*—metaphysically independent beings—or whether we are states or aspects of something else. Think of a car with a dent in it. The dent is not a part of the car: you couldn't take it away from the car, or move it to another car, as you could a wheel. The dent seems to be a state or an aspect of the car—a way that the car is. It is not a substance: not a *thing* in the most robust sense. The car, by contrast, is not a way that the dent is. Nor does it appear to be a state or an aspect of anything else: there is nothing, it seems, that stands to the car as the car stands to the dent. It is a good candidate for being a substance. Our question, then, is whether you are like a car or like a dent. Are you a state or an aspect of something other than yourself? Or an event or process that something else is undergoing, like the car's cooling off? Is there something—an organism or a lump of matter, perhaps—that stands to you as the car stands to the dent in it?

We can ask whether we persist through time. Do we literally continue existing for seventy years or more? Or is the sober truth that we exist only for a moment? Some say that you appear to persist only because you are instantly replaced by a being so much like you that no one can tell the difference—not even that being himself, for he inherits all of your mental features. Could they be right?

This is the sort of thing I have in mind when I ask what, metaphysically speaking, we are. There are many more such questions. We can ask, for instance, what our persistence conditions are: what is necessary and sufficient for a past or future being to be you. We can ask which of our properties are essential to us and which are accidental, or more generally which properties it is in any sense possible for you or me to have or lack. We can ask how exactly we relate to those biological organisms that we sometimes call our bodies. And so on. Answers to these questions would tell us what we are.

1.2 Some Answers

In understanding a question, it often helps to see what would count as an answer to it; and often the answers are easier to grasp than the question itself. (Understanding the questions is the hardest thing in philosophy.) Here, then, are some accounts of what we might be: views that would, if they were true, at least begin to tell us what we are.

One view is that we are animals: biological organisms. It may seem as evident that we are animals as it is that we are made of matter. We are certainly not plants, or angels, or stones. But few philosophers say that we are animals. It may be evident that we are in *some* sense animals—that we have animal bodies, for instance. (We will consider the meaning of this claim in §2.1.) But our having bodies that are animals does not by itself tell us whether *we* are animals. Saying what sort of thing my body is would tell me what sort of thing I am if I *am* my body—if my body and I are one and same thing—but whether this is so is much disputed, even among materialists.

How could we be material things other than animals? Well, we might be parts of animals: brains, for instance. Or we might be temporal parts of animals rather than spatial parts: you might be spatially the same size as the animal we call your body but temporally shorter, in that the animal extends further into the past or the future than you do. Many views are possible about what spatial or temporal parts of animals we might be. These two thoughts can also be combined: we might be temporal parts of brains.

Some philosophers deny that we are either animals or parts of animals but insist that we are nonetheless material things. They say that the same matter can make up two different objects at once. Specifically, the matter making up a typical human organism also makes up a certain nonorganism. These nonorganisms, they say, are what we are. So another possible answer to our question is that we are material things made of the same matter as or "constituted by" our animal bodies.

Hume once suggested that each of us is "a bundle or collection of different perceptions, which succeed each other with an inconceivable rapidity, and are in a perpetual flux and movement" (1978: 252). In that case we are not material things at all. Our bodies may be made of matter, but we ourselves are made up of perceptions—'perceptions' being Hume's word for mental states and events generally. Our parts are not organs or cells or atoms, but memories, wishes, and dreams. We are concrete particulars, but not substances: we are like dents—or, as Hume himself suggests, like theater performances.

A view with a long tradition has it that we are simple immaterial substances—simple meaning without parts. We are not made of matter, or of perceptions, or indeed of anything else. We have no mass or shape or any other physical property. Our bodies may have such properties, but they are not what we are or even parts of us. A related view says that each of us is a compound object made up of both an immaterial substance and a material organism.

Some people seem to think that we are something like novels or computer programs: abstract universals that can be embodied in flesh or stored on magnetic disks or written down on paper. The concrete beings that walk and talk and sleep in our beds are mere instances or "hard copies" of us.

There is even the paradoxical view that there is nothing that we are. There are no such beings as you and I. We don't exist. Strictly speaking, this book has no author. The atoms we call mine may be real enough; perhaps even the thoughts and actions we call mine exist; but they are not parts or states of any thinking, acting being.

None of these views offers a complete account of what we are. None purports, by itself, to answer all of my questions. The view that we are animals, for instance, does not by itself tell us whether we have parts, or which of our properties are essential to us and which are accidental. It is even disputable whether it implies that we persist through time. For that, we should need to know whether animals persist, whether they have parts, and which of their properties are essential to them and which are accidental; and here there is disagreement. The same goes for the other accounts. Even so, they each tell us a good deal about what we are. They are mutually incompatible: if we are animals, then we are not parts of animals, immaterial substances, bundles of perceptions, or any of the other sorts of things I have mentioned; if we are immaterial substances, then we are not animals or parts of animals; and so on. Moreover, once we know which of them is correct, questions about our metaphysical nature become questions about the metaphysical nature of animals, bundles of perceptions, or what have you; and with any luck those questions will be easier to answer than the original question about our own metaphysical nature.

By way of contrast, here is a view that does not answer the question of what we are: that we are *people*. (In this book I follow ordinary English, and depart from academic usage, in using 'people' as the plural of 'person'. This is purely for stylistic reasons.) Although in many contexts it may be a perfectly good answer to the question "What is *x*?" to be told that *x* is a person, the claim that we are people tells us nothing about our metaphysical nature. No one, no matter what her view of our metaphysical nature, thinks that we are *not* people. More to the point, the claim that we are people tells us nothing about the metaphysical nature of people: whether they are material or immaterial, abstract or concrete, and so on.

Nor does it answer our question to say that we are *essentially* or *most fundamentally* people. To say that we are essentially people is to say that we could not possibly exist without being people. To say that we are most fundamentally people is to say, roughly, that we have our identity conditions by virtue of our being people and not, say, by virtue of our being organisms or concrete objects or sentient beings. Not everyone agrees that we are essentially or most fundamentally people. And the view that we are essentially or most fundamentally people may rule out certain accounts of what we are, such as the view that we are organisms (see §2.9). So this view may tell us something about what we are. But it doesn't tell us much. It doesn't by itself tell us whether we are material or immaterial, or concrete or abstract.

There are many other possible accounts of what we are, but this incomplete list ought to give some idea of what I am after. In particular, it shows what level of generality I have in mind. The bulk of this book is devoted to examining these views and a number of others. I will try to divide my attention among them in proportion to their interest and importance. The rest of this chapter, meanwhile, looks more closely at the question itself.

1.3 'We'

Our question is what sort of things we are, most generally and fundamentally. I have tried to say what I mean by 'what sort of things'. What do I mean by 'we'?

Consider first its scope. By 'we' I mean you and me and the people we know—we *human* people. I don't mean nonhuman people, if there are any.

So our question is not about the basic metaphysical nature of people as such, but only of ourselves.

Why this restriction? I don't want to consider the metaphysical nature of people in general because for all I know there might be people of metaphysical kinds different from our own. Suppose for the sake of argument that we are biological organisms. That doesn't rule out the possibility that there are also angels or gods: rational, intelligent, self-conscious beings that are wholly immaterial. Nor does it deny that there could be inorganic artifacts with mental features just like ours. Assuming that being rational, intelligent, and self-conscious suffices for being a person, all of these beings—gods, inorganic machines, and we organisms—would count as people. For that matter, there are philosophers who believe that many human people acting together can compose a larger "group" or "corporate" person: Apple Computer Inc. might be a person in the same sense as we are. I see no reason to suppose that all the items on this list would have to share the same basic metaphysical nature. That is, I am not convinced that there *is* any one metaphysical sort of thing that people in general are or must be. Or if there is, we cannot know it until we have either ruled out the possibility of some of the items on this list—gods, thinking machines, or the like—or else shown that despite appearances people of all these sorts would share the same basic metaphysical nature. It is in order to avoid this complication that I limit the inquiry to ourselves. That will leave us with more than enough to think about.

This approach is unorthodox. Most discussions of personal identity take for it granted that claims about what *we* are—about our identity over time, for instance—necessarily apply to all people (see §2.9). Insofar as they consider our metaphysical nature at all, they take it to derive from our being people, rather than from our being organisms or material objects or anything else. It follows from this assumption that we must share our most basic properties with all people, including gods and inorganic thinking machines, if there could be such things.

That strikes me as dogmatic. Not only is it unwarranted, but it rules out accounts of what we are that might otherwise be attractive. It is incompatible with the view that we are organisms, for instance. I doubt whether the basic metaphysical nature of any organism derives from its being a person. Organisms seem to have the basic metaphysical nature they have by virtue of being organisms—a nature they share with snails and trees (which I assume are not people). It is even less likely that any organisms have the same basic metaphysical nature as gods or angels or intelligent computers would have. But if there could be people whose metaphysical nature is different from that of organisms, and all people must necessarily have the same metaphysical nature, it follows that no person could be an organism. Assuming that *we* are people, we ourselves could not be organisms. This seems a poor argument for the claim that we are not organisms. Its premises were these: (1) there could be inorganic people; (2) inorganic people would not have the same metaphysical nature as organisms; (3) necessarily all people have the same metaphysical nature; and (4) we are people. The most doubtful of these premises seems to me to be the third. Let us not assume it.

In any case, this unorthodox stance can do no harm. I am not assuming that different people *could* have different metaphysical natures. I am merely declining to assume that they couldn't. If people really must all have the same metaphysical nature, then the question of what sort of things we are and the question of what sort of things people in general are will have the same answer, so we lose nothing by asking the first rather than the second.

I said that in asking what we are I was asking about the basic metaphysical nature of us human people. By *human* people I don't mean simply those people who are human beings—not, at least, if a human being is a kind of organism. Whether we are human beings in that sense, or indeed whether any people are, is disputed: it is one of the questions we want answered, not something we can assume at the outset. (Despite its homely attraction, the phrase 'human being' is too slippery to be of much use in metaphysics.) Still, there is a sense in which you and I are undoubtedly human. Setting aside the possibility that some of us might be Martian foundlings, anyway, it is clear that each of us relates in an intimate way to an animal that is biologically human. When we see you, we see a human animal; when you move, a human animal moves; you perceive the world via a human animal's sense organs; and so on. That makes you human—rather than, say, bovine or angelic or divine. A human person is a person who relates to a human animal in this way. It is, we might say, someone with a human body. Even if in the final analysis there are really no human animals (as, for instance, some idealists say), there must still be some real feature of the world—something about sense impressions or whatever—that makes it true to say that when you look in a mirror, you see a human animal and not an angel or a cow. Our question is about the fundamental nature of human people in this sense.

1.4 Rephrasing the Question

So much for the intended scope of the word 'we'. Further issues about what I mean by 'we' arise if we shift from the material to the formal mode—from asking, What are we? to asking, What does the word 'we' refer to? To avoid irrelevant worries about plural reference, we can put this by asking what a human person refers to when he or she says 'I'. I take it that I am whatever I refer to when I say 'I'—just as London is the thing we refer to when we say 'London'. And presumably what I refer to when I say 'I' is what others refer to when they address me as 'you' or speak of me as 'he' or as 'Olson'. So anyone who finds the question, What sort of things are we? puzzling could replace it with the question, What sort of things do our personal pronouns and proper names refer to?

These two questions—What are we? and What do our personal pronouns and proper names refer to?—are not entirely equivalent. We sometimes use personal pronouns to refer to dogs or ships, even though none of *us* are dogs or ships. But they come to almost the same thing. The view that we are organisms (say) amounts, near enough, to the view that our personal pronouns, in their most typical uses at least, refer to organisms. The view that we don't exist—that there is nothing that we are—amounts to the view that our personal pronouns don't refer to anything because there is nothing for them to refer to.

Now this way of rephrasing the question assumes that the word 'I' and other first-person pronouns are referring expressions: expressions that purport to refer to something, expressions that refer to something if there is anything "there" to be referred to. Anscombe (1981) has denied this. According to her, the word 'I' in 'I am walking' no more purports to refer to something that walks than the word 'it' in 'it is raining' purports to refer to something that rains. If she is right, then I am not the thing I refer to when I say 'I', for I don't refer to anything when I use that word. But it doesn't follow from this claim that I don't exist, or that there is nothing here speaking that *could* be referred to. So on Anscombe's view it is a mistake to ask what we are by asking what we refer to when we say 'I'. This suggests that it is equally mistaken to ask what sort of thing *I* am, or what sort of things we are: that would be like asking what sort of thing it is that rains.

This view seems to me to have no plausibility whatever.[1] Consider these apparent facts: (1) That I am hungry entails that something or other is hungry, just as that London is a city entails that something is a city. (That it is raining, by contrast, does not seem to entail that something is raining.) These inferences appear to be licensed by the rule of existential generalization: they have the form 'this particular thing is so; therefore something is so'. Thus, 'I', like 'London', appears to be a referring expression. (2) The sentence 'I am hungry' expresses a truth just when the being who utters it is hungry. The one who utters it is the one who must be hungry in order for it to be true. The obvious explanation for this is that 'I' refers to the being who utters it. (3) If Rinka says, 'I am hungry', we can

[1] I draw here on Garrett 1998: chap. 7; and van Inwagen 2002b.

report this by saying, 'Rinka says that she [Rinka] is hungry'. This seems to imply that the word 'I' in Rinka's mouth refers to same thing as the name 'Rinka' refers to—that is, to Rinka. (4) On solemn occasions we say such things as 'I, Alice Margaret Buggins, hereby promise ...' What could the inserted name be doing, if not specifying which person the pronoun refers to? (5) If I am Olson, and Olson is the author of this book, it follows that I am the author of this book. The most obvious explanation for the validity of this inference appeals to the principle that if $x = y$ and y is so, then x is so. This assumes that 'I am Olson' is an identity sentence—one in which the identity sign is flanked by two referring expressions—in which case 'I' is a referring expression. Those who deny that 'I' is a referring expression need to account for these facts in a way that is consistent with their view. More generally, they need to explain what the word 'I' does do, if it doesn't refer to the person who utters it. I have never seen such an account.

But no matter: even if Anscombe is right, we can still put our question by asking what sort of things Olson and Thatcher and Socrates are, or what sort of things our second- and third-person personal pronouns and personal proper names refer to. No one denies that *those* words are referring expressions.

What if I refer to more than one thing when I say 'I' or 'Olson'? Then there would be no one thing that I am. Asking what sort of thing I am would be like asking about the nature of the planet between the earth and the sun. The question would have no straightforward answer, since it would embody the false presupposition that there is only one being asking it. So perhaps we ought rather to ask, What sort of thing *or things* does a personal pronoun or proper name typically refer to?

It would be especially inconvenient for our inquiry if words like 'I' and 'Olson' referred in their typical uses not just to more than one thing, but to more than one *kind* of thing. We cannot rule this possibility out a priori. But perhaps we can dismiss one distracting version of it. Some people suggest that the personal pronouns are systematically ambiguous, referring sometimes to one's mind and sometimes to one's body, so that in one sense of the word 'I', I am a mind (and not a body), and, in another sense of the word, I am a body (and not a mind). It follows that we cannot ask what sort of thing I am without specifying which sense of 'I' (or 'Olson') we mean: Do we mean what I am in the "mental" sense of 'I', or what I am in the "bodily" sense of that word?

This view—call it *linguistic dualism*—seems to me scarcely more plausible than the view that 'I' is not a referring expression. Linguistic dualists are not very clear what sorts of things "one's mind" and "one's body" are supposed to be, but presumably they take the mind to be the bearer of one's mental properties, such as consciousness and intelligence, and the body to be the bearer of one's brute physical properties, such as height and weight. Further, the mind is supposed to have no physical properties (or at any rate none like height or weight), and the body is supposed to have no mental properties. Otherwise, why call one of them the mind and the other the body? Linguistic dualism therefore implies that in the mental tone of voice, where 'I' refers to my mind, I can say truly I am conscious but have no height or weight—indeed I am entirely invisible and intangible. And it implies that in the bodily tone of voice, where 'I' refers to my body, I can say truly that I weigh 150 pounds but am no more conscious or intelligent than a stone. The most I can say about my mental properties while speaking in the bodily tone of voice is that I relate in some intimate way to a conscious, intelligent being other than myself—a being that is not even a part of me, for the mind is not, on this view, a part of the body. There would be no tone of voice in which I could say that I am both visible and aware of this fact, for none of the referents of my first-person pronoun would have both the property of being visible and the property of being aware of anything. Saying that I am both visible and aware of it would be like pointing to Fred and Ginger and saying, "That person is both male and female." It is tempting to call this a reductio ad absurdum of linguistic dualism.

Nor is there any reason, even for those who believe that "the mind" is a purely mental thing and "the body" is something purely physical, to hold such a view. It would be far better for them to say that we are purely mental things. Then there would be no sense in which we are as stupid as stones. Our being invisible "minds" need not imply that such statements as 'I am visible' are always false: in ordinary contexts this may mean not that I have the property of being visible, but that I have the property of having a body that is visible—a property that a purely mental thing can have.

Linguistic dualism looks false. But again, I needn't insist on it. If the word 'I' in my mouth really does refer sometimes to a thinking thing and other times to an unthinking thing, then our concern is with the thinking thing. Never mind the referential role of the personal pronouns. This is an essay in metaphysics, not the philosophy of language. Our question is about the nature of the beings holding the inquiry. So we can rephrase our question in yet another way: What sorts of beings think our thoughts and perform our actions?

1.5 Must There Be an Answer?

Let me make a few remarks about the status of the question.

I take it that the question of what we are must have an answer, whether or not it is within our power to discover or even to understand it. There must be *some* sort of thing that we are, if we exist at all. When we say 'I' or 'you' or 'Socrates', we either refer to something or we don't. If we do, that thing (or those things) must have some general and fundamental properties or other: it must be concrete or abstract, material or immaterial, simple or composite, and so on. If we don't refer to anything, that is presumably because there are no human people to be referred to. Again, if any beings think our thoughts, they must have some metaphysical nature or other; if nothing thinks our thoughts, then we don't exist.

What if eliminative materialism is true, and there is no such thing as thinking? What then becomes of the question of what we are? Well, we could still ask what sort of being wrote this book, and what sort of being is now reading it. And we could ask what sorts of beings our personal pronouns denote.

A more worrying possibility is that there are no hard facts about which things think. Suppose, as instrumentalists about the mental say, that it is merely useful, in explaining and predicting the behavior of certain entities, to "take up the intentional stance" toward them—that is, to ascribe to them beliefs and other mental properties (Dennett 1981). It is more useful to attribute mental properties to chimpanzees than to amoebas or daisies: you are better off explaining the behavior of daisies in nonmental terms, whereas with chimpanzees psychological explanation will get you further. But the question of which things *really* have mental properties, the idea goes, has no answer. There may not even be a straightforward answer to the question of what sort of thing it is most useful to ascribe our mental properties to, for it may be most useful to ascribe them to one sort of thing for some purposes and to other sorts of things for other purposes. That would suggest that our question has no answer.

If this really were so, then I suppose all we could say about the metaphysical nature of the beings that think our thoughts would be that it is most useful for certain purposes to attribute our thoughts to beings of one kind (organisms, say), and most useful for other purposes to ascribe them to other beings (bundles of perceptions, perhaps)—supposing that such beings actually exist, anyway. That would be at least a sort of answer to the question of what beings think our thoughts, though a rather unsatisfying one. It would make our inquiry a good deal less interesting than it would otherwise be. But I don't think there is any compelling reason to accept instrumentalism about the mental.

In asking what we are, I am not asking about our conception or our understanding of ourselves—about what we take ourselves to be. This is metaphysics, not anthropology. What we ordinarily take ourselves to be may be wildly mistaken.

Why suppose that we can discover what we are, as opposed to what we think we are? Well, why suppose that we can discover the answer to any philosophical question? All we can do is to try and see how it goes. If we seem to make progress—if many proposed answers turn out to be incoherent, or to conflict with apparently well-established facts, or to have consequences that just look plainly false, whereas a small number of views stand up well to interrogation—that will be a reason to think that we might be able to know what we are, or at least to muster some rational grounds in support of a partial answer. Alternatively, if our best efforts turn up no strong grounds for preferring one answer over any other, or if the more we think about the possible answers the less well we seem to understand them, we may have to admit that the question is too hard for us. But there is no obvious reason to suppose at the outset that we cannot learn anything about what we are. (Kant thought he had a reason. He thought we could not know the metaphysical nature of anything, but only how things appear to us and the conditions necessary for this appearance. If he is right, our project is doomed from the start—as is the whole of metaphysics as we know it. I hope I can be forgiven for omitting a critical discussion of Kant's philosophy from a book that is more than long enough already.)

1.6 How the Question Differs from Others

Our question may not sound quite like any of the philosophical problems we learn about as students. But it probably won't seem completely new either: it sounds a bit like the traditional mind-body problem, and a bit like familiar problems of personal identity. How exactly does it relate to those problems?

Those who speak of the mind-body problem are usually thinking of questions about the basic nature of mental phenomena, such as belief and conscious experience, and how they relate to such nonmental phenomena as brain chemistry and bodily movements. Our question, by contrast, is about the nature of the *subjects* of mental phenomena: the beings that think or are conscious. The two topics are of course related: some accounts of what we are may rule out some views on the mind-body problem and vice versa. But we could know a good deal about mental phenomena and their relation to the physical while knowing little about the basic metaphysical nature of mental subjects. If all mental events turned out to be physical events in another guise, for instance, that might rule out the view that we are immaterial substances, but it would not tell us whether we are organisms, parts of organisms, or bundles of perceptions, or even whether we exist at all. Having a "theory of mind"—an account of the nature of mental phenomena and their relation to the physical—would not tell us what we are. Likewise, knowing our basic metaphysical nature is likely to tell us little about the nature of mental phenomena. Suppose it turned out that we are temporal parts of organisms. That would leave it almost entirely open which account of the mind-body problem is true: it would be compatible with behaviorism, functionalism, property dualism, various psychophysical identity theories, and eliminative materialism, for instance.

It is especially important to distinguish the question of what we are from traditional questions of personal identity. Three questions have dominated discussions of personal identity since the time of Locke. One is what it takes for us, or for people in general, to persist through time: the *persistence question*. What sort of thing is it possible, in the broadest possible sense, for you to survive, and what sort of event would necessarily bring your existence to an end? What determines which past or future being is you? A second question, not always distinguished from the first, is how we find out who is who: the *evidence question*. What evidence bears on the question of whether the person here now is the one who was there yesterday? How do different sorts of evidence about who is who relate to one another? A third question asks what it is to be a person, as opposed to a nonperson: the *personhood question*.

The question of what we are is more or less completely unrelated to the personhood question. What qualifications a thing needs in order to count as a person is one thing; what sort of thing meets those qualifications—organisms, immaterial substances, bundles of perceptions, or what have you—is another. Suppose for the sake of argument that something is a person if and only if it is, as Locke put it, "a thinking intelligent being, that has reason and reflection, and can consider itself as itself, the same thinking thing, in different times and places" (1975: 335). I take this to be a paradigmatic answer to the personhood question. Yet for all it says, "thinking intelligent beings" might be material or immaterial, simple or composite, persisting or momentary;[2] they might be organisms, brains, bundles of thoughts, immaterial substances, or what have you. Locke's definition doesn't answer any of the questions we want answered. It doesn't even tell us whether we exist at all—that is, whether *anything* satisfies the conditions for being a person. One could have a view about what it is to be a person without having any idea what sort of thing, metaphysically speaking, we are. (This is more or less Locke's own position.)

[2] How could something momentary "consider itself as itself in different times and places"? Well, a thing might *consider* itself as existing at different times even if it doesn't exist at different times—just as I might consider myself rich and famous without being rich and famous.

To know what it is to be a person is therefore not to know what we are. Likewise, to know what we are is not to know what it is to be a person. Suppose we are human animals. That does not imply that to be a person *is* to be a human animal—even assuming that we ourselves are people. It is consistent with there being gods or angels or Martians who are people but not human animals. Nor does it imply that all human animals are people: it is consistent with the view that human animals in a persistent and irreversible vegetative state don't count as people. An account of our metaphysical nature implies nothing at all about what it is to be a person.

Nor is the evidence question the question of what we are. One is epistemic; the other is metaphysical. One is about how we find out who is who; the other concerns our metaphysical nature. They could hardly be more different.

If any familiar question about personal identity is the question of what we are, it is the persistence question. Some philosophers seem to think that to say what it takes for us to persist through time *is* to say what we are.[3] It is certainly one aspect of our metaphysical nature. Knowing our persistence conditions would tell us something about what we are. But it would tell us less than you might think.

Consider some examples. The most popular view about our identity over time is that it consists in some sort of psychological continuity: you are, necessarily, that future being that in some sense inherits its mental features—personality, beliefs, memories, and so on—from you; and you are that past being whose mental features you have thus inherited. There is dispute over the precise nature of this inheritance. Some say that your mental life must be (as Unger puts it) "continuously physically realized": your brain or something like it must remain intact and capable of supporting thought and consciousness in order for you to survive. Some also add a "nonbranching" clause to deal with cases where two past or future beings are psychologically continuous with you at once: they say that you are identical with a past or future being who is psychologically continuous with you as you are now only if no one else is then psychologically continuous with you as you are now.

Imagine these matters settled: let us say that our identity over time consists in nonbranching, continuously physically realized psychological continuity. Call this the *conservative psychological-continuity view*. Would it tell us what we are? Not by itself, it wouldn't. It may have implications about what we are, such as ruling out our being immaterial substances—it is hard to see how any sort of physical continuity could be necessary or sufficient for the persistence of an immaterial substance. It may also imply

[3] Wiggins (1980: 60) and Shoemaker (1995: 60) come close to saying this.

that we are not organisms, for it seems possible for any organism, even a human animal, to persist without any sort of psychological continuity whatever (see §2.8). The information that we are neither immaterial substances nor organisms would certainly tell us something about what we are. But it would also leave a lot open. Moreover, the conservative view doesn't actually *say* that we are not immaterial substances or organisms, and the implication might be disputed.

So the conservative view gives, at best, a radically incomplete picture of what we are. Even if we can derive some of our most general and fundamental properties from it, few of those derivations will be straightforward, and even then the picture will be fragmentary. Yet it is a paradigmatic answer to the persistence question. Saying what it takes for us to persist does not tell us what we are.

Other answers to the persistence question teach the same lesson. Consider what Parfit calls the *simple view*, that our identity through time does not consist in anything other than itself but is "simple and unanalyzable": *no* nontrivial conditions are both necessary and sufficient for a person existing at one time to be identical with something existing at another time. The simple view appears to be compatible with almost any account of what we are. Its advocates have said that we are simple immaterial substances, compounds of a simple immaterial substance and a physical organism, organisms, things constituted by organisms, microscopic physical parts of our brains, and partless material objects physically indiscernible from organisms.[4]

These examples show that we could know our persistence conditions and yet know little about our other properties of metaphysical interest. The converse also holds: we could know a great deal about our basic metaphysical nature without knowing our persistence conditions. For example, Ayers, Merricks, van Inwagen, and Wiggins[5] agree that we are biological organisms, and agree to a large extent about the metaphysical nature of those organisms, yet diverge widely about what it takes for us to persist.

To say what our identity through time consists in is only to begin to say what sort of thing we are, just as describing a country's coastline only begins to tell us about its geography. What it takes for a person to persist through time is one thing; what beings *have* those persistence conditions, or indeed whether any do, is another matter.

[4] These views are advanced by Reid (1975), Swinburne (1984: 27), Merricks (1998), Baker (2000), Chisholm (1989: 126), and Lowe (1996: 32–44), respectively. We will consider all of them in due course.

[5] Ayers 1991: 222–225; Merricks 1998 and 2001b: 85; van Inwagen 1990b: 142–158; Wiggins 1980: 160, 180.

1.7 Why It Matters

The question of what we are is often neglected. It is common practice to defend an account of our persistence conditions at great length without saying a word about what we are, except perhaps to rule out our being immaterial substances; Grice, Perry, Nozick, Parfit, and Unger are notable examples.[6] When the matter is addressed at all, it is frequently little more than an afterthought. For example, near the end of his well-known debate with Swinburne, Shoemaker mentions that the account of our identity conditions he has been developing rules out our being organisms. He suggests instead that we are each "physically realized in" an organism and share our matter with it. But he says little about how we are to understand this, and he considers no objections. It apparently seemed to him little more than an interesting corollary of his view of our identity over time (1984: 113–114; his 1999 paper attempts to remedy this defect). Rovane's book on personal identity is silent about what we are for 200 pages before mentioning in passing, as if it were rather obvious, that a person is "a set of intentional episodes" (1998: 212). Although Rovane says a good deal about which intentional episodes go to make up a given person, she says nothing about what sort of thing a set of intentional episodes is supposed to be; nor does she consider the thought that we might not be sets of intentional episodes at all.

Does it matter? Why should those concerned with traditional questions of personal identity worry about what we are? Haven't we just seen that they are different questions? Well, they are different in that one could know the answer to any of the traditional questions without knowing what we are and vice versa. Yet they are also connected, in that an answer to one may constrain the range of available answers to another. In particular, accounts of what it takes for us to persist may have troublesome implications for what we are. Those who ignore our metaphysical nature may end up with a view of our identity over time that seems attractive in itself but is incompatible with any plausible account of what we are.

Earlier I mentioned the conservative psychological-continuity view: that we persist by virtue of nonbranching, continuously physically realized psychological continuity. Many would omit the qualification about continuous physical realization. They say simply that you are that future

[6] Grice 1941; Perry 1972, 1975b; Nozick 1981: chap. 1; Parfit 1984: part 3; Unger 1990. Garrett 1998 and McMahan 2002: 66–94 are further examples. A refreshing exception is Hudson 2001: 113–148. Although for reasons given in chapter 4 I cannot accept Hudson's account of what we are, I recommend his discussion as a model of how the issue ought to be debated.

being who inherits the mental features you have now, and that past being whose mental features you have inherited. How these mental features are passed on is irrelevant, or at any rate need not involve the continuous existence of any physical object capable of supporting thought and consciousness. Call this the *liberal psychological-continuity view*.

Imagine a device that records the total psychological state of your brain ("erasing" or destroying that organ in the process) and then imposes that state, or a state with the same content, onto a new brain in another head (thereby obliterating any psychological content already present there). I take this device to be logically possible, even though it will never be within our technological capability; if you like, imagine that the machine simply destroys both brains and makes a duplicate of the first out of the remains of the second. The liberal view seems to imply that this "brain-state-transfer procedure" would move *you* from one human organism to another (Shoemaker 1984: 108).

What sort of thing might you and I be if this were true? What sort of thinking being could the brain-state-transfer machine move from one animal to another? It is hard to see how it could move any *material* thing (van Inwagen 1997). The machine doesn't move any matter from one head to another. So how could it move a material thing? Surely you cannot send a concrete material object as a message by telegraph. At most the machine would seem to cause one material thing to lose its mental properties and another material thing to acquire them. What it does is analogous to reading a message written on one sheet of paper, erasing it, and then writing a message with the same content on another sheet. This process of reading, erasing, and writing doesn't move any material thing from one sheet of paper to the other. Nor, for that matter, does it move any *non*-material thing. No persisting, concrete object of any sort is located or "realized" first in one sheet of paper and then in another one. So it seems, anyway. Likewise, it is hard to see how the brain-state transfer machine could move anything, let alone a thinking being, from one head to another. On the face of it, at least, the liberal view looks incompatible with *anything* we could be.

I don't say that the problem is insoluble: one could turn for help to the ontology of temporal parts (§5.5). But not all advocates of the liberal view would welcome this serious metaphysical commitment; and without serious metaphysics it really is insoluble.

Nor do the problems end there. The liberal view clearly rules out our being biological organisms. Whatever the brain-state transfer machine does, it doesn't move an *animal* from one place to another. If you are in Paris, and I am in London, and the machine erases your total brain state and copies it onto my brain, no biological organism thereby moves from

Paris to London. Rather, an animal in Paris has its brain erased or destroyed, and another animal in London has its brain remodeled to resemble that of the animal in Paris. If you are an animal, you stay in Paris. But if the liberal view is true, you move to London. If it is possible for you to leave your animal behind in this way, then you are not an animal: nothing can leave itself behind. Not only are you not *essentially* an animal, but you are not an animal at all: nothing that is even contingently an animal could move from Paris to London via brain-state transfer. In our story there is only one animal in Paris, and it stays in Paris.

But there *is* an animal that we call your body. And human animals with normal functioning nervous systems would seem to be able to think. Or at least they think if any material thing can think, and most friends of the liberal view believe that material things can think. So an animal thinks your thoughts. Yet according to the liberal view, that animal is not you—even if our imaginary brain-state transfer procedure never takes place. It follows that there are two beings thinking your thoughts: you and the animal. That is one thinker too many. How could you ever know which one you are?

For that matter, an animal that was psychologically indistinguishable from you would satisfy any ordinary definition of 'person': for instance the Lockean view that a person is an intelligent, rational, self-conscious being. (Surely there could not be intelligent, rational, self-conscious *non*people.) So the liberal view implies that there are two *people* now thinking your thoughts, an animal and a nonanimal. That is not merely absurd, but also incompatible with the liberal view. Human animals don't persist by virtue of psychological continuity. If your animal body counts as a person, it follows that some people don't persist by virtue of psychological continuity. Yet the liberal view is ordinarily taken to assert that *all* people, not just you and I, must persist by virtue of psychological continuity (§1.3). The liberal view appears not only to have repugnant consequences but to be inconsistent.

Again, I don't want to claim that these problems are insoluble. But they are problems. In fact they afflict not only the liberal psychological-continuity view but the conservative view as well, for it too appears to imply that we are not animals; no animal persists by virtue of nonbranching, continuously physically realized psychological continuity.

I will say more about all this in the next chapter. My point here is that these popular views about our identity over time have troubling consequences. Though some psychological-continuity theorists have tried to address the problems, many more appear to be unaware of them. The reason, I think, is that they have not asked what we are. They have not asked, for instance, whether their view about our identity over time is compatible with our being animals. More generally, they have not asked what sorts of things we could be if their view is true. If they had, the difficulty of finding a good answer might have led them to think again.

Why it is that so many philosophers have felt entitled to theorize about personal identity without thinking about what we are, is an interesting question. The answer probably lies in the general neglect of metaphysics throughout the history of English-speaking philosophy. But I don't want to speculate about history here.

That completes my discussion of the meaning and importance of our question. Let us turn now to the answers.

2

Animals

2.1 Animalism

What sort of things might we be? Let us begin our study of answers to this question with the view that we are animals: biological organisms, members of the primate species *Homo sapiens*. This has a certain immediate attraction. We *seem* to be animals. When you eat or sleep or talk, a human animal eats, sleeps, or talks. When you look in a mirror, an animal looks back at you. Most ordinary people suppose that we are animals. At any rate, if you ask them what we are and indicate that "animals" is one of the possible answers, they typically say that it is obviously the right answer. No one is going to feel immediately drawn to any of the alternative views—that we are bundles of perceptions, or immaterial substances, or nonanimals made of the same matter as animals, say. Compared with those proposals, the idea that we are animals looks like plain common sense.

But things are not so simple. As we saw earlier, the appearance that we are animals may owe merely to our relating in some intimate way to animals—to our having animal bodies, if you like—rather than to our actually being animals. The weight of authority is overwhelmingly opposed to our being animals. Almost every major figure in the history of Western philosophy denied it, from Plato and Augustine to Descartes,

Leibniz, Locke, Berkeley, Hume, and Kant. (Aristotle and his followers are an important exception.) The view is no more popular in non-Western philosophy, and most of those writing about personal identity today either deny outright that we are animals or say things that are incompatible with it. We will come to the reasons for its unpopularity later.

The view that we are animals has become known as *animalism*.[1] Because animalism is easily confused with similar-sounding claims, I will say something about how I understand it. Animalism says that each of us is numerically identical with an animal: there is a certain organism, and you and it are one and the same. This would not bear stating but for the fact that some philosophers who deny that we are identical with any animal nonetheless insist on saying that we are animals. What they mean is that we "are" animals in some loose sense: in the sense of having bodies that are animals, or of being "constituted by" animals, or the like. We are animals in something like the sense in which an actor playing Lear is a king. That is not animalism.

This terminological point calls for a brief comment. I wish I could persuade philosophers not to state views according to which we are non-animals by saying that we are animals. It forces us to express the view that we are *really* animals—that we are animals in the ordinary, straightforward sense in which we are people—with the ugly phrase 'we are numerically identical with animals'. This is linguistically perverse: the most obvious interpretation of the sentence 'That is an animal' is surely that the denoted object really is an animal, and not that it relates in some way to something else that really is an animal. It is also tendentious: it makes animalism sound complicated and difficult when it ought to be simple and intuitive. Likewise, stating the view that we are nonanimals constituted by animals (for instance) by saying, 'We are animals', makes it sound simple and intuitive when it ought to be complicated and difficult. I, for one, refuse to play this mug's game. When I discuss the view that we really are animals, I will state it by saying, 'We are animals'. And I will state the view that we are nonanimals constituted by animals by saying, 'We are nonanimals constituted by animals'. I encourage others to do the same.

Anyway, animalism says that *we* are animals, not that people in general are; so it is compatible with the existence of people who are not animals (gods or angels, say), and of animals—even human animals—that are not people. Animalism is not an account of what it is to be a person, and it implies no answer to the personhood question of §1.6.

[1] Advocates of animalism include Carter (1989), Ayers (1990: 283–285), Snowdon (1990), van Inwagen (1990b), Hoffman and Rosenkrantz (1997), and Merricks (2001a, 2001b). See also Olson 1997a and 2003a.

The view that we are animals may call to mind the idea that we are identical with our *bodies*. What does animalism say about this? Is it the same as the view that we are our bodies? Does it at least entail that we are? I find these questions hard to answer. Suppose that a person's body, or at least a human person's body, must always be a sort of animal: none of us could possibly have a nonanimal body. And suppose also that none of us could ever be an animal other than the animal that is his body. If these assumptions are true, then our being animals amounts to our being identical with our bodies. But are they true?

I don't know. Someone might doubt whether a person's body must always be an animal. It is often said that we could have partly or wholly inorganic bodies: "bionic" bodies with plastic or metal parts, say, or even entirely robotic bodies. But no biological organism could come to be partly or wholly inorganic. If you cut off an animal's limb and replace it with an inorganic prosthesis, the animal only gets smaller and has something inorganic attached to it. It doesn't acquire prosthetic parts. If you were to replace *all* an organism's parts with inorganic prostheses, it would no longer be there at all. You couldn't point to an inorganic machine and say truly, "That machine developed in its mother's womb." So it seems to me, anyway. If this is right—if we could acquire inorganic bodies, but no organism could become inorganic—then replacing some or all of your parts with inorganic gadgets could give you a body that was not an organism: a body that was at most partly organic. In that case you could be identical with your body without being an animal—or else be an animal without being identical with your body. Being an animal would be something different from being your body, even if ordinarily, when our bodies are wholly organic, the two conditions coincide.

What it is right to say here depends on whether having some of your parts replaced by inorganic bits could give you a partly inorganic body (one that was not an animal), or whether it would only cause your body to shrink and become attached to those inorganic bits (as the animal would). And that depends in turn on what thing someone's body *is*. It depends, in other words, on what it is for a thing to be someone's body. For any objects x and y, what is necessary and sufficient for x to be y's body? What does it *mean* to say that a certain thing is your body, or that your body is an animal, or that someone might have a robotic body? Unless we have some idea of how to answer these questions, we shall have no way of saying whether someone might be identical with his body without being an animal or vice versa.

I have never seen a good account of what makes something someone's body (see Olson 1997: 144–150, 2006a; van Inwagen 1980). I am unable to complete the formula 'necessarily, x is y's body if and only if . . . '. Because of this, I don't know what would happen to someone's body if some of a human animal's parts were replaced with inorganic prostheses; and I therefore have no idea whether someone could be his body without being an animal or vice versa. So I cannot say how animalism relates to the thesis that we are our bodies. More generally, I find the word 'body' unhelpful and frequently misleading in metaphysical discussions (§2.5 gives an example of the sort of confusion it can cause). For the sake of convenience, I will sometimes use the term 'x's body' to mean the human animal intimately connected with x: the animal we point to when we point to x, the animal that moves when x moves, the animal that x would be if x were any animal at all, and so on. This is merely a stipulation, however, and does not pretend to reflect the way other philosophers use the word 'body'.

Here is another delicate matter. Suppose someone said, "We are animals, but not *just* animals. We are more than mere biological organisms." Is that compatible with animalism? Does animalism say that we are nothing more than animals? That we are *mere* animals?

The answer depends on whether being "not just" or "something more than" an animal is compatible with being an animal. And that in turn depends on the import of the qualifications 'not just' and 'more than'. If a journalist complains that the cabinet is more than just the prime minister, she means that the cabinet is *not* the prime minister: it has other members too. If we are more than just animals in something like that sense, then we are not animals at all; at best, we may bear some intimate relation to those animals we call our bodies. That may be because we have parts that are not parts of any animal, such as immaterial souls. On the other hand, we say that Descartes was more than just a philosopher: he was also a mathematician, a Frenchman, a Roman Catholic, and much more. That is of course compatible with his being a philosopher. We could certainly be more than just animals in this sense, yet still be animals. We could be animals, but also mathematicians or Frenchmen or Roman Catholics. There is nothing "reductionistic," in the pejorative sense of the term, about animalism. An animal can have properties other than being an animal and properties that do not follow from its being an animal. At least there is no evident reason why not. Despite its ugly name, animalism does not by itself imply that our behavior is determined by a fixed, "animal" nature, or that we have only crudely biological properties, or that we are no different in any important way from other animals. We could be unique among animals, and yet be animals.

Finally, animalism does not say that we are animals essentially; for all it says, our being animals might be only a contingent or perhaps even a temporary feature of us, like our being philosophers. Whether we could be animals contingently depends on whether human animals are animals contingently: whether it is possible for something that is in fact a human animal to exist without being an animal. Animalism implies that we have the metaphysical nature of human animals; but what that nature amounts to is a further question (see below). My own view, and that of most philosophers, animalists or not, is that animals are animals essentially; but few arguments for or against our being animals turn on this claim.

2.2 What Is an Animal?

Saying that we are animals will tell us little about what we are unless we have some idea of what sort of thing an animal is. I mean by 'animal' what biologists mean by it: animals are biological organisms, along with plants, bacteria, protists, and fungi. Animals are what zoologists study. Someone might say that 'animal' in the ordinary sense of the word means nothing more than 'animate being'—a thing that can move and perceive—and that whether animals in this sense must be biological organisms is an open question. If that is the case, then my use of the word 'animal' is not the ordinary one, and I ought to have used the term 'organism' or 'animal in the biological sense' instead.

Anyway, here is a brief sketch of what I take to be the metaphysical nature of animals. The view I will offer has controversial elements, but it is nonetheless widely held. (More detailed accounts more or less consistent with mine are found in Hoffman and Rosenkrantz 1997: chap. 4; van Inwagen 1990b: §14; and Wilson 1999: chap. 3.)

As I see it, animals, including human animals, have more or less the same metaphysical nature as other biological organisms. This is not to deny that some animals may have properties of considerable metaphysical interest—rationality and consciousness, for instance—that no plant or fungus could ever have. But if we ask what organisms are made of, what parts they have, whether they are concrete or abstract, whether and under what conditions they persist through time, and the like, I believe that the answer will be more or less the same for human organisms as it is for plants and fungi. So we need an account of the metaphysical nature of organisms generally.

I take it that organisms are concrete particulars. They are substances, and not events or states or aspects of something else. They persist through time; moreover, they continue to be organisms when they persist. I will assume for the present that they do not have temporal parts, though we will revisit this assumption in chapter 5. I also assume that organisms are made up entirely of matter: they have no immaterial or nonphysical parts. Descartes thought that each normal human animal was somehow attached to an immaterial substance that is necessary for a thing to think rationally, but not necessary for it to be alive in the biological sense. If this were true, I take it that the animal would be the material thing, and not the object made up of the material thing and the immaterial one.

Organisms differ from other material things by having *lives*. By a life I mean more or less what Locke meant (1975: 330–331): a self-organizing biological event that maintains the organism's complex internal structure. The materials that organisms are made up of are intrinsically unstable and must therefore be constantly repaired and renewed, or else the organism dies and its remains decay. An organism must constantly take in new particles, reconfigure and assimilate them into its living fabric, and expel those that are no longer useful to it. An organism's life enables it to persist and retain its characteristic structure despite constant material turnover.

There may be things besides organisms that are in some sense alive: certain parts of organisms, such as arms, and things made up of several organisms, such as packs of wolves. They are not organisms because they lack lives of their own. My arm's tissues are kept alive by the vital processes of the human animal it is a part of: there is no self-organizing biological event of the right sort to be a life going on throughout my arm and nowhere else.

Organisms have parts: vast numbers of them. A thing is alive in the biological sense by virtue of a vastly complex array of biochemical processes, and the particles caught up in these processes are parts of the organism. (If Aristotle thought that organisms were mereologically simple, that is presumably because he thought that matter was homogeneous and not particulate.) Owing to metabolic turnover, organisms are made up of different parts at different times.

What are the parts of an organism? Where does an organism leave off, and its environment begin? Where an organism's boundaries lie has presumably to do with the spatial extent of its life. But just how its life determines its boundaries is not obvious. It is tempting to say that an organism is made up at a given time of just those particles that are caught up in its life—its metabolic activities—at that time. If you are an organism, you extend all the way to the surface of your skin and no further because that is the extent of your biological life. Your clothes, or a prosthetic limb, are not parts of you because damage to them is not repaired in the way that damage to your living fabric is repaired, because they are not nourished by your blood supply, because their parts are not renewed and replaced in the way that parts of your kidneys are, and so on. Neat though this view is, however, some find it too restrictive. They say that the particles in an animal's hair or in the dead heartwood of an aging tree are parts of the organism, despite no longer being caught up in its life (Ayers 1991: 225). We needn't settle this matter for present purposes.

As for identity over time, I am inclined to believe that an organism persists if and only if its life continues. This has the surprising consequence that an organism ceases to exist when the event that maintains its internal structure stops and cannot be restarted—that is, when the organism dies. Whatever is left behind—the organism's lifeless remains or its corpse or what have you—is something other than the organism. Strictly speaking, there is no such thing as a dead organism: no organism can be alive at one time and dead at another. I believe this because I have never seen a plausible alternative account of what it takes for an organism to persist (Olson 2004: 269–271). It is not a wholly eccentric view: in addition to Aristotle (see Furth 1988: 156–157) and Locke (1975: 330–331), it has several contemporary advocates (Hoffman and Rosenkrantz 1997: 159; van Inwagen 1990a: 142–158; Wilson 1999: 89–99). It is controversial, however, and nothing I say in this book turns on it. The persistence conditions of human animals will concern us again in §§2.8 and 7.7.

2.3 The Thinking-Animal Problem

Why suppose that we are animals? Well, there are about six billion human animals walking the earth—the same as the number of human people. For each of us there is a human animal, and for every human animal (pathological cases aside, perhaps) there is one of us. Those animals are very like ourselves: they sit in our chairs and wear our clothes; they do our work and read our newspapers and chat with our friends. They appear to be *so* like us, both physically and mentally, that it is hard to tell the difference. These apparent facts pose a formidable obstacle to anyone who would deny that we are animals: the *thinking-animal problem*.

There is a human animal intimately related to you, which some call your body. Now consider that animal's mental properties. It would seem to *have* mental properties. You have mental properties, and the animal has the same brain and nervous system as you have (and the same surroundings too, if that is relevant). It went to the same schools as you did, and it had the same teachers. It shows the same behavioral evidence of mentality as you show. What more could be required for a thing to have mental properties? In fact the animal seems to be mentally exactly like you: every thought or experience of yours appears to be a thought or experience on the part of the animal. How could you and the animal have *different* thoughts? But if the animal thinks your thoughts, then surely it *is* you. You could hardly be something other than the thing that thinks your thoughts.

Consider what it would mean if you were not the animal. The animal thinks. And of course you think. (We can't suppose that the animal thinks and you don't think. Nor can we suppose that you don't exist, when your animal body thinks.) So if you were not that thinking animal, there would be *two* beings thinking your thoughts: there would be the thinking animal, and there would be you, a thinking nonanimal. We should each share our thoughts with an animal numerically different from us. For every thought there would be two thinkers.

Or perhaps the animal located where you are doesn't think, or doesn't think in the way that you do. Something might prevent it from thinking. Or someone might suppose that it was a mistake to concede the existence of an animal sitting there in the first place: maybe there is, strictly speaking, no such thing as your body. In any case, there are just three alternatives to your being an animal: (1) there is no human animal where you are; (2) there is an animal there, but it doesn't think in the way that you do; or (3) there is an animal there, and it thinks exactly as you do, but you are not it. There is no fourth possibility. The repugnancy of these alternatives seems to me a powerful reason to suppose that you are an animal. Let us consider them.

2.4 Are There Animals?

If you are not an animal, the reason may be that there is no animal that you or anyone else could be. How could there be no human animals? What reason could anyone have for believing this?

A number of general metaphysical principles are incompatible with the existence of animals. For instance, some versions of idealism entail that there are no material objects at all (so I should describe those views, anyway); and if there are no material objects, there are no biological organisms. But let's not discuss idealism. Another example is the principle that nothing can have different parts at different times. According to this principle, whenever something appears to exchange an old part for a new one, the truth of the matter is that the object composed of the old parts ceases to exist (or else begins to disperse) and is instantly replaced by a new object composed of the new parts. Yet organisms by their very nature constantly exchange old parts for new ones. If nothing *could* ever survive a change of any of its parts, then organisms are metaphysically impossible; what we think of as an organism is in reality only a series of "masses of matter" that each take on organic form for a moment—until a single particle is gained or lost—and then pass that form on to a numerically different mass.

The principle that nothing can change its parts is at once theoretically elegant and strikingly implausible (we will return to it in §§7.3–7.4). But few opponents of animalism deny the existence of animals. They have good reason not to: anything that would rule out the existence of animals would also rule out the existence of most of the things we might be if we were not animals. If there are no animals, then there are no beings constituted by animals, for instance, and no temporal or spatial parts of animals. And if nothing can change its parts, then persisting bundles of perceptions are no more possible than animals. If there are no animals, there will be few items remaining among the furniture of the earth that we might be.

2.5 Can Animals Think?

The second alternative to our being animals is that the animals we call our bodies exist but don't think in the way that we do. (Let any sort of mental activity or state count for present purposes as thinking.) There are two possibilities here: that human animals don't think at all, and that they think but not as we do.

Consider first the idea that they don't think at all. *You* think, but the animal sitting there doesn't. The reason for this can only be that the animal cannot think: it would certainly be thinking now if it were able to. And if that animal cannot think now, no human animal can ever think, for no human animal is better suited for thinking than it is. Presumably no biological organism of any sort could think. The claim, then, is that animals, including human animals, are no more sentient or intelligent than stones; in fact they are *necessarily* incapable of thought. It may still be that most human animals relate in some intimate way to thinking beings—to us—and stones do not; and it might be appropriate for certain purposes to describe this fact loosely by saying that human animals are more intelligent than stones. But strictly speaking, human animals would have no mental properties whatever.

That would be surprising. Human animals *seem* to think. Could this really be only a misleading appearance? If human animals and other organisms cannot think, there must surely be some impressive explanation of why they can't—that is, some account of what prevents them from using their brains to think.

One possible explanation is that nothing can think: there is no such thing as thinking, any more than there is such a thing as phlogiston (a chemical substance once thought to be a constituent of solid matter and released in combustion). This is eliminative materialism. But no opponents of animalism that I know of accept it. If it were true, it could not be the case that our identity through time consists in psychological continuity, or that we have our mental properties essentially. That would leave little reason to suppose that we are anything other than animals (see §§2.8 and 2.9).

Suppose eliminative materialism is false. In that case, the reason why human animals cannot think must presumably be that they have some property that prevents them from thinking—a property that we, who clearly can think, lack. (Or maybe they lack a property of ours that is necessary for thought.) The most obvious candidate for such a property is being material. If any material thing could ever think, surely it would be some sort of animal; so if animals cannot think, we should expect the reason to be that only an immaterial thing could think. You and I must therefore be immaterial. Of course, simply denying that any material thing could think does nothing to explain *why* it couldn't; but those who hold this view have said many things that would, if they were true, explain why no material thing could think. So you might expect anyone who denies that you and I are animals to deny that we are material things of any sort. But this is not so: many opponents of animalism claim to be materialists. They cannot explain human animals' inability to think by appealing to the fact that animals are material.

They might say that human animals cannot think because they are mere *bodies*, and mere bodies cannot think. It could only be some sort of joke, the idea goes, to say that Newton's body believed in absolute space, while Leibniz's body disagreed. Since *we* think, it would follow that we are not our bodies, and therefore not animals. But that wouldn't mean that we are immaterial: we might be material things other than our bodies.

Now even if this is a reason to believe that animals cannot think, it does nothing to explain why they can't. That a human animal is someone's body and that it is somehow absurd to say that someone's body thinks tells us nothing about *why* a human animal, call it what you will, should be unable to think. It makes that claim no less surprising or easier to believe. (Compare: if Professor Hawking tells us that light cannot escape from a black hole, that is a reason to believe it, but no explanation of why it is so.)

In any case, it is hardly an impressive argument against animal thought. I grant that there is something odd about the statement that Newton's body believed in absolute space. But a statement can be odd without being false. Though it sounds preposterous to say that there is a liter of blood in my office, it is nevertheless true: I am in my office, and there is a liter of blood in me. The statement is odd because it suggests that blood is stored in my office in something like the way it is stored in blood banks, which really would be preposterous. The statement that Newton's body believed in absolute space might be odd for a similar reason. For instance, the reason it sounds wrong might be that it suggests the false claim that believing in absolute space is in some sense a "bodily" property.

In any case, the oddness of saying that Newton's body believed in absolute space should not lead us to infer that the phrase 'Newton's body' denotes something of Newton's—a certain human organism—that was unable to think. Compare the word 'body' with a closely related one: *mind.* It is just as odd to say that Newton's mind was tall and thin, or indeed that it had any other size or shape, as it is to say that Newton's body believed in absolute space. But no one would conclude from this that Newton had some mental thing with no size or shape. That would be a poor argument for substance dualism. We cannot always substitute the phrase 'Newton's mind' for the name 'Newton' without something going wrong; but it is doubtful whether any important metaphysical conclusion follows from this. We ought to be equally wary of drawing metaphysical conclusions from the fact that we cannot always substitute the phrase 'Newton's body' for the name 'Newton' without something going wrong.

Anyone who wants to explain why some material objects can think but animals cannot has his work cut out for him. I know of just two possible explanations worth considering. The first says that animals cannot think because they are too big. The true thinkers are brains, or perhaps parts of brains. A whole animal can be said to think only in the derivative sense of having a thinking brain as a part, much as a car is powerful in the sense of having a powerful engine as a part. Animals are stupid things inhabited by clever brains. I will take up this idea in chapter 4.

Shoemaker proposes a far more interesting explanation: animals cannot think because they have the wrong identity conditions (1984: 92–97; 1999; 2004). Mental properties, he says, have characteristic causal roles. For you to be hungry, for instance, is for you to be in a state that, among other things, is typically caused by your having low blood sugar, and which tends to cause you to act in ways you believe would result in your eating something nourishing. That is, your hunger is a state that tends to combine with *your* beliefs—not mine—to cause *you*, and no one else, to behave in certain ways. That is part of the nature of hunger. More generally, for you to have any mental property at all is at least in part for you to be in a state disposed to combine with certain of your other states to cause you, and no one else, to do certain things.

How does this rule out animal thought? Well, if your cerebrum gets put into my head tomorrow, your current mental states will have their characteristic effects in the being who ends up with that organ, and not in the empty-headed thing left behind. By Shoemaker's reasoning, the subject of those states–you–must therefore be the being who ends up with your transplanted cerebrum. Any being whose later states or actions are caused in the appropriate way by your current mental states must be you. In other words, psychological continuity of a sort must suffice for you or any other mental being to persist through time. Since no sort of psychological continuity suffices for any organism to persist—no human animal would go along with its transplanted cerebrum (§2.8)—it follows that no organism could have mental properties. The nature of mental properties makes it metaphysically impossible for animals to think. However, material things with the right identity conditions would be able to think. Shoemaker believes that human organisms typically "constitute" such things.

It is important to see just how surprising this view is. Suppose you and I are physically just like human animals. (Shoemaker more or less accepts this.) Then the view implies that beings with the same physical properties and surroundings can differ radically in their mental properties. In fact this happens regularly: every human person coincides with an animal physically indistinguishable from her—a perfect physical duplicate—that has no mental properties whatever. There are physically identical beings, in identical surroundings, that differ as much in their mental properties as we differ from trees. Mental properties fail to supervene on physical properties in even the weak sense that any two beings with the same physical properties will have the same mental properties. A thing's having the right physical properties and surroundings does not even reliably *cause* it to have any mental properties.

I find Shoemaker's argument against animal thought unpersuasive. It doesn't seem absolutely necessary that the characteristic effects of a being's mental states must always occur in that very being. In fact it seems that it would not be so in fission cases. Suppose your cerebrum is removed from your head and each half is implanted into a different empty head. Then your mental states have their characteristic effects in two different people. If the nature of mental states entails that the donor must be identical with the recipient in the "single" transplant case, it ought to entail that the donor must be identical with both recipients in the double transplant. But that, as Shoemaker himself agrees, is impossible.

There is more to say about Shoemaker's argument, but this is not the place for it (see Olson 2002c). What if human animals do think, but not in the way that we do? There are two possibilities here. One is that human animals have mental properties different from our own: for instance, they are conscious but never self-conscious. The other is that they have the same mental properties as we have, but they have them in a different way: for instance, they think only in the derivative sense of relating in a certain way to us, whereas we think in a straightforward and nonderivative sense.[2] By itself, however, neither of these suggestions does anything to

[2] Baker combines these proposals (2000: 12–18, 68n.; and 2002: 42). She says that human animals have thoughts requiring a "first-person perspective" only in the derivative sense of constituting nonanimals (ourselves) that have them nonderivatively, whereas the opposite is the case for other thoughts: human animals have them nonderivatively, and we have them derivatively.

solve the thinking-animal problem. If human animals were incapable of having the sorts of thoughts that we have, or if they could not think in the sense that we do, that would be just as surprising as it would be if they could not think at all. It would demand the same sort of explanation, and the prospects for finding one would be similar. It is hard to see what opponents of animalism would gain by proposing such a view.

2.6 Too Many Thinkers

Suppose human animals think in just the way that we do: every thought of yours is a thought on the part of a certain animal. How could that thinking animal be anything other than you? Only if you are one of at least two beings that think your thoughts. (Or maybe you and the animal think numerically different but otherwise identical thoughts. Then you are one of at least two beings thinking exactly similar thoughts.) If you think, and your animal body thinks, and it is not you, then there are two thinkers sitting there and reading this book. Call this the *cohabitation view*. It is unattractive in at least three different ways.

Most obviously, it means that there are far more thinking beings than we thought: the *overcrowding problem*. Defenders of the cohabitation view—and it has its defenders—typically respond by proposing linguistic hypotheses. They claim that the things we ordinarily say and believe about how many people there are do not mean or imply what they appear to mean or imply. They interpret, or reinterpret, our ordinary, nonphilosophical statements and beliefs in a way that would make them consistent with the cohabitation view. When I write on the copyright form that I am the sole author of this book, for instance, I might seem to be saying that every author of this book is numerically identical with me, which according to the cohabitation view is false. But it may not be obvious that that is what I mean. Perhaps I mean only that every author of this book bears some other close relation to me: that they all share their thoughts with me, say, or that they exactly coincide with me. In that case, the ordinary statement that I am the sole author of this book comes out true, even if, strictly speaking, the book has at least two authors. My wife is not in any ordinary sense a bigamist, even if she is married both to me and to this animal. It would be badly misleading to describe our relationship as a *ménage à quatre*.

The general idea is that whenever two thinking beings relate to one another in the way we relate to our animal bodies, we "count them as one" for ordinary purposes (Lewis 1993). Ordinary people—people not engaged in metaphysics—have no opinion about how many *numerically different* thinkers there are. Why should they? What matters in real life is not the number of numerically different thinkers, but the number of *nonoverlapping* thinkers. Human people and thinking human animals don't compete for space. The world is overcrowded only in a thin, metaphysical sort of way and not in any robust quotidian sense.

If this is right, the cohabitation view is consistent with everything we ordinarily say and believe about how many of us there are. But that does not entirely deprive the overcrowding problem of its force. Philosophers of language who know their business can take *any* philosophical claim, no matter how absurd, and come up with a linguistic hypothesis according to which that claim is compatible with everything we say and think when we're not doing philosophy. If I say that I had breakfast before I had lunch today, there is no doubt something I could be taken to mean that would make my statement compatible with the unreality of time. But that would not make it any easier to believe that time is unreal—not much, anyway. For the same reason, the mere existence of the hypothesis that we "count" philosophers by a relation other than numerical identity does little to make it easier to believe that there are two numerically different philosophers sitting there and reading this now. That is because that linguistic hypothesis seems to most of us to be false.

In any case, the troubles for the cohabitation view go beyond mere overcrowding. The view makes it hard to see how we could ever *know* that we were not animals. If there really are two beings, a person and an animal, now thinking your thoughts, you ought to wonder which one you are. You may think you're the person—the one that isn't an animal. But since the animal thinks exactly as you do, it ought to think that *it* is a person. It will have the same grounds for thinking that it is a person and not an animal as you have for believing that you are. Yet it is mistaken. If you *were* the animal and not the person, you would still think you were the person. So for all you know, you are the one making the mistake. Even if you are a person and not an animal, it is hard to see how you could ever have any reason to believe that you are.[3] Call this the *epistemic problem*.

The cohabitation view is unattractive in a third way as well. If your animal thinks just as you do, it ought to count as a person. It satisfies every ordinary definition of 'person': it is, for instance, "a thinking intelligent

[3] Someone might think that this problem arises only on an "internalist" epistemology. If you are the person and not the animal, the idea would go, then your belief that that is what you are is guaranteed to be true, and so is reliably formed, and so counts as knowledge. I don't think any serious epistemologist would endorse this reasoning. Suppose I come to believe, in an insane delusion, that I am Napoleon. And suppose I am in fact Napoleon reincarnated. Finally, suppose that who I am has no influence on who, in my demented state, I believe myself to be. Then my belief is guaranteed to be true; yet it has no epistemic virtue whatever and certainly doesn't count as knowledge.

being, that has reason and reflection, and can consider itself as itself, the same thinking thing, in different times and places,'' as Locke put it. But no one supposes that your animal body is a *person* numerically different from you—that we each share our thoughts with *another* person. If nothing else, that would contradict the popular claim that people—all people—have properties incompatible with those of animals (see §§2.7–2.9). It would also mean that some human people *are* animals, even if others are not. And if human animals are not only psychologically indistinguishable from ourselves but are also people in their own right, it is even more difficult to see how anyone could have any reason to believe that she was not one of the animal people.

If ordinary human animals are not people, on the other hand, despite having the same mental properties as people, all familiar accounts of what it is to be a person are too permissive. There could be nonpeople whose inner life was entirely indistinguishable from ours; indeed, there would be at least one such nonperson for every genuine person. That would deprive personhood of any psychological or moral significance. For that matter, it would make it a real epistemic possibility that *we* are not people. I can verify easily enough that I am rational, self-conscious, and so on; but how could I assure myself that I have that extra feature required for personhood that rational human animals lack? Call this problem—that our animal bodies would be people different from ourselves—the *personhood problem.*

2.7 Creative Linguistics

Some say that the epistemic problem has a linguistic solution (Noonan 1998, forthcoming). They make two surprising claims. First, they say, not just any rational, self-conscious being, or more generally any being with our mental capacities, is a person. To count as a person, a thing must have not only the appropriate mental qualities, but something else as well: it must persist by virtue of psychological continuity, or have those mental qualities essentially, or the like. Call this extra feature *F*. That beings must have *F* in order to fall within the extension of the word 'person' is supposed to be a contingent fact about how we use that word. Human animals lack *F* and therefore do not qualify as people, despite their being psychologically indistinguishable from ourselves. That is the first claim. The second is that the word 'I' and other personal pronouns, at least in their most typical uses, refer only to people: that's why we call them *personal* pronouns. A being that says 'I' in normal circumstances refers thereby to the *person* who says it. This too is supposed to be a contingent fact about how we use language.

These two claims, together with the cohabitation view, yield the startling conclusion that first-person utterances (and presumably first-person thoughts as well) do not always refer to the beings that utter or think them. In particular, when your animal body says 'I', it doesn't refer to itself, as it isn't a person. But presumably you have *F*; so you are a person, and when you say or think 'I', you do refer to yourself. Since your animal body says and thinks just what you say and think, its first-person utterances and thoughts therefore refer to you—the person who produces them—rather than to itself. If it says, "I am hungry," it means not that it itself is hungry but that you are. More to the point, if the animal says or thinks, "I am a person and not an animal," it does not say falsely that *it* is a person and not an animal, but truly that you are. So neither you nor the animal is mistaken about which thing it is.

Call this linguistic hypothesis—that personal pronouns refer only to people and that people by definition have *F*—*personal-pronoun revisionism*. How would it solve the epistemic problem? Suppose there are two beings thinking your thoughts: an animal, and also a nonanimal that has psychological persistence conditions—a *psychological continuer* for short. Better, suppose that you know this. Suppose further that having psychological persistence conditions is the extra person-making feature *F*. Now imagine wondering which of the beings thinking your thoughts you are, the animal or the psychological continuer. How could you work out the answer to this question?

Well, as a competent speaker of English you would know at least implicitly (1) that each occurrence of the word 'I' refers only to the person who utters it. You would also know, or be able to work out, (2) that something counts as a person only if it is a psychological continuer, which according to pronoun revisionism is true by definition. And of course you know (3) that you are whatever you refer to when you say 'I'. These are supposed to be linguistic and conceptual facts that we can know a priori. Given that a psychological continuer thinks your thoughts, it follows from these claims (4) that you are a person and a psychological continuer. If you know that animals are not psychological continuers, you can infer from this that you are not an animal—even if you share your thoughts with an animal psychologically indistinguishable from you. You can therefore know that you are a psychological continuer and not an animal. You can know which of the beings thinking your thoughts you are. That would solve the epistemic problem.

There is much to be said about this proposal (I discuss it at greater length in Olson 2002b; see also Zimmerman 2003: 502–503). I will make just one comment. We are supposing that the human animals that walk and talk and sleep in our beds have the full range of human attitudes and emotions and are psychologically indistinguishable from ourselves.[4] (We discussed the view that human animals differ psychologically from us in the previous section.) Now consider your understanding of the word 'person'. In particular, think of the sense of the word that informs your use of the personal pronouns. What features must a being have for you to call it a person in that ordinary sense? What must it have in order to be a some*one* rather than a some*thing*, a *he* or a *she* rather than an *it*? If something were psychologically indistinguishable from yourself or from one of your close friends, would you refuse to call it a person or a someone until you were told whether it persists by virtue of psychological continuity? That seems to be no part of what we ordinarily mean by 'person'. If human animals really are psychologically just like ourselves, they will count as people in any ordinary sense of the word. It couldn't turn out that half of the rational, self-conscious, human-sized beings that we know and love and interact with in daily life are *not people*. Human animals may fail to satisfy some specialized philosophical sense of 'person', owing to their having the wrong persistence conditions or on some other trivial grounds. But they are surely people in the sense of the word that informs our ordinary use of the personal pronouns.

Maybe it isn't always clear to us what we mean by our words. Some ordinary words may mean something very different from what they seem to mean. Perhaps we cannot dismiss personal-pronoun revisionism as absurd. But it is not very attractive.

2.8 Animalism and Our Identity over Time

Those who say that we are not animals will probably want to argue either that human animals cannot think in the way that we can or that we can somehow know that we are not the human animals that share our thoughts. Neither prospect looks promising. That, to my mind, is the principal case for our being animals. What is the case against it?

[4] Could a being that cannot refer to itself in the first person be self-conscious? Well, pronoun revisionists agree that human animals have first-person thoughts just like our own. All that prevents those animals from referring to themselves in the first person, the idea goes, is the contingent linguistic fact that we (and they) use the personal pronouns to refer only to psychological continuers. We could change the way we talk, so that our personal pronouns referred only to beings with animal persistence conditions. If we did that, *we* should be unable to refer to ourselves in the first person, though our mental lives would otherwise remain unchanged. Would that deprive us of self-consciousness? Not in any important sense, surely. Someone might point out, however, that according to pronoun revisionism, a human animal could not "think of itself as itself," and would therefore fail to satisfy Locke's definition of 'person'.

Historically, the main reason for denying that we are animals is hostility to materialism. The conviction that no material thing, no matter how complex, could ever think in the way that we do is clearly incompatible with our being animals. But few philosophers set much store by it nowadays. The main contemporary objection to animalism has to do with our identity over time, the most popular account of which is that we persist by virtue of some sort of psychological continuity. That rules out our being animals, for no sort of psychological continuity is either necessary or sufficient for a human organism to persist.

To see that it isn't necessary, consider the fact that each human animal starts out as an embryo incapable of any mental activity. There is no psychological continuity of any sort between an adult human animal and the embryo it once was: the adult animal's mental properties cannot derive in any way from those of the embryo, for the embryo had none. The embryo *is* the adult human organism, yet there is no psychological continuity between the embryo as it started out and the full-grown animal as it is today. A human animal can therefore persist without any psychological continuity whatever. Or consider what would happen if you were to lapse into a persistent and irreversible vegetative state. The result of this would be a human organism that was clearly alive, in the biological sense in which an oyster is alive: it would breathe spontaneously, digest its food, fight infection, heal wounds, and so on. It would presumably be the very human organism that was once able-bodied: no one supposes that a human animal that lapses into a persistent vegetative state thereby ceases to exist and is replaced by a new animal. But the animal would no longer be capable of any mental activity. Again, a human animal can persist despite complete psychological discontinuity. If any sort of psychological continuity is necessary for *you* to persist, then your animal body existed before you did, and it could outlive you. But nothing existed before it itself existed, and nothing can outlive itself. It follows that you are not that animal.

Now the claim that psychological continuity is necessary for us to persist may sound unattractive. Those who have actually suffered the misfortune of having a loved one lapse into a persistent vegetative state do not often believe that that person has literally ceased to exist, and that the living thing lying on the hospital bed is a numerically different being. (They may say that their loved one's life no longer has any value or that he ought to be allowed to die, but that is another matter.) Nor does this attitude appear to rest on the mistaken belief that there is some sort of psychological continuity in these cases. And when we see an ultrasound picture of a 12-week-old fetus, most of us are inclined believe that we are seeing something which, if all goes well, will come to be a full-fledged human person, even though it now has no mental properties. (This is something that most parties to debates over the morality of abortion agree on.) We don't ordinarily suppose that the fetus cannot itself become a person, but can only give rise to a person numerically different from itself.

In fact animalism appears to be compatible with everything we believe about our persistence in real-life situations. In every *actual* case, the number of people we think there are is the same as the number of rational human animals. Every actual case in which we take someone to survive or perish is a case where a human animal survives or perishes. Or at least this is so if we leave aside religious beliefs—our being animals may be incompatible with our being resurrected or reincarnated (though some leading philosophers of religion disagree: see Merricks 2001a; van Inwagen 1978; Zimmerman 1999).

But animalism conflicts with things we are inclined to say about science fiction stories. This appears to show a deep and widespread conviction that some sort of psychological continuity is *sufficient* for us to persist.

Imagine that your cerebrum is put into another head The being who gets that organ, and he alone, will be psychologically continuous with you on any account of what psychological continuity is: he will have, for the most part anyway, your memories, beliefs, and other mental contents and capacities; he will have your "first-person perspective"; he will take himself to be you; all these mental properties will have been continuously physically realized throughout the process; and there are no troublesome rival claimants. If any psychological facts suffice for you to persist, that being would be you: you would go along with your transplanted cerebrum. And many people are convinced that you would indeed go along with your transplanted cerebrum.

What about your animal body? Would *it* go along with its cerebrum? Would the surgeons pare that animal down to a lump of yellowish-pink tissue, move it across the room, then supply it with a new head, trunk, and other parts? Surely not. A detached cerebrum is no more an organism than a detached arm is an organism: if the animal went along with the cerebrum, it would have to cease being an organism for a time and then become an organism once more when the transplant is complete. Or think of the empty-headed thing left behind when your cerebrum is removed. It *is* an organism. If the surgeons are careful to leave the lower brain intact, it may even remain alive. It seems to be the very animal that your cerebrum was a part of before the operation. The empty-headed being into which your cerebrum is to be implanted is also a living human organism. And putting your cerebrum into its head surely doesn't destroy that organism and replace it with a new one.

So there appear to be two human animals in the transplant story. One of them loses its cerebrum and gets an empty head. That organ is then fitted into the empty cranium of the other animal, which is thereby made whole again. The surgeons move an organ from one animal to another, just as they might do with a liver. No animal moves from one head to another. Even though there is full psychological continuity between the cerebrum donor and the recipient, they are not the same animal. Thus, no sort of psychological continuity suffices for a human animal to persist through time. One human animal could be psychologically continuous in the fullest possible sense with another human animal.[5]

The conviction that you would go along with your transplanted cerebrum is therefore incompatible with your being an animal. Your animal body would stay behind if your cerebrum were transplanted. If *you* would go along with your transplanted cerebrum, then you and that animal could go your separate ways. And of course a thing and itself can never go their separate ways. It follows that you are not that animal, or indeed any other animal. Not only are you not essentially an animal. You are not an animal at all, even contingently: nothing that is even contingently an animal would move to a different head in a cerebrum transplant.

So the standard case against animalism is this: If we were animals, we should have the persistence conditions of animals, conditions which have nothing to do with psychological facts. Psychology would be completely irrelevant to our identity over time. Cerebrum transplants would be no different, metaphysically, from liver transplants: you could donate your cerebrum to someone else, just as you could donate your liver. But that is absurd. Psychology clearly *is* relevant to personal identity. You would go along with your transplanted cerebrum; you wouldn't stay behind with an empty head. Therefore we are not animals.

Taken in isolation, the transplant argument may look strong. Why deny that we should go along with our transplanted cerebrums? Isn't it *obvious* that that is what would happen? But we have seen how this "transplant conviction" could be wrong: it would be wrong if we were animals. Would it really be so surprising if it were wrong? To my mind, it would be surprising if it were *right*. That would mean either that human animals cannot think or that you are one of two beings thinking your thoughts. *That* would be surprising.

In any case, there are other reasons to doubt the transplant conviction. For one thing, the sort of psychological continuity that would hold between you and the recipient of your cerebrum could hold between you and two future beings. If your cerebrum were divided and each half

[5] Although I am not sure whether I have understood them, Wiggins (1980: 160–163) and McDowell (1997: 237) seem to disagree with me about this. For more on this matter, see Olson 1997a: 109–119; and §7.7 below.

implanted into a different head, at least one of the resulting beings would be mistaken in thinking that she was you, for the simple reason that one thing (you) cannot be numerically identical with two things.[6] Someone can be fully psychologically continuous with you and yet not be you: psychological continuity is not sufficient for us to persist. That undermines the judgment that the one mentally continuous with you in the original transplant story would be you. If the claim that anyone psychologically continuous with you must be you fails to hold in fission cases, it might fail to hold in cerebrum transplants too.

For another, the transplant conviction gets much of its support from a questionable assumption about our practical attitudes—"what matters in identity," as the jargon has it. Imagine that your cerebrum is about to be transplanted into my head. The empty-headed being left behind will then get a new cerebrum. The hospital has only enough morphine for one of the two resulting people; the other will suffer unbearable pain. If we asked you before the operation who should get the morphine, how would you choose? (Imagine that your motives are entirely selfish.) Most people say that you would have a strong reason to give the morphine to the one who ends up with your cerebrum, and little reason, if any, to give it to the other person. This may lead us to infer that you would be the one who ends up with your cerebrum.

But this inference is questionable. Many philosophers doubt whether your selfish interest in the welfare of the person who gets your cerebrum must derive from the fact that he or she is you. In the double-transplant case, they say, you would have a selfish reason to care about the welfare of both offshoots. Better, you would have the *same* reason to care about the fission offshoots as you would have to care about the one who got your whole cerebrum. Yet neither of the fission offshoots would be you. In that case, the concern you would have for the person who got your cerebrum in the single transplant case would not support the claim that he or she would be you, thus depriving the transplant conviction of what appears to be its principal support.[7]

If the transplant conviction is false, why did anyone ever accept it? Well, someone's being psychologically continuous with you is strong evidence for her being you. Conclusive evidence, in fact: no one is ever psychologically continuous with anyone other than herself in real life. That makes it easy to suppose that the one who gets your cerebrum in the transplant case would be you, even if, because we are animals, it isn't so.

[6] Advocates of the temporal-parts view have a way of denying this claim: see §5.5.

[7] I say more about this in Olson 1997a: 52–70. Whether any of these claims about what matters in identity are true is another matter.

Here is another reason why someone might find the transplant argument a conclusive refutation of animalism. Suppose there *are*, in addition to human animals, thinking nonorganisms that would go along with their transplanted cerebrums, or more generally beings that persist by virtue of some sort of psychological continuity. And suppose that such a being thinks your thoughts. Then there are two beings that are otherwise equally good candidates for being you, except that one has the persistence conditions we believe you to have and the other (the animal) doesn't. Would it not be perverse, in that case, to suppose that you are the second being? Such reasoning can make animalism look plainly wrong. I believe that many advocates of the transplant argument do assume that certain nonanimals think our thoughts. Few of them give any reason to accept that metaphysical claim, however, and some such reason is surely needed. We will consider some reasons for it in chapters 3 and 5. But even if assuming that human animals coincide with thinking nonanimals would make the transplant argument an irresistible attack on animalism, it would not make it a strong argument for any positive view about what we are. That is because of the thinking-animal problem: the difficulty of knowing that we are anything other than the animals thinking our thoughts.

2.9 Further Objections

We have seen that animalism conflicts with traditional thinking about our identity over time. Here are some further objections.

First, animalism seems to imply that you and I are only temporarily and contingently people. At least this is so on most proposed accounts of what it is to be a person. Every human animal was once an embryo with no mental properties. If being a person implies having certain mental properties—rationality and self-consciousness or the like—then each human animal was once a nonperson. Even if a thing need only have the capacity to *acquire* the relevant mental properties to count as a person, so that unthinking embryos might be people, human animals in a persistent vegetative state will not count as people, and any human animal could end up in such a state.

I don't want to argue about what it is to be a person. (I don't find it an interesting question.) The important fact is that our being animals would make our having mental features of any sort a temporary and contingent condition of us—even if it is our normal or proper condition. It would mean that any of us could exist at a time without having any mental properties whatever at that time, or even the capacity to acquire them. What is more, any of us could have existed without having any mental properties at *any* time: any of us could have died six weeks after conception. Your being able to think or experience would be no more essential to you than your being a philosopher. It would not, so to speak, be part of your being.

Second, animalism appears to entail that there are no persistence conditions for people as such: no persistence conditions that necessarily apply to all people and only to people. The persistence conditions of human animals presumably derive from their being animals, or organisms. That makes their persistence conditions no different from those of oysters, which are not people by anyone's lights. If so, then our being animals implies that we have the same persistence conditions as some nonpeople. Animalism is also consistent with there being people whose persistence conditions are different from ours: inorganic people such as gods or angels, for instance. If there could be such beings, it would not be necessary that all people have the same persistence conditions. People's persistence conditions, and for that matter their metaphysical nature in general, would derive not from their being people, but from their being animals, or immaterial substances, or whatever metaphysical *sort* of person they are. *Person* would not be a kind that determines the identity conditions of its members.

Some philosophers see in these implications a grave objection to animalism (Baker 2001: 218–220). They find the claim that I might be a person only temporarily and contingently as absurd as the idea that the moon might be only temporarily and contingently a material object. This thought looks incompatible with our being animals.

The claim that there are no persistence conditions for people as such is said to conflict with the very idea of personal identity (Baker 2001: 124). To think about personal identity, the objection goes, is to inquire into the identity conditions of people as such—identity conditions that things have by virtue of being people. That, they say, is why we call it *personal* identity. If there are no such conditions, as animalism seems to imply, then there is no such thing as personal identity—an implication that is also taken to be absurd.

I suppose these objections have some force. That you and I are people essentially is an attractive claim. But it doesn't seem obvious. If we take seriously the idea that a person could be an organism, and we accept that organisms have mental properties only contingently, and we take being a person at a time to entail having mental properties at that time, then we can understand well enough how someone might be a person only contingently And if nothing else, the thinking-animal problem shows that our being organisms is a claim that we must take seriously.

That we must have our persistence conditions by virtue of being people, so that there must be persistence conditions for people as such, is another interesting conjecture. Here is how I see it. You and I have many important properties. We are people. We are also (let us suppose) material, composed of parts, biologically alive, sentient, and awake. For that matter, we might also be philosophers, Hindus, women, or Ukrainians. What principle dictates that our being *people* must determine our identity conditions, rather than any of these other properties? None that I know of. It may be plausible on the face of it; but its incompatibility with our being animals looks like an excellent reason to doubt it.

One further objection to animalism is that it implies the wrong account of what determines how many of us there are at any one time (Lowe 1996: 31), a topic sometimes called "synchronic identity." If we are animals, then the number of human people at any time will always be equal to the number of human animals that have whatever it takes to be a person at that time. And what determines the number of animals is presumably a matter of brute biology. Perhaps it is determined by the number of biological lives in the sense sketched in §2.2. But many philosophers, beginning with Locke, have assumed that the number of people or thinking beings at any given time is determined not by brute biology but by psychological facts: facts about mental unity and disunity.

My mental states are *unified* in the sense of being disposed to interact with one another, and not with any others, in an especially direct way. For instance, my desire to get a train to London will tend to combine with my belief that this train goes to London to cause me to board it. My desires don't interact with *your* beliefs in this way to produce action. That, the idea goes, is what makes it the case that my desires and my beliefs are the states of a single person, whereas my desires and your beliefs are not. More generally, mental states belong to the same person or thinking being just when they relate to one another in this way (Shoemaker 1984: 94–97). So the number of people, or thinking beings generally, is necessarily equal to the number of unified systems of mental states. Call this the *psychological individuation principle*.

This principle looks incompatible with animalism. It seems possible for an animal to have disunified mental states—supposing that an animal can think at all, anyway. It may even be possible for an animal to have a mental life that is no more unified than yours is with mine: perhaps a single human animal could be the home of *two* unified mental systems. This might happen in an extreme case of multiple personality—not in any actual case, but in a case that we could imagine by extrapolating from actual cases. The psychological individuation principle implies that such an animal would be the home of two people.

This doesn't yet show that the psychological individuation principle conflicts with animalism. Animalism doesn't say that all people are animals. Why couldn't we normal human beings be animals, and people with extreme split personality be something else? But that would be an uncomfortable view. What sorts of things would the people in those unusual cases be? They must be *something*. Perhaps they would be bundles of mental states, or parts of brains. But if an animal with split personality could house two or more such nonanimal people, we should expect your animal (which I take to be normal and mentally unified) to house *one* nonanimal person. And if there is a nonanimal person within you, it will be hard to maintain that you are the animal. How could you ever know which person you are? Animalism at least strongly suggests that for every animal there can be at most one human person, no matter how disunified that animal's mental states might be. And that appears to be incompatible with the psychological individuation principle.

As I see it, the psychological individuation principle is yet another debatable conjecture (Olson 2003b). In §6.3 I will argue that it is incompatible with our being material things of any sort, and is best combined with the view that we are bundles of mental states.

I believe that the most serious worries for animalism are very different from those we have considered here. We will come to them in chapter 9.[8] In the meantime, let us turn to the other views of what we are.

[8] For more objections to animalism see Baker 2001: 12–18 and 122–124; Snowdon 2003; Olson 2004; and Hershenov 2005.

3

Constitution

3.1 Material Things Constituted by Animals

It is easy to suppose that we have properties incompatible with those of animals: that we are essentially capable of thinking, say, or that what it takes for us to persist is different from what it takes for an animal to persist. These claims rule out our being animals. Yet we appear to be material things. Not only that, but each of us appears to be made of just the same matter as a certain animal. We are no larger or smaller than our animal bodies and are located just where they are.

The idea that we are not animals, but are nevertheless material things made of the same matter as our animal bodies and located in the same place, may sound strange. We can increase the tension by noting the apparent truism that no two material things can be in exactly the same place at once. If we know anything about material things, we know that they compete for space and exclude one another. So we find ourselves drawn to each of four inconsistent claims: (1) we are material things; (2) each of us has the same location as an animal (which is also a material thing); (3) we are not animals; and (4) two material things can never be in the same place at once.

What to do? Those who think that we are partly or wholly immaterial deny the first claim. Those who think that we are spatial or temporal parts of animals deny the second: they say that our animal bodies are not located precisely where we are, but occupy larger regions. We will come to these views in due course. Animalists deny the third claim. But some deny the fourth: they say that two material things *can* be in the same place. Not just any two material things, of course: you will never get a dog and a cat into the same place. Material things can be in the same place only if they are made of the same matter. That, the thinking goes, is the truth behind the idea that material things compete for space.

The claim, then, is that two or more things can be made entirely of the same matter at the same time. For technical reasons it will be useful to recast this idea in slightly different terms.[1] Let us say that some things, the *x*s, *compose* something *y* if and only if each of the *x*s is a part of *y*, no two of the *x*s share a part, and every part of *y* shares a part with at least one of the *x*s.[2] So when a child builds a castle of Lego bricks, the castle is composed of those bricks. If each brick is itself composed of atoms, then the castle is also composed of atoms, for a part of a part of something is itself a part of it. So our suggestion is that the same things can compose two different objects. In other words, different material objects can *coincide materially*, where *x* coincides materially with *y* if and only if *x* and *y* are material objects and some things, the *z*s, compose *x* and also compose *y*. Applied to ourselves, the idea is that we coincide materially with animals, even though we are not animals ourselves. One can be made of the same matter as one's animal body while having properties that no animal could have.

If the relation between you and your animal body is not identity but material coincidence, we should expect to find more examples of material coincidence without identity; and indeed those who hold this view take it to be ubiquitous. The particles that compose a clay statue, they say, also compose a lump of clay; yet the lump and the statue are numerically

[1] The technical reason is this: "Four-dimensionalists" say that two things can be made of the same matter at once, but they don't mean it in the sense that is relevant here. They mean only that two material things can share a temporal part. They deny that two things can coincide materially in the sense defined below. I will return to this point in §§5.3 and 7.4.

[2] The term 'the *x*s' is a plural variable, standing to the singular variable '*x*' as the plural name 'the Marx Brothers' stands to the singular name 'Groucho', and as the plural pronoun 'they' stands to the singular pronoun 'it'. Here I follow van Inwagen 1990b: 22–27. It might be better to define the phrase 'the *x*s compose *y* at a time *t*' rather than 'the *x*s compose *y*', as the claim we are exploring is that things can compose two different objects at the same time. I have not done this because four-dimensionalists agree that atoms (say) can compose two different objects at the same time in the sense that the thing the temporal parts of those atoms located at that time compose can be a temporal part of two different objects that diverge elsewhere in space-time. This sort of "coincidence," which consists only in sharing temporal parts, is not the idea explored in this chapter.

different because the lump will ordinarily have existed before the statue did (before it was statue-shaped), and because squashing it would destroy the statue but not the lump. The bricks that compose the child's castle might also compose a material object called an "aggregate" of bricks, which predated and will outlive the castle. If we replaced a brick, the castle would come to coincide with a different aggregate. Owing to metabolic turnover, an organism coincides with a different mass of matter or aggregate of atoms every fraction of a second. And so on.

In each of these examples, our proposal says, numerically different objects not only coincide materially, but also differ in important qualitative respects—where by 'qualitative' I mean any property that doesn't specify the identity of its bearer (*being Stan Getz* would be a nonqualitative property). The objects differ in kind: one is a statue and not a lump, the other is a lump and not a statue; one is a person and not an animal, the other is an animal and not a person. They differ in their modal properties: statues are essentially statue-shaped, but statue-shaped lumps are only contingently statue-shaped; people are essentially able to think, but the animals coinciding with them think, at best, only contingently. They have different persistence conditions: statues and people can survive things that lumps and organisms cannot, and vice versa. There is no point in saying that coinciding objects are numerically different but qualitatively identical. No one will say, for instance, that we are animals coinciding with *other* animals exactly like us. The attraction in saying that statues are not lumps or that we are not human animals is that statues and people have properties that lumps and human animals lack. These are not merely historical properties: a statue and its coinciding lump are supposed to differ not only in that the lump existed before the statue did. They are supposed to differ *while they coincide*: for instance, while they coincide, the lump but not the statue is capable of surviving squashing. A statue and its coinciding lump, or a person and her animal body, would differ qualitatively even if they coincided throughout their entire careers.

The view that qualitatively different things can coincide materially is called the metaphysic of constitution or *constitutionalism*. The name alludes to the fact that whenever two things coincide materially, one of them is supposed to "constitute" the other. Few of those who speak of constitution bother to say what they mean by it, and those who do say different things.[3] But most agree that constitution is necessarily asymmetric and irreflexive: two things cannot constitute each other, and nothing can constitute itself. (Material coincidence, by contrast, is an equivalence

[3] Compare Doepke 1982 and 1996: chap. 7; Thomson 1998: 157; Baker 2000: 27–46 and 2001: 163; and Lowe 2002: 73. I say more about constitution in §7.6.

relation.) And when constitutionalists take two things to coincide materially, they usually agree about which constitutes which: people are constituted by their bodies, for instance, which in turn are constituted by masses of matter, and not vice versa. (Do not confuse constitution with composition. Constitution by definition relates one thing to one thing, whereas many things can jointly compose something.)

Constitutionalism is a principle about material things in general, and not about ourselves in particular. It doesn't say what you and I coincide with, or even whether we coincide with anything. For all it says, we might be animals coinciding with masses of matter (Thomson 1997), or material objects that do not coincide with anything else, or even wholly immaterial things. Most constitutionalists, though, say that we are nonanimals coinciding materially with human animals. Or at least this is the usual situation. Although we are all nonanimals, they say, we may not all coincide with animals. Perhaps some of us coincide with a thing made up of a human animal and a plastic knee (see §2.1). Someone who had a cerebrum transplant might coincide with different animals at different times, and briefly coincide with a naked cerebrum. Perhaps, by gradual replacement of parts, someone might one day come to coincide with a wholly inorganic machine. If we are lucky, we might be constituted in the next world by something glorious and indestructible but not in any sense biological. In this regard, the idea goes, we are like statues, which by careful replacement of parts can coincide with different lumps of matter at different times. Coinciding with a particular human animal is supposed to be only a contingent and perhaps a temporary feature of us. But most constitutionalists say that we must always coincide with *some* material thing other than ourselves, be it animal, machine, or what have you: we could not become immaterial.

Most constitutionalists say that we have certain mental properties essentially, or that some sort of psychological continuity is necessary for us to persist through time. It follows that we come into being later than our animal bodies do: you appeared when a human animal reached a certain point in its development—perhaps when it acquired those mental features that distinguish people from nonpeople. Depending on what those features are, this could happen at any time between the appearance of the first mental capacities five or six months after fertilization and the onset of full self-consciousness a year or more after birth. And you ordinarily cease to exist when your animal body ceases to support the relevant mental features, as it would if it lapsed into a persistent vegetative state. Here again we are like clay statues, which constitutionalists say come into being when a lump of clay is modeled in a certain way, and perish, outlived by the lump, when squashed.

I will call the view that you and I are nonanimals coinciding with animals—as opposed to constitutionalism in general—the *constitution view*.[4]

3.2 The Clay-Modeling Puzzle

Whether the constitution view is right depends largely on the truth of constitutionalism in general. If constitutionalism is false, so is the constitution view. If constitutionalism is true, on the other hand, and if we are material things, it will be hard not to accept the constitution view.

Suppose constitutionalism is true. Then statue-shaped lumps of clay in the right circumstances constitute things that are essentially statue-shaped: statues. Likewise, lumps of matter in the appropriate organic configuration constitute things that are essentially living: organisms. These are supposed to be paradigm cases of constitution. Now it doesn't strictly follow from this that human animals in the right state and the right circumstances constitute things that are essentially able to think. It could be that statue-shaped lumps constitute things that are essentially statue-shaped but human animals never constitute things that are essentially thinkers. But that would be surprising. We should expect there to be an explanation for this important difference. The most likely explanation, it seems, would be that no material thing of any sort could think, essentially or otherwise: thinking beings are immaterial and are not constituted by anything. (Remember, constitutionalism in general does not imply that we are material things.) The claim that thinkers *are* material, but don't stand to human animals as clay statues stand to lumps of clay, sounds rather unprincipled.

If human animals of the right sort do constitute essential thinkers, it is but a short step to the constitution view. Those essential thinkers would not themselves be animals, for no animal is essentially able to think. And it would be hard to find any reason to suppose that we were the animals and not the essential thinkers. On the contrary, the apparently widespread and deeply held conviction that we are essentially able to think will be a reason to suppose that we are things constituted by animals.

So the truth of constitutionalism in general would provide a fair case for our being nonanimals constituted by animals. (Someone might say that we are constituted by brains or other parts of animals, rather than by whole animals. I see this as a near variant of the constitution view, and most of what I will say about the view that we are constituted by animals

[4] Advocates of the constitution view include Johnston (1987), Sosa (1987), Doepke (1996: chap. 9), Shoemaker (1999), and Baker (2001, 2002, 2003).

applies equally to the view that we are constituted by brains.) The constitution view and constitutionalism in general are likely to stand or fall together. In effect, then, any argument for constitutionalism is an argument for the constitution view. If we can find *any* case where qualitatively different objects coincide materially, that will be a reason to suppose that we are constituted by animals (or perhaps by brains). And there are plenty of arguments for constitutionalism.

Consider first the *clay-modeling puzzle* (Wiggins 1968). Take a lump of clay of nondescript shape and knead it into the form of, let us say, Margaret Thatcher. (Iron might be a more appropriate material in this case, but clay suits our purposes better.) Then squash the lump and model it into a cube. We seem to have here a material object—a lump or mass or portion of clay—that is first shapeless, then Thatcher-shaped, then cubical. There also seems to be, for a time, a statue of Thatcher. During that time the lump and the statue coincide materially. Yet we wouldn't say that *the statue* starts out shapeless and ends up cubical. We wouldn't say, "See that statue? It was nothing but a shapeless lump this morning. Tomorrow it will be a cube." The statue doesn't seem to start out as a nonstatue, become a statue for a while, and then revert to being a nonstatue. It doesn't merely cease to exist *as a statue* when we squash it. It seems to go out of existence altogether.

It is easy enough to make this into an argument for constitutionalism. The story invites us to accept these claims:

1. There is a lump of clay that is first shapeless, then Thatcher-shaped, then cubical.
2. There is a statue that is never shapeless or cubical.
3. The statue coincides materially, while it exists, with the lump.

1 and 2 imply that there are two different clay objects in the story. They have to be two because they exist at different times, and because one is shapeless for a time and the other is never shapeless. It follows, given 3, that two different things can coincide materially.

Now this is not yet constitutionalism—not quite. Constitutionalism says that different things can not only coincide materially, but also differ qualitatively while they coincide. If the statue and the lump were qualitatively exactly alike while they coincided—if both were statues and both were lumps, and they shared all the same dispositions, essential properties, and so on—then the clay-modeling puzzle would support only the claim that you and I coincide materially with human animals numerically different from us. That is not yet the constitution view, since it doesn't imply that we are in any way qualitatively different from those animals.

To make the clay-modeling puzzle into an argument for constitutionalism we need to establish that the statue and the lump in the story differ qualitatively while they coincide. But that is just what the story suggests. According to the story it is no accident that the lump persists throughout the various changes of shape whereas the statue does not. If we took a thousand shapeless pieces of clay and kneaded each of them first into the shape of Thatcher and then into a cube, it would always be the lump—the thing that was first shapeless—that survived the loss of its human shape and became cubical. The statue—the thing that comes into being when the lump becomes Thatcher-shaped—would always pass away when it loses that shape. That is because lumps have the *capacity* to survive those changes and statues lack it: lumps, but not statues, have the modal property of possibly surviving radical changes of shape. If that is right, then the lump and the statue in our story have different qualitative properties while they coexist. In fact they would differ in this way even if they were to coincide throughout their careers. So the story suggests a fourth claim as well:

4. The lump has a qualitative property, while it coincides with the statue, that the statue then lacks.

Grant this, and constitutionalism follows.

There is no easy way to avoid this conclusion. If constitutionalism is false, one of the four claims must be false; yet they all seem to be true.

We have already considered affirming the first three claims while denying the fourth—the view that the lump predates and outlives the statue but is qualitatively identical with it while they coincide. It is unsurprising that no one holds that view.

A more likely way out would be to accept the first claim but deny the second: to say that there is a lump that changes its shape twice, but there is no statue that is always Thatcher-shaped. The only large clay object in the story is the lump, which simply happens to be temporarily Thatcher-shaped. No new material object comes into being when we knead the lump into that shape, and none ceases to be when we squash it. No two things coincide materially. Call this suggestion *lumpism*.

Another possibility is that the second claim might be true and the first false: there is, if you like, a statue but no lump. Perhaps, when we knead the clay into the shape of the former prime minister, a new object, a statue, comes into being, and perishes when we squash it. But no clay object persists through these changes: nothing is first shapeless, then Thatcher-shaped, then cubical. (What about *the clay*? Isn't *it* first shapeless, then Thatcher-shaped, then cubical? Maybe so; but that doesn't obviously imply that any material object changes its shape. Perhaps the expression 'the clay' refers not in the singular to any one thing, but in the plural to a lot of particles[5]—particles that never compose anything that can survive radical changes of shape. That is, perhaps the clay is merely a lot of particles and not a large composite object.) Call the view that 1 is false and 2 is true *statuism*.

The trouble with these proposals is that they are hard to generalize (Olson 1996). Though they may sound attractive in the case of the statue and the clay, they are implausible in other cases.

Take lumpism, the idea that statues are merely statue-shaped lumps. If there are such things as lumps of clay, there ought to be such things as lumps of flesh and bone as well. Why should clay particles stuck together compose lumps, but not flesh particles stuck together? But although it may sound attractive to say that clay statues are just special lumps of clay, it is not plausible to say that living things are just special lumps of flesh.

Lumps of flesh ought to be able to survive crushing if lumps of clay can. So the lump composed of the flesh particles of a dog ought to be able to survive the same sorts of radical changes of shape as a lump of clay can survive. But the dog cannot survive that. If something analogous to squashing the statue and making the clay into a cube were to happen to a dog, it would not merely change its shape. It wouldn't just cease to be a dog and come to be a cubical piece of meat. Surely the dog would cease to be altogether. Or consider that dogs can survive wholesale changes of parts, owing to metabolic turnover. Lumps of flesh cannot survive this: if you take away half a lump's particles and replace them with new ones—even if you do it gradually—you end up with a lump that is numerically different from the one you began with. So say those who believe in lumps, anyway. If there are such things as lumps of flesh, the lump now coinciding with a dog is not the one that coincided with it a year ago. A dog is not a lump of flesh. If there is only a lump of flesh in the dog story, in the way that (according to lumpism) there is only a lump of clay in the statue story, then there are really no dogs or other organisms at all: what appears to be a persisting organism is reality a series of numerically different lumps, each taking on organic form only briefly.

Those who would avoid constitutionalism by saying that statues are just lumps are likely to end up concluding that *all* material things are lumps—things that can survive radical changes of shape but cannot be composed of different particles at different times. They will arrive at a general "lump ontology." Because most familiar material objects—organisms, artifacts, and ourselves as well, if we are material—are not lumps, the

[5] Zimmerman (2003) argues against this proposal. But he is no constitutionalist; he endorses the "lump ontology" mentioned below.

lump ontology implies that there are no such things. That may not be a reductio ad absurdum of the lump ontology, but it shows how tough-minded you have to be to accept it. Lumpism offers no easy way round the clay-modeling argument.

Now consider statuism, the idea that the only Thatcher-shaped object in the story is the statue, which has that shape throughout its career. What's wrong with that? Well, if clay particles arranged in the shape of Thatcher compose a clay statue, we should expect the organic particles that compose Thatcher herself to compose something analogous to a statue—not a statue, exactly, but something of the same metaphysical sort as a statue, with the same persistence conditions: a "statue-type object." (If you believe that Thatcher is immaterial, consider her animal body.) What principled reason could there be to suppose that clay particles arranged in the shape of Thatcher compose a statue-type object whereas flesh particles arranged in that way do not?

But Thatcher can survive things that no statue-type object could survive. She grew in size enormously in the course of her development. She could become a good deal smaller as well. She could survive the loss of her arms and legs. Given enough life-support machinery, she could probably even survive as a severed head. No one thinks that a clay statue could have that sort of history. Thatcher herself is therefore no statue-type object. If the only Thatcher-sized material thing in the story is a statue-type object, then there is no such thing as Thatcher. Or if Thatcher really is a statue-type object, her history and persistence conditions are radically different from anything anyone ever thought. Those who would avoid constitutionalism by saying that lumps are really statue-type objects are likely to end up with something at least as repugnant as the lump ontology.

You might find my attempts to generalize lumpism and statuism too crude. Maybe the clay-modeling story is disanalogous to the stories of dogs and prime ministers that I have tried to compare it with. Perhaps clay particles arranged in human or in canine form compose lumps of clay, but organic particles arranged in human or canine form don't compose lumps of anything. Or maybe clay particles arranged statuewise compose clay statues but organic particles arranged in human form do not compose fleshy statue-type objects. That might enable us to resist the clay-modeling argument and avoid constitutionalism without going to such loony extremes as the lump ontology. The trouble with these suggestions is that they sound unprincipled. One would like to think that there was some reason *why* clay particles arranged in human form compose lumps or statue-type objects whereas organic particles arranged in that way do not. Claims like these ought to fit into some broader and more systematic picture of the ontology of material objects. Otherwise we ought to worry that they are more wishful thinking than reliable insight. And it is hard to draw up any such picture.[6]

A more radical response to the clay-modeling puzzle is to reject both 1 and 2: there are neither lumps of clay nor clay statues. Of course, there is *something* there that sculptors work and that has aesthetic value. Perhaps there are clay particles. Sculptors arrange some of these particles in special ways, with certain intentions and in special circumstances. We describe this situation loosely by saying such things as, "She has made a clay statue of Margaret Thatcher." But really there are no clay objects, but only particles. Clay particles never *compose* anything: there is nothing that has many clay particles as parts and every part of which overlaps at least one of those particles. There is never any larger thing for clay particles to be parts of. The clay particles in our story start out stuck together in a nondescript fashion, then get arranged in a way that we describe as Thatcher-shaped, and end up arranged cubically. But nothing in the story is literally Thatcher-shaped or cubical. This would enable us to describe the clay-modeling case without committing ourselves to constitutionalism. We might call this proposal *the sparse ontology*.

Some philosophers have trouble understanding the sparse ontology. What is the difference, they ask, between things' being lumped together and their composing a lump? Given that some clay particles cohere together and don't cohere with any other clay particles, how can it be a *further* question whether there is a lump of clay there? We might as well say that there are many people gathered in the street but there is no crowd, or that there is a left shoe and a matching right shoe but no pair of shoes. How could that be a serious view?

Well, consider the claim that any objects whatever, no matter what they are like in themselves or how they are arranged, always compose something. That is, for any things at all, there is something that has all those things as parts, and all the parts of which share a part with one or more of those things—something numerically different from any of those parts, unless there is just one of them. Call this *compositional universalism*. Those who don't understand the sparse ontology appear to be assuming this principle. In fact they seem to think that it cannot intelligibly be doubted or denied: it is true solely by virtue of the meanings of the words used to state it, and in such an obvious way that anyone who understands the words 'thing', 'compose', and 'something' must see, on reflection, that it is true. Their view is apparently that it is a logical principle, like the principle of noncontradiction. Given that there are

[6] Hoffman and Rosenkrantz (1997: 87–88, 99–100) may have such a reason; see §9.5. Burke (1994, 1996) denies 1 and accepts 2; I say a bit about his view in §7.4.

such things as your left leg, St. Paul's Cathedral, and the planet Mars, anyone who fails to see that there is also an enormous disconnected material thing composed of those three objects is simply confused.

That is not how it seems to me. *I* find it eminently doubtful whether there is anything made up of your left leg, St. Paul's Cathedral, and the planet Mars. It is not only doubtful whether those three things compose a "genuine object" or a thing with natural boundaries or anything of the sort that we have reason to pay any mind to. It is doubtful whether they compose anything at all. Universalism looks to me like a substantive metaphysical principle. It is not at all like the principle of noncontradiction. It is more like the claim that God exists. It might be true, and then again it might not be. But if we can meaningfully ask whether just any things compose a larger thing, how could it be meaningless to ask whether clay particles lumped together compose anything?

This is not going to satisfy those who have tried hard and failed to understand the sparse ontology. I can refer them to other sources (for instance, Merricks 2001: 12–28; van Inwagen 1990b: 6–12, and 1994). And we will see in chapter 9 that what we say about composition has important implications for what we are.

Even if we can understand the claim that there are no lumps or statues, though, we may find it hard to believe. The result of kneading some clay into the shape of Thatcher certainly *appears* to be a medium-sized clay object. At any rate it takes some doing to get people to take seriously the idea that there might be nothing there but particles. The proposal also raises difficult theoretical questions. For instance, if the particles in our story don't compose a lump of clay or anything else, when *do* particles compose something? What *would* it take for particles to compose something, if not their being lumped together? More to the point, if clay particles arranged in the form of a human being never compose anything, why suppose that organic particles arranged in human form compose something? Surely there is no ontologically significant distinction between clay particles and organic particles. If there are no lumps or statues, how could there be any people—unless people are immaterial? We will return to these matters in §9.5.

Other opponents of constitutionalism accept that the statue and lump exist and have different careers, but deny that they coincide materially. Despite appearances, they say, there are no smaller things that compose both the lump and the statue. The lump has *temporal* parts that do not overlap with any parts of the statue, such as the cubical part of it located later than its statue-shaped part. If a statue and a lump *were* to have all the same parts, including temporal parts—if the god of the philosophers were to create a clay statue out of nothing and then annihilate it without changing its shape, for instance—they would be one and the same. This proposal at least provides a systematic way of avoiding material coincidence. However, it requires the contentious assumption that statues and lumps, and presumably all persisting objects, including ourselves, are made up of temporal parts. We will return to it in chapter 5.

3.3 The Replacement Puzzle and the Amputation Puzzle

The clay-modeling puzzle is just one of many considerations about the ontology of material objects that support constitutionalism. Here are two more.

The *replacement puzzle*, like the clay-modeling puzzle, suggests that each ordinary material object coincides materially with something of a different sort (Thomson 1998). Suppose we break off an arm of our clay statue and burn it in a very hot fire, then replace it with a new arm made of different clay. Then the argument is this: There is a clay statue that persists throughout the story and has first one arm and then another. There is also a statue-shaped lump of clay coinciding with the statue before the replacement, and *another* statue-shaped lump of clay coinciding with it afterward. I say another lump because the original lump doesn't get smaller when we destroy part of it, as the statue does, and then regain its original size when a new part is provided. Rather, the lump ceases to exist when the arm is destroyed. And when the new arm is attached, a new lump comes into being. Or perhaps a previously disconnected lump—one existing in two detached pieces—comes to be a connected lump—one that is all in one piece. Either way, the new lump is not the old one. Since the statue coincides first with one lump and then with another, it cannot be identical with either. More generally, every clay statue has a property that no lump of clay has, namely the capacity to have different clay parts, or to be made of different clay, at different times. It follows that no clay statue is identical with any lump of clay—not even a clay statue that never has any of its parts replaced. Once more we have qualitatively different material objects coinciding materially. The alternatives to this conclusion are similar to those in the clay-modeling puzzle.

Then there is the ancient *amputation puzzle*. Consider an ordinary human organism, Peter. Presumably there is such a thing as Peter's left hand. And if there is such a thing as his left hand, there ought to be such a thing as his "left-hand complement": something composed of all of Peter's particles save those that compose his left hand. Call it Pete. Pete and Peter are not the same thing: Peter is bigger. Pete would seem to be one of Peter's parts. Now imagine that Peter loses his left hand. Better, let the hand be entirely destroyed. This is surely something that Peter could survive. Suppose he does. Then he gets smaller by a hand. But what about Pete? What happens to *it* when Peter loses his hand? If the loss is clean and quick, Pete need not be directly affected. Only its surroundings would change. So it seems that both Peter and Pete would exist after the amputation. How would they then relate to one another? It seems that they would coincide materially: the very atoms that compose Peter would compose Pete as well. But they cannot be the same thing, for they were different things before they coincided. If these assumptions are all correct, then this is another case of material coincidence (Thomson 1983). (It will be a genuine case of constitution only if Peter and Pete differ qualitatively while coinciding; but those who accept the rest of the story are unlikely to deny this.) Again, there is no easy way of avoiding the constitutionalist conclusion. We will return to the amputation puzzle in §§7.3–7.4.

3.4 Thinking Animals Again

The constitution view promises to combine the apparent fact that we are living material things with the conviction that we have identity conditions or essential properties different from those of human animals. It claims to have all the virtues of animalism with none of its vices. And it is part of a package that appears to solve a number of vexing metaphysical puzzles. This might make the constitution view sound like a gift from the gods.

But it is too good to be true. For one thing, the constitution view shares some of the objections leveled against animalism. In §2.9 we saw that animalism was incompatible with the widely held claim that facts about mental unity determine how many of us there are at any one time. I will argue in §6.3 that the constitution view is also incompatible with that claim. (We will consider another objection to both animalism and the constitution view in §9.3.)

The constitution view also has troubles of its own. The most obvious is the thinking-animal problem. The constitution view says that we are not identical with our animal bodies. As we saw in §2.3, this implies that one of three things must be the case: there are no human animals at all, or human animals cannot think in the way that we do, or each of us shares all our thoughts with another being. Which of these unsavory consequences should friends of the constitution view accept?

They cannot deny that there are human animals. That such an animal constitutes you is part of their view. Someone might deny that there are animals and say that we coincide with lumps of flesh or masses of matter instead. (Though this is not strictly a version of the constitution view as I have stated it, it is a close relative.) In that case, there would be no thinking-animal problem, but there would still be a thinking-lump problem. It might perhaps be easier to explain why a lump of flesh in human form could never think than to explain why a human animal couldn't. But even so, advocates of this view face the considerable challenge of explaining why there are no human animals in a way that is compatible with their view of what we are. Why might there be no human animals? It might be because there are no material things at all: the physical world is an illusion. Or maybe there are no composite material things, but only elementary particles (§8.5). Or it might be because nothing can have different parts at different times (§§7.3–7.4). None of these claims are compatible with anything like the constitution view. Any account of why there are no animals will also do away with any "constituted" material things that we could be.

So according to the constitution view, there are human animals coinciding materially with us. What if those animals think in the way that we do? Then there are two beings thinking your thoughts, you and the animal. And that is too many. We saw the problems this raises in §2.6. The human animals coinciding with us ought to count as people. Human people would then come in two kinds: animal people and the nonanimal people they constitute. That makes it hard to see how we could know whether we are the nonanimal people or the animal people.

Baker seems to think that these problems dissolve once we see that the animal constitutes the person (2000: 169–179, 191–204; 2002: 42). If we state the constitution view correctly, she claims, the question of how we know we are not our animal bodies does not arise. She says that I am an animal as well as a person, and that the animal constituting me—call it *A*—is a person as well as an animal. But *A* and I are animals and people in different senses. I am an animal only derivatively, she says, insofar as an animal constitutes me. *A*, however, is an animal nonderivatively: it is an animal independently of its constituting or being constituted by anything. Contrariwise, *A* is a person only insofar as it constitutes a person, whereas I am a person nonderivatively, independently of any constitution relations I enter into. How does that help? In particular, how does it enable me to know that I am not *A*? Well, I can know that I am a person, Baker says, because I can think first-person thoughts, and only a person can think first-person thoughts (that is her definition of 'person'). Yet *A* is also a person. How do I know *which* person I am? Baker says that although I am a person, and *A* is a person, and we are numerically different, we are not *two* people. Whenever one thing constitutes another, she says, they are one thing. And because there are not two people there, it makes no sense to ask which one I am.

I don't know what Baker means when she says that *A* and I, though numerically different, are one person. But whatever it means, I do not see how it could help me to know that I am not *A*. There is *A*, Baker says, and there is the person *A* constitutes—Olson—and they are numerically different. So I ought to be able to ask whether I am identical with Olson or with *A*. If I *am* identical with Olson and not with *A*, as Baker claims, how can it be impossible to ask whether I am Olson or *A*? And if I can ask whether I am Olson or *A*, I can also ask what grounds I have for accepting one answer to this question rather than another—just the problem Baker's account was supposed to do away with.

Friends of the constitution view will want to solve the thinking-animal problem by denying that human animals can think, or that they can think in the way that we think.[7] But as we saw in §2.5, this is a hard thing for a materialist to maintain: if you say that *some* material things can think, you will find it hard to argue that biological organisms cannot. It is especially hard to argue that physically indistinguishable things in the same surroundings—and according to the constitution view you and I are indistinguishable in this way from our animal bodies—can nonetheless differ radically in their mental capacities. There appears to be no difference between you and your animal body that could account for any psychological difference.

Someone might say that what prevents human animals from thinking is not any defect in their physical structure or surroundings or history, but that they belong to the wrong metaphysical kind. The kind might be *biological organism*: perhaps human animals cannot think because they are organisms. We, by contrast, are able to think because we are not organisms (as well as having the right microstructure, surroundings, history, and so on).

Why should a thing's being a biological organism prevent it from thinking (or from thinking in the way that we think)? Maybe organisms can't think because they have the wrong persistence conditions. We considered this rather unlikely view in §2.5. Even if it were true, though, it would not yet explain why we can think and human animals can't. That is because it doesn't explain why we are not animals ourselves. Of course, it is part of the constitution view that we are not animals. But even if we coincide materially with animals numerically different from ourselves, the question remains: What *makes* us nonanimals? We are physically identical with human animals. We have the same developmental and evolutionary history as those animals have (we weren't cooked up in the lab by mad

[7] This seems to be Baker's view: human animals, she says, can think first-person thoughts only derivatively, whereas we think them strictly speaking. So human animals and human people differ psychologically. But she does not explain why human animals cannot think in the way that people can. Zimmerman 2002 is an illuminating discussion of Baker by a philosopher with more patience than I.

scientists). How could things like that—beings that no biologist could ever distinguish from animals—not be animals?

Perhaps we are not animals because we lack the identity conditions of organisms: maybe our identity over time, but not that of organisms, consists in some sort of psychological continuity. But this raises a further question: What could give us identity conditions different from those of human animals? How could material things with the same physical properties (or at least the same microstructure) in the same surroundings differ in the sort of thing they can survive? What is it about human animals that enables them to survive in a persistent vegetative state (for instance), when we—beings otherwise exactly like them—cannot survive it?

I have asked why we can think but the animals coinciding with us cannot, what makes us nonorganisms despite being physically indiscernible from organisms, and what could give us identity conditions different from those of the animals coinciding with us. We might also ask what could make one object a statue and another object, physically indiscernible from it and with the same surroundings, a mere statue-shaped lump. These are all instances of a more general question, which we might call the *indiscernibility problem*: How can putting the same parts together in the same way in the same circumstances give you qualitatively different wholes? If the same atoms can compose two things at once, what could make those two things qualitatively different? What could give them different mental properties, or different persistence conditions, or different modal properties? If atoms really could compose more than one object at once—if numerically different objects could coincide materially—should we not expect those objects to be qualitatively identical?

Constitutionalists evidently do not expect this. They are not surprised that two objects that are otherwise indiscernible should differ systematically in their mental or modal properties. Why not? Presumably it is because they take these differences to be primitive or brute: not explainable in terms of other differences. There is no saying *why* you would go along with your transplanted cerebrum and your animal body would not, or why you can think but the animal can't, because there is no other difference between you and the animal that *could* explain it. A human animal's inability to think is a primitive and basic feature of it. It just can't, and that's all there is to be said. Asking why a human animal cannot think is like asking why an electron is negatively charged: there is no more basic level of properties underlying it in terms of which it could be explained. Or maybe animals cannot think because they have the wrong persistence conditions to think (as Shoemaker argues), and their persistence conditions are brute. Each pair of coinciding objects must have some brute difference that explains the other differences between them.

Constitutionalists will point out that all things must have some brute properties or other: a thing cannot have every property it has by virtue of its having some other property. So why shouldn't a thing's persistence conditions and mental properties be brute?

Not many philosophers would agree that mental properties are brute. That would mean that there is no explanation of why some beings are conscious or intelligent and others aren't. At any rate, there would be no explanation in many cases. It may be that having a certain sort of brain is necessary for being intelligent or conscious. But only some of the beings with that sort of brain would be intelligent and conscious, and there would be no saying why those beings with that sort of brain that are intelligent and conscious *are* intelligent or conscious, and why those that are not intelligent or conscious are not. No amount of information about a being's brain structure, history, or surroundings would suffice to explain why it is conscious or intelligent. It would not even suffice to explain why a thing is *likely* to be conscious or intelligent, in the way that someone's being dealt three aces explains why she is likely to win the poker game. This would make mental properties deeply mysterious.

Constitutionalists may want to say that things' mental properties are not primitive, but only their modal properties—their persistence conditions, for instance—and use the difference in the modal properties of coinciding objects to explain their other differences. But it will not be easy to say how the modal properties of human animals prevent them from having mental properties.

And there seems to be something fishy in the claim that things' modal properties are primitive and entirely independent of their nonmodal properties. Suppose someone said that every person located in the Northern Hemisphere coincides materially with a being that is *essentially* in the Northern Hemisphere: an "essential northerner." (Perhaps Antipodeans coincide with essential southerners; perhaps not.) If you were to cross the equator from the North, the essential northerner coinciding with you would necessarily perish. Now it might occur to someone to ask *why* that being cannot cross the equator. You can cross the equator. And your essential northerner is otherwise just like you. What stops *him* from crossing? This seems to me to be a legitimate question—a question we should expect to have an answer. But if the modal properties that coinciding objects don't share are primitive, as constitutionalists are apparently committed to saying, it is not a legitimate question. That your essential northerner cannot exist outside the Northern Hemisphere would be a brute property of him, not explainable in terms of his having any other properties. Why can't he get across the equator? He just can't. Not even God could say why. That strikes me as an absurd thing to say.

Constitutionalists may say that it is absurd because essential northerners are absurd: it is absurd to suppose that any material object is essentially located in the Northern Hemisphere. And the existence of such things in no way follows from the claim that human animals coincide with beings that are essentially able to think in a certain way. That is fair enough—but then we shall want to know why human animals coincide with essential thinkers but not with essential northerners. What's the difference between the two cases? What makes one absurd and the other respectable? This is the topic of the next section.[8]

3.5 When Does Constitution Occur?

Let me mention two further worries about the constitution view. They may appear trifling compared with the thinking-animal problem. But many philosophers say that there is no such problem, or that it can be solved, or that it is troubling but outweighed by the constitution view's advantages. So these further worries may be important. In any case, they are interesting in their own right.

The first has to do with when one thing constitutes another. Constitutionalists say that certain qualitative properties have the following feature: necessarily, when an object acquires one of them, a new object comes into being which coincides materially with the first and has that property essentially. So when a sculptor models a lump of clay into the shape of Thatcher, the lump comes to coincide with a new object—a statue—that has that shape essentially. The lump could have any shape you like, but the statue—that particular statue—could not exist without having that shape. (Perhaps it is only an approximate shape.) Or again: when, in the course of its development, a human organism acquires a certain mental property (the capacity for self-awareness or for first-person thought or what have you), it comes to coincide with a new being—a person—that has that property essentially. Because most constitutionalists say that in these cases the original object constitutes the new object, we might call such properties *constitution-inducing*.

There is a complication. Constitutionalists deny that constituting objects always share the properties of the things they constitute. For instance, human organisms that come to constitute people never become self-aware themselves (or at least not in the way that the people are self-aware); otherwise human animals and human people would hardly be

[8] For more on the indiscernibility problem see Burke 1992; Levey 1997; Rea 1997b; Baker 2000: 27–58 and 167–90; Olson 2001b; and Bennett 2004.

worth distinguishing. Rather, the organism comes to constitute a being having the capacity for self-awareness essentially when it acquires some *other* property: perhaps a property, the having of which suffices for a thing to be self-aware if it belongs to the right kind or has the right identity conditions or the like. This other property might be the neural substrate of self-awareness, or the conjunction of the right neural substrate and appropriate surroundings.[9] And of course some properties that constituted objects are said to have essentially are properties that nothing could *acquire*: having certain persistence conditions, for instance. (Nothing can start out having one set of persistence conditions and later exchange them for a new set, incompatible with the first.) If a thing's acquiring a property P suffices for it to come to constitute a new object that has a property Q essentially, let us say that P and Q are *constitutional correlates*. So a property P is constitution-inducing if and only if, necessarily, whenever an object acquires P, it comes to coincide with a new object that has a constitutional correlate of P essentially. (This allows that a property might be a constitutional correlate of itself.)

A general question now arises: What properties are constitution-inducing? What properties are such that when a thing acquires one of them, it comes to constitute a new object that has that property or a constitutional correlate of it essentially? In other words, under what circumstances does constitution occur? What alterations in a previously existing material thing call a new material thing into being? I take it that this question must have an answer. At any rate, it must have an answer if constitutionalism is true.

I am not asking for a definition of 'constitution'—an account of what it would be for one thing to constitute another. That would not tell us when constitution occurs. Suppose we agree that, by definition, x constitutes y if and only if x and y coincide materially and it is possible for y to cease to exist while x endures and retains the same parts, but it is not possible for x to cease to exist while y endures with the same parts. Clearly we could still disagree about when these conditions obtain: you might take many properties to be constitution-inducing, whereas I might say that few are, or none. We could be like people who agree about what absolute moral rights would be but disagree about which such rights there are.

[9] I assume here that properties are, as the metaphysicians say, "abundant": that for more or less any description of a thing, there is a property that something has if and only if it satisfies that description. I therefore beg the indulgence of those who think that properties are sparse—that there are only "natural" properties, or only those properties that figure in ultimate basic physics, for instance. They may want to imagine my 'property' replaced by 'description' or 'condition'. I don't think anything in my discussion turns on this point.

There are three broad sorts of answers to this question. One is that no properties are constitution-inducing; that's what opponents of constitutionalism say. Another is that all properties are constitution-inducing: any alteration to any material object, no matter how trivial, necessarily results in its coming to constitute a new object that has the property thereby acquired, or a constitutional correlate of it, essentially. Third, it may be that some properties are constitution-inducing and others are not.

Call the claim that all properties are constitution-inducing the *generous view*.[10] It has the important advantage of being principled. If some properties are constitution-inducing, and others aren't, it seems fair to ask why the ones that are are, and why the others aren't—just as, if some people are rich and others aren't, we can ask why the rich ones are rich and the others aren't. The generous view can tell us why a given property is constitution-inducing: because all properties are necessarily constitution-inducing.

But the generous view is hard to believe. For one thing, every persisting material object has properties that change continuously: at every moment you acquire, among other things, a new shape and a new distance from the moon. So the generous view implies that you come to constitute a new being at every moment. During the time it takes you to blink your eyes, you pass through an uncountable infinity of shapes, and each of those minute alterations brings forth a new being, coinciding with you, that has that shape essentially.

Now this sort of ontological extravagance is not unique to the generous view: the ontology of temporal parts has a similar consequence. But the generous view is infinitely more extravagant than the ontology of temporal parts. Suppose you stand up, thereby coming to constitute a being, *S*, that is essentially standing. And suppose that as you are in the process of standing up, you also begin to frown, thereby coming to constitute a being, *F*, that is essentially frowning. Are *S* and *F* the same object, or different? (Suppose, if you like, that *S* and *F* go out of existence at the same time.) Do the things that have their posture essentially also have their facial expression essentially? We could ask the same questions about a thing's mass, age, distance from the moon, pH, net electric charge, and so on. Any material object acquires a vast number of new properties at any moment—perhaps an infinite number. How many new objects does it thereby come to constitute? And how are the properties a thing acquires (or their constitutional correlates) distributed essentially across the objects it then comes to constitute?

As far as I can see, the only principled way of answering this question is to be generous once more (Bennett 2004: 354): when you stand and

[10] It may be the view of Yablo (1987). Matthews (1982) thinks Aristotle held something like it. Bennett (2004: 354–359) argues that constitutionalists must accept it.

frown at once, you coincide with a being that essentially stands and contingently frowns, with a second being that contingently stands and essentially frowns, and with a third being that essentially stands and essentially frowns. More generally, for every nonempty subset of the set of qualitative properties you have at a given time, there is a being coinciding with you that has the members of that subset (or constitutional correlates of them) essentially and has the other properties you have at that time (or constitutional correlates of them) contingently. So if the number of properties you have at a given moment is n, the number of material things you coincide with at that moment will be a bit less than 2^n. That's a lot.

Worse yet, suppose you begin to think about Vienna. The generous view implies that you thereby come to constitute a being different from yourself that thinks about Vienna essentially (*you* don't think about Vienna essentially). It follows that whenever you think about Vienna, you are one of at least two beings thinking about Vienna (far more than two if the suggestion of the previous paragraph is right, but never mind that). You ought to wonder which one you are. Are you the one who was absorbed with things other than Vienna a moment ago, or the one that thinks about Vienna throughout the whole of its brief career? How could you ever know? This problem arises even if constitutionalists can explain why the animals that constitute us are unable to think in the way that we do; it has nothing to do with the mental properties of animals.

It is not surprising that most constitutionalists want to say that only some properties are constitution-inducing. But which ones? You might think that all and only *intrinsic* properties are constitution-inducing. But this is hardly better than the generous view. Many mental properties appear to be intrinsic; so it suggests that you coincide with many mental beings besides yourself. What's more, some constitutionalists say that constitution-inducing properties can be extrinsic (Baker 1997).

Baker proposes that a thing x constitutes something y just when "y has whole classes of causal properties that x would not have had if x had not constituted anything" (2000: 41).[11] If we use an anvil as a doorstop, she says, it holds open the door merely by virtue of properties it would have even if it didn't constitute anything. It acquires no new classes of causal properties. A person, by contrast, has many properties that a mere organism would not have if it didn't constitute a person, such as the capacity to

[11] For a proposal along similar lines, see Doepke 1996: chap. 8. Unlike Baker's proposal, Doepke's appears to have real implications about when constitution occurs. What those implications are, however, is unclear to me. His proposal deserves further development.

think about the future. That, she says, explains why certain organisms constitute essential people, but anvils never constitute essential doorstops.

Baker concedes that this is not a satisfactory account of when constitution occurs, but she thinks it is a helpful guide. As far as I can see, it is no help at all. Does the human organism now sitting in your chair constitute something? According to Baker's proposal, it does if there is something now coinciding with it that has certain causal properties that the animal wouldn't now have if it didn't constitute anything. Well, what causal properties *would* the animal now have if it didn't constitute anything? One answer is that it would have precisely the causal properties that you now have, including your mental properties. Another is that the animal would lack many of the mental properties you now have unless it constituted something that had certain mental properties essentially. How can we decide between these two answers? Only, it seems, by finding out whether the animal constitutes something. Those who think it doesn't will say that the animal would have all the causal properties that you have; those who think the animal constitutes an essential thinker will say that it would lack some of your causal properties. But whether the animal constitutes something is just what we wanted to find out. Those who have no idea when constitution occurs will be none the wiser for all Baker's proposal tells them. The same goes for other putative cases of constitution.

You might think that Baker's proposal gives at least a *necessary* condition for constitution, even if it is no good as a sufficient condition. That is, even if it tells us nothing about when constitution does occur, it might tell us something about when it doesn't—ruling out the generous view that all properties are constitution-inducing, if nothing else. It might imply that an anvil doesn't come to constitute an essential doorstop when we use it to prop open a door, because it thereby acquires no new classes of causal properties.

But I cannot see that it helps even here. Whether the anvil constitutes an essential doorstop depends on what causal properties the anvil would have if it didn't constitute anything. Baker says that an anvil used as a doorstop has the same causal properties whether it constitutes anything or not. But why suppose that? Someone *might* think that putting an anvil in front of an open door necessarily causes it to constitute an essential doorstop, and infer from this that if the anvil didn't constitute anything, it wouldn't keep the door open. Baker's proposal would give her no reason to change her mind. Those who deny that anvils ever constitute essential doorstops will find Baker's proposal equally consistent with their own view. Those who have no idea whether this is a case of constitution and want to find out will get no help.

Of course, it might be *silly* to suppose that putting an anvil in front of a door causes it to constitute an essential doorstop, with causal powers that the anvil lacks. But then some philosophers find it silly to suppose that the normal development of a human organism causes it to constitute an essential thinker, with causal powers that the organism lacks. Baker's proposal does nothing to help resolve these disputes. If essential doorstops are silly and essential thinkers are not, we should like to know why this is so, and Baker's proposal doesn't say. It implies nothing at all about when constitution occurs.

I have never seen a serious answer to the question of which properties are constitution-inducing, apart from 'all' and 'none'. Does it matter? Every philosophical claim raises questions that no one knows how to answer. Is this a problem for constitutionalism or merely an interesting topic for further research?

I think it is a problem. For one thing, if we have no idea what sorts of properties are constitution-inducing and no idea how to find out, it ought to undermine our confidence in the claim that any particular property is constitution-inducing—all the more so given that constitutionalists disagree widely among themselves about these matters. That would cast doubt on constitutionalism generally and on the constitution view of ourselves in particular.

More seriously, it is hard to combine the constitution view with any acceptable answer to this question. Most friends of the constitution view say that a human animal comes to constitute a person when it acquires a certain mental capacity (or its constitutional correlate). Suppose it is the capacity for first-person thought: when an animal acquires it, it comes to constitute a person that has that capacity essentially. This has the implausible consequence that we were never fetuses and that human beings in a persistent vegetative state are not, and do not constitute, the people by whose names we continue to call them. But never mind that. A human animal acquires all sorts of mental capacities (or their constitutional correlates) in the course of its development from a fetus into an adult. For instance, it acquires the capacity to have bodily sensations. It also acquires the capacity to have beliefs and desires, the capacity to think about the future, the capacity to do arithmetic, and many more. Friends of the constitution view say that just one of these capacities is constitution-inducing. (Otherwise each of us would coincide with a different thinking being for each constitution-inducing mental capacity.) They say, for instance, that a being can acquire the capacity to have sensations without thereby coming to constitute anything that has that capacity essentially, but no being can acquire the capacity to think in the first person without coming to constitute anything that has *that* capacity essentially. What is it about first-person thought that makes it, alone among mental properties, constitution-inducing?

If there is to be any answer to this question, it will involve the claim that the capacity to think in the first person is somehow uniquely special among mental capacities. But there doesn't seem to be anything uniquely special about it. Constitutionalists may point out that the capacity for first-person thought is a prerequisite for a wide variety of other mental capacities, such as the capacity to plan for the future. But many other mental capacities are equally special: the capacity to think at all, for instance, is a prerequisite for an even wider variety of mental capacities. The claim that the capacity for first-person thought, but no other mental property, is constitution-inducing seems arbitrary and unprincipled. It isn't just that we don't know what makes it constitution-inducing, but that it looks impossible to say.

Well, maybe it isn't the capacity for first-person thought that is constitution-inducing, but rather the capacity to think at all. (This seems to be Shoemaker's view.) That might sound less arbitrary. But is it? We have all sorts of capacities, some mental and some not. Why should that one in particular be constitution-inducing? Why not the capacity for sense experience? Or the capacity to move? Or the capacity to breathe? I cannot see any way of answering these questions. The constitution view looks inconsistent with any principled account of what properties are constitution-inducing—short of the generous view, anyway.

Someone might wonder whether there has to *be* any principled account of what properties are constitution-inducing. There must be some answer to that question if constitutionalism is true, but why suppose that the answer must be intellectually satisfying and not simply arbitrary? Could it not be that the capacity for first-person thought is constitution-inducing, and no other capacity is, and there is *no* reason why? Well, maybe. But if the facts about which properties are constitution-inducing are arbitrary, it is hard to see how anyone could ever know them.

3.6 What Determines Our Boundaries?

Here is the second worry. The constitution view says that I coincide materially with a certain animal. Its parts are my parts, and my parts are its. We share our spatial boundaries. This may be only contingently true—maybe I could come to coincide with something partly or wholly inorganic—but it is the usual situation. Why should this be so? *Why* is my boundary the boundary of this animal? What makes all and only the animal's parts my parts? What is it about my feet, for instance, that makes them, but not my shoes, or *your* feet, parts of me?

I am not asking for a causal or historical explanation of how my boundaries came to lie where they do, in the way that we might ask how

Texas came to be a part of the United States. Never mind history. I want to know what it is about the way I relate to my feet *now* that makes them parts of me now. This is analogous to asking what current geopolitical facts make it the case that Texas is a part of the United States rather than, say, a part of Mexico or an independent state. We could not understand how historical events affect a thing's current boundaries unless we understood what sorts of facts fix things' boundaries in the first place.[12]

I take it that this question must have an answer. Our boundaries may be indefinite—there may be things that are neither definitely parts of me nor definitely not parts of me—but even so we must *have* boundaries. And where they lie is no accident. According to the constitution view, they ordinarily coincide precisely with those of a particular animal and, moreover, continue to coincide with those of a human animal for the whole of our lives. This fact deserves an explanation.

If we were animals, what fixes our boundaries would be whatever fixes the boundaries of an animal. And we know what that is: an animal extends as far as its biological life extends (more or less; see §2.2). My feet are parts of this organism because they are caught up in its life; my shoes are not parts of it because they are not caught up in its life: they don't respond in the right way to the organism's metabolic activities. If I am not an animal, though, the mere fact that something is a part of this animal cannot make it a part of *me*. Nor can the fact that something is caught up in a certain animal's life, by itself, make it a part of me.

What might determine where our boundaries lie if the constitution view were true? It is not easy to say. Locke suggested that we extend spatially as far as our "consciousness" extends. Those particles, he said, that are "vitally united to this same thinking conscious self, so that we feel when they are touch'd, and are affected by, and conscious of good or harm that happens to them, are a part of our selves" (1975: 336). The idea is that my feet are parts of me because I can feel them or, more generally, because changes in them have an immediate effect on the nature of my experience. Of course, I cannot feel any particular atom, and no single atom is such that changes in it have an immediate effect on my experience, yet on Locke's proposal many atoms are parts of me. But an atom can be a part of a larger thing that I can feel, and any part of a part of me is itself a part of me. So we could say that our proper parts are those things that we can feel in this way, and the parts of those things. Most friends of the constitution view think that psychological facts fix our temporal boundaries—when we

[12] I speak indiscriminately here of what determines my boundaries and of what makes something a part of me. Though these are not strictly the same question (§1.1), in this context the difference is immaterial.

begin and end. This may lead them to think for similar reasons that psychological facts fix our spatial boundaries, just as Locke's proposal has it.

But a moment's reflection shows that this will not do. It implies that a limb that was completely numb would not be a part of you. An accident that left you numb and paralyzed from the neck down would literally reduce you to a head (or perhaps to something constituted by a head). An event that left you *entirely* numb, depriving you of all sensory input, would leave you with no parts at all. Since you could not exist without having any parts (even yourself, your "improper" part), this means that you could not survive in such a state, even for a moment. I take that to be absurd. For that matter, Locke's proposal implies that even in ordinary circumstances our boundaries are not the boundaries of a human animal. The reason is that you can't feel the whole of your animal body. You can't feel the blood flowing through your aorta, for instance. On Locke's proposal, neither your blood cells nor the atoms composing them are parts of you: you are smaller than a human animal. It follows that no animal constitutes you. So Locke's proposal is actually incompatible with the constitution view. Locke's proposal may seem like a straw man. There is probably a better account of what determines our boundaries that is compatible with the constitution view. But I have no idea what it might be.

You may suspect that there is really no problem here. It follows from most definitions of constitution that whenever one thing constitutes another, the two things share their boundaries and their parts (or at any rate there are things that compose each of them). Thus, given that we are constituted by human animals, as the constitution view says, our boundaries will be the boundaries of those animals. Those people who come to be constituted by things other than organisms will share their boundaries with whatever it is that constitutes them then. Friends of the constitution view might therefore seem to have a perfectly good account of what determines our boundaries: they are the boundaries of whatever it is that constitutes us.

Our being constituted by animals would indeed imply that our boundaries are those of our animal bodies. But rather than answering the question of what determines our boundaries, this proposal merely relocates it. The question is now what makes it the case that animals constitute us. Why not things a bit larger or smaller than animals? Granted, it *seems* to be human animals that constitute us if anything does, and not something bigger or smaller. But that appearance is nothing more than the fact that we appear to extend all the way out to our skin and no further. It does nothing to explain *why* we are constituted by things that extend all the way out to our skin and no further, rather than by things with a greater or lesser extent. This is a question that friends of the constitution view need to answer. At any rate, they are committed to its having an answer. And it will be no easier to answer than the original question of what determines our boundaries.

This problem might not seem unique to the constitution view. The question of why animals constitute us rather than bigger or smaller things may be a good one. But don't other accounts of what we are face a similar question? Take animalism. What could make it the case that we are animals, rather than things bigger or smaller than animals? Don't animalists need to answer this question? And won't their answer suit the constitution view equally well? Suppose animalists can say why we are animals and not bigger or smaller things. Wouldn't that also explain why we are constituted by animals and not by bigger or smaller things, if indeed that is the case?

It is true that both animalists and constitutionalists face similar questions—animalists about what makes it the case that we are animals and constitutionalists about what makes it the case that animals constitute us. We will consider how animalists might answer their question in §9.3. But the constitutionalists' question will be harder to answer than the animalists' question. There are two things animalists can say about why we should be animals rather than bigger or smaller things: they can deny that those bigger and smaller things can think, or they can deny that such things exist. (A third option would be to accept that such things exist and can think, and appeal to the "personal-pronoun revisionism" discussed in §2.7 to account for our ability to know that we are not those bigger or smaller things. I take it that neither animalists nor constitutionalists will be happy with this.)

What might prevent something bigger or smaller than a human animal from thinking? If anything, we should expect it to be the fact that it is not an organism. That only an organism could think is sometimes said to belong to the very idea of thinking (see §4.2). But whatever merits this may have as an explanation of why you are an animal rather than something bigger or smaller than an animal, it cannot explain why you are *constituted by* an animal rather than by something larger or smaller than an animal. In fact it is incompatible with the constitution view, which says that non-animals do think.

The second possible reason for supposing that we are animals rather than things larger or smaller than animals is that there simply *are* no such larger or smaller things. The only material thing that is even a candidate for thinking your thoughts—the only one that includes the neural machinery that makes your thought possible—is the animal. You are not your left-hand complement, for instance, because there is no such thing; those of your particles not located in your left hand do not compose anything. There are fewer material objects in the world than some philosophers have supposed. The animal is the only thing there that *could* be you.

Of course, if there is nothing bigger or smaller than the animal that could *be* you, there is also nothing bigger or smaller than the animal that could constitute you; so this story would also serve the constitutionalist as an account of what determines our boundaries. But no constitutionalist would touch it. Even if this sort of sparse ontology of material objects is consistent with the letter of constitutionalism, it goes completely against its spirit. One of constitutionalism's main attractions is that it provides a supply of objects rich enough to make true almost any metaphysical view about material things. Are you inclined to think that clay statues and lumps of clay, organisms and masses of matter, and people and organisms all exist, yet are numerically different, owing to their different essential properties? Constitutionalism will give you those objects. It is designed precisely to squeeze more things than you would have thought possible into the same place. It is an ontological shoehorn, the metaphysical equivalent of high-rise building. Once we start economizing with material objects, and especially if we have to economize on such a scale as to deny the existence of any parts of human beings big enough to include brains, constitutionalism loses its appeal.

We can illustrate this conflict by recalling the metaphysical puzzles about material objects that we considered earlier in this chapter. A sparse ontology of material objects can solve those puzzles by denying the existence of one or more of the entities whose apparent coincidence was puzzling—the statue, the lump, the person's hand complement, and so on. That solution has a high intuitive cost: the sparse ontology is hard to believe. (See §§7.4 and 9.5 for more on the sparse ontology.) Constitutionalism was supposed to solve those problems without that cost. It has a cost of its own, of course: something must be done about the thinking-animal problem, not to mention the problem of when constitution occurs. But you might still prefer it to the sparse ontology. If constitutionalism requires a sparse ontology as well, this benefit is lost; there is no point in paying twice for the same thing, especially if the price is high. That would be a good reason to consider accepting the sparse ontology without constitutionalism.

So neither of the things animalists can say about what determines our boundaries is any good for the constitution view. Constitutionalists need to give another account; or at least they are committed to there being one. But I cannot see what account they could give.

4

Brains

4.1 The Brain View

If we are neither animals nor material things constituted by animals, we might be parts of animals. This chapter is devoted to the view that we are spatial parts of animals; the next asks whether we are temporal parts. The only spatial parts of animals that I can think of any reason to suppose we might be are brains, or something like brains—parts of brains or perhaps entire central nervous systems. Call the view that we are something like brains the *brain view*.

The brain view says that we are identical with brains, not that we "are" brains in some looser sense. It is not the view that our brains are important to our being in a way that none of our other parts are. (That is not an account of what we are.) Nor is it that our brains constitute us, or that we are temporal parts of brains (views I will briefly discuss in §4.3). The brain view is that we are literally brains. So it implies that you are about four inches tall and weigh less than three pounds. You are located entirely within your cranium and made up mostly of soft, yellowish-pink tissue. In normal circumstances we never strictly see ourselves or each other. (Most of us would not want to.) This might sound like something out of a comic book. Some readers will already be thinking of jokes. Is it really a serious view?

One could defend the brain view by pointing out that even if you are a brain, it may still be true to say, in ordinary circumstances, that you are five or six feet tall, that you weigh more or less what the scales say when you step on them, and that you see yourself when you look in a mirror. These things might be true because your animal body has those properties. A brain can be six feet tall in the sense of having a six-foot-tall body. And that sense may be all we mean when we say, in ordinary contexts, that some of us are six feet tall. If so, the ordinary belief that some of us are six feet tall is perfectly compatible with the brain view. Those who believe that we are immaterial and have no physical properties at all have been saying this sort of thing for centuries: an immaterial thing can "be six feet tall" in the same sense as a brain can.

Whether such linguistic hypotheses make the brain view any easier to believe is debatable. It may only combine an absurd view about what we are with an implausible view about what we mean. When we say that Haroun is six feet tall, we don't *seem* to mean merely that he relates in a certain way to something or other that has the property of being six feet tall. We seem to mean that Haroun himself has that property. And there doesn't seem to be any sense in which Haroun is four inches tall.

In any case, the brain view is the sort of thing that only a philosopher would think of, and only at the end of a long chain of argument. That may be why it is hard to find anyone who seriously advocates it.[1] But even if no one thinks that we are brains, the view raises important issues that bear on other accounts of what we are. So we cannot avoid discussing it.

Why suppose that we are brains? Well, it would support the conviction that you could survive the loss of your fingers, legs, abdominal organs, and so on, but not the loss of your brain—that you could be pared down to a naked brain (or a part of a brain) but no further. (I don't say that this conviction is true, but it is widely held.) Of course, you couldn't survive for very long as a naked brain—at any rate, not without life-support machinery far beyond anything now in existence. But it may seem that you couldn't survive even for a moment without a brain. If you *are* your brain, the reason for this would be simple: destroying your brain would literally destroy you, whereas cutting away your limbs and other organs would only change your surroundings, albeit in a drastic way.

[1] Puccetti (1973) takes each of us to be a cerebral hemisphere, and Hudson (2001: 143) says we are temporal parts of brains. Tye (2003: 142) says that we are brains, but he appears to take it back on the next page. (His view may be that we are material things constituted by brains.) Though the view that we are brains is often attributed to Nagel, this does not appear to be his considered view (see Nagel 1986: 40). As far as I can see, Nagel has no account of what we are.

Likewise, the brain view fits nicely with the conviction that you would go along with your transplanted brain. According to the brain view, to transplant your brain is literally to transplant *you*: to cut you out of your head, move you across the room, and then re-house you in a new head. If you were any material thing other than your brain (or a part of it), the view that transplanting your brain would transplant you would appear to have the awkward implication that the surgeons would move *two* brain-sized things across the room—you and your brain—raising the awkward question of what the relation would be, in mid-transplant, between those two objects. (Friends of the constitution view have an answer to this question; but we have seen that it has its faults.) The brain view has the virtue of offering an entirely straightforward account of what happens in brain transplants.

Better yet, it offers a solution to the thinking-animal problem (Persson 1999: 521). Anyone who believes that we are not animals needs to say something about those human animals that appear to think our thoughts. Why don't they count as people? And what reason could we have to suppose that we are not those animals? Friends of the brain view can answer that in the strictest sense human animals don't think our thoughts: they think only in the derivative sense of having brains that think. The existence of *un*thinking animals, or of animals that think only in a loose sense, is no threat to the claim that you and I are not animals. To my mind, this line of thought offers the best argument for the brain view. More important, perhaps, it poses a problem for anyone who believes that we are not brains: What grounds could you have for supposing that you are something other than your thinking brain? Call it the *thinking-brain problem*.

4.2 The Thinking-Brain Problem

The brain is our organ of thought. We think with our brains, and not with our lungs or kidneys or any other parts of our bodies. The brain produces thought, much as the liver produces bile. So it seems, anyway. This suggests that the brain thinks. Just as the heart's function is to pump our blood, the brain's function is to think. (As before, let us take 'thought' and 'thinking' as broadly as possible, to include not only active cogitation but mental activity and states generally.) Philosophers of mind often say that if any material thing thinks, it is the brain; they ask whether a material thing could be conscious by asking whether a brain could be conscious. They ask whether mental states are physical states by asking whether they are brain states. But what could a brain state be, if not a state of a brain? And if a mental state is a state *of* something, that something ought to be the subject of that state, or at any rate *a* subject of it—that is, a thinking or conscious being. What more could it take for a thing to be conscious than for it to be in conscious states?

But if the brain thinks, that suggests that anything larger than a brain—a human animal, a thing constituted by a human animal, or what have you—could be said to think only in the derivative sense of having a part that thinks. Brains, by contrast, would think in the strictest sense. They would have the property *thinking*; larger things could, at best, have the property *having a thinking part*. But having a thinking part doesn't seem to be a way of thinking. The solar system, if there is such a thing, has many people as thinking parts. Yet *it* doesn't think. Not in any interesting sense, anyway. Maybe a human organism that thinks by virtue of having a thinking brain as a part bears a more intimate relation to the property of thinking than the solar system does by virtue of having a thinking person as a part, and this difference explains why we say that human organisms think and the solar system doesn't. Even so, if it is the brain that thinks, it looks as if nothing larger than a brain could think in the strictest and most straightforward sense. Anything larger than a brain could think only in a derivative sense—in the sense of having a special sort of part that thinks in the strictest sense. But isn't it obvious that *I* think in the strictest sense? Surely it couldn't turn out that it is something other than me that thinks my thoughts, whereas I myself think them only in some loose, second-rate sense. It follows that I could not be anything other than my brain. If the true thinkers of our thoughts—the beings that bear our mental properties in the most robust sense—are brains, then we must conclude, however reluctantly, that we are brains.

We can summarize this reasoning like this: (1) There is such a thing as my brain. (2) My brain thinks my thoughts in the strictest sense. (3) If my brain thinks my thoughts in the strictest sense, then anything else that thinks my thoughts does so only in the derivative sense of having a part that thinks in the strictest sense. (4) If anything thinks my thoughts in the strictest sense, I do. It follows from these four premises that I am my brain. Those who think that we are not brains are committed to denying one of them. Let us consider the prospects for resisting the argument.

Start with the fourth premise. Could it be that in the strictest sense I *don't* think? Surely not. If I know anything at all, I know that I think—not merely that it is correct to say in ordinary, nonphilosophical contexts that I think, but that I think in the strictest possible sense. At all events, I think my thoughts if anything does. It could hardly be the case that something *does* think my thoughts—some one thing—but I am not it. As Chisholm once said in another context:

> There is no reason whatever for supposing that *I* hope for rain only in virtue of the fact that some *other* thing hopes for rain—some stand-in that, strictly and philosophically, is not identical with me. . . . If there are thus two things that now hope for rain, the one doing it on its own and the other such that its hoping is done for it by the thing that now happens to constitute it, then I am the former thing and not the latter thing. (1976: 104)

That is how it seems to me. But I needn't insist on this point. Those who say that you and I—the beings we refer to with our personal pronouns—don't think in the strictest sense disagree with me only about words. As I said in §1.4, if the beings that think our thoughts are different from the beings our personal pronouns and proper names denote, the important matter is the nature of the beings that think our thoughts.

What about the first premise, that there is such a thing as my brain? This might seem hard to deny, unless we are idealists and deny the existence of material things generally. But some philosophers concede that there are particles "arranged cerebrally" within my skull, yet deny that those particles compose anything. There is nothing, they say, that has all those particles as parts, and all the parts of which overlap one or more of those particles. We encountered this sort of sparse ontology of material objects in the previous chapter, and we will return to it in §§7.4 and 9.5.

The third premise was that if my brain thinks, then anything else that thinks my thoughts does so only in the derivative sense of having a part that thinks. Though this looks right to me, I wouldn't defend it to the death. It is not generally true that whenever an object has a part that is *F*, that object itself is *F* only in the sense of having an *F* part. If my foot is injured, then I am injured, and not, it seems, merely in a loose and derivative sense. It seems that I am injured in the same sense as my foot is: I really do have the property *being injured*, and not merely the property *having an injured part* (though I have that too). Thinking might be like that: perhaps both my brain and I think in the strictest possible sense. If so, then the fact that my brain thinks provides no reason to suppose that I am a brain rather than, say, an organism, and the argument for the brain view fails.

Even if this is right, though, it would offer little comfort to those who think that we are not brains. If I am something other than my brain, yet my brain thinks in the same strict sense as I do, then I am one of at least two beings thinking my thoughts. That makes it hard to see how I could have any reason to suppose that I am the nonbrain that thinks my thoughts rather than the brain that thinks them. And we can hardly assert that we are not brains if we have no reason to suppose that this is the case. So even if the thinking-brain problem doesn't show that we are brains, it may show that we have no reason to suppose that we're not, and that would be trouble enough for anyone who rejects the brain view. We will return to this matter in §9.3.

Those who deny that we are brains are most likely to say that our brains don't think at all, contrary to premise 2. We *use* our brains to think, they will say, just as we use our eyes to see, but our brains no more think than our eyes see. Our brains do something necessary but insufficient for us to think. We think not by having thinking brains, but by having brains that do something other than thinking. Our brains may have neural structures that in some sense underlie mental properties, but they themselves lack those mental properties. We might call what the brain does "subthinking," as opposed to genuine thinking.

This attractive thought is surprisingly hard to defend. It is plain enough why our eyes don't see: the existence of open eyes in good working order in the presence of visible objects in good lighting is not enough for seeing to take place. What the eyes do is only a small part of the activity of seeing. You need more than just eyes in order to see: you need something like a brain as well. But you don't *seem* to need anything more than a working brain to think. It is a philosophical commonplace that a brain removed from someone's head and kept alive in a vat could think. (It may of course be false, but it is no less commonly held for all that.) Some doubt whether a brain that had *always* been in a vat could think, as it is unclear what could give its states any content—what could make them thoughts about Vienna, say, rather than about something else or about nothing at all—but this wouldn't prevent a brain that was removed from someone's head yesterday from thinking. And if a brain in a vat can think, why not a brain in a head?

Some say that thinking is a biological property that only an organism could have. This is the opposite of Shoemaker's claim (§2.5) that it belongs to the nature of mental properties that biological organisms *cannot* have them. If this is right, then our brains cannot think because they are not organisms. Now maybe a detached brain, kept alive in a vat, would actually *be* a biological organism: maybe you could make a human organism smaller by removing all of it except its brain, much as you can make a human organism smaller by amputating a finger (van Inwagen 1990b: 172–181). That would make the suggestion that thinking can be a property only of organisms compatible with the claim that a brain in a vat could think. But the brain view is not that we are detached brains in vats but that we are undetached brains in heads, and they are not organisms.

If it were absolutely impossible for anything but a biological organism to think, it would be big news. It would rule out the possibility of artificial intelligence, or at any rate inorganic artificial intelligence. The only way to create artificial intelligence would be to create an artificial biological organism that was intelligent. Gods, angels, and immaterial thinking substances would be impossible. For that matter, the view that only organisms could think would rule out every account of what we are apart from animalism and the view that we don't exist at all. That would make it a good deal easier to work out what we are! Until we see an impressive argument for this bold claim, we had best be on our guard.

Others say that it belongs to the very idea of thinking that no thinker can be a proper part of another thinker. Thinking, in other words, is *maximal*.[2] Given that I think, and that my brain is a part of me, it follows that my brain cannot think—though a naked brain that wasn't a part of a larger thinker might be able to think. A thing that was otherwise ideally suited to be a thinker might be unable to think merely because it had the wrong neighbors. I don't myself find this idea at all plausible. I find it hard to believe that an embodied brain should be prevented from thinking by its fleshy surroundings, and would blossom instantly into a thinker if only the flesh were removed. In any case, the maximality of thought would not explain why our brains cannot think. It implies that *if* a whole human being can think, then its brain cannot. But it also implies that if the brain can think, the human being cannot. And by itself it provides no support for one starting point over the other.

It may be that we don't ordinarily *call* what brains do 'thinking'. At any rate, we commonly apply the word 'thinking' to things the size of human animals, and we don't (it seems) commonly apply it to brains. And someone might wonder whether it is really possible for us to be mistaken about this. Surely it couldn't turn out that all the things we call 'cats' were really dogs and all the things we call 'dogs' were really cats. We can occasionally mistake a dog for a cat, but we couldn't all be thoroughly and systematically mistaken about which things are cats (assuming, at least, that there really are material things we call 'cats'). If none of the furry domestic animals that purr and chase mice were cats, what would give the word 'cat' its meaning? This might suggest that we could not be thoroughly and systematically mistaken about which things are thinkers either. Don't we *mean* by 'thinking' whatever it is that things the size of human animals do, and not whatever it is that brains do? What brains do may be very like thinking, but the way we speak shows that it does not fall within

[2] Burke 2003: 112–113. More precisely, Burke's view is that if x thinks, then no proper part of x whose particles would come to compose x if the rest of x's particles were annihilated can think. The complication is designed to make the maximality of thought compatible with the possibility of a thinker's being composed of many smaller thinkers in the way that a human organism is composed of cells. I will ignore it in the sequel.

the extension of the word 'thinking' or the concept it expresses. Therefore, the argument would go, brains don't think.

But the concept of thinking, or the meaning of the word 'thinking', does not appear to have built into it any restriction on the size or shape (or surroundings) of the things it applies to. The hypothesis that brains think and things the size of human animals don't think does not appear to conflict with the meaning of 'thinking' in the way that the hypothesis that all the things we call 'cats' are really dogs and all the things we call 'dogs' are really cats appears to conflict with the meaning of 'cat'. Many people have believed that the thinkers of our thoughts are immaterial souls rather than things the size of human animals. That view has its faults, but it doesn't appear to be internally inconsistent on account of the meaning of the word 'thinking'. It isn't like saying that wholly unconscious beings might think. The same appears to go for the hypothesis that brains think. Nor can anyone argue that if things the size of human animals don't think, we lose our grip on the meaning of the word 'think'. We can say a good deal about what thinking involves—for instance that it has to do with inner representational states mediating between sensory stimulation and behavior—without saying anything about the intrinsic nature of the beings that engage in it. That, indeed, is the main insight of the functionalist theory of mind.

Someone may doubt whether there is any hard fact of the matter as to whether brains think and human animals (or things the size of animals) merely have thinking brains as parts, or whether animals think and brains merely have neural properties that underlie thinking. Brains, the idea goes, have a property that is a good candidate for being called 'thinking', and animals have another property that is an equally good candidate, and that's all there is to it. To ask whether the brain property or the animal property is *really* thinking, or whether both are, is to ask an unanswerable question.

I don't think this idea is forced on us, though it is certainly a possible view. It would imply that it is indeterminate which things think our thoughts: whether it is brains, or things the size of human animals, or perhaps things of intermediate size—heads, say. Given that *we* think our thoughts, it would follow that it is indeterminate which things we are. It would not be definitely true that we are brains, but not definitely false either; and likewise it would be neither definitely true nor definitely false that we are animals, or things the size of animals. How big I am—six feet tall or small enough to fit into a shoe box—would therefore be indeterminate. And it would be indeterminate whether anyone has ever seen me. We might call this rather untidy account of what we are the *indeterminate-size view*.

The indeterminate-size view would appear to share most of the disadvantages of the brain view: troubles for the view that we are brains will equally be troubles for the view that we are not definitely not brains. (We will come to these troubles presently.) So we gain little if we try to resist the claim that our brains think by arguing that it is indeterminate whether brains or whole organisms think.

These reasons for supposing that our brains cannot think, or that they cannot think in the way that we can, are disappointing.[3] And the other ways of solving the thinking-brain problem aren't very nice either. This is bad news for those who suppose that we are not brains, and good news for those, if there are any, who suppose that we are. For all that, I believe we can resist the claim that the true thinkers are brains. First, though, I will consider objections to the brain view itself.

4.3 The Brain View and Our Identity over Time

What is the case against the brain view? We have already noted its implication that we are far smaller than we thought and that we never really see anyone. It also appears to have repugnant implications about our identity over time. For example, it would make it impossible for anyone to have different brains at different times: you cannot exchange your old brain for a new one if you *are* your brain. If Shoemaker's brain-state transfer machine were to copy the contents of your brain onto another brain while erasing the contents of the original brain (§1.7), then according to the brain view you would remain the original brain. The new brain would of course believe that it was you, but it would be mistaken.

The brain view would seem to make it impossible for us to become wholly inorganic. Many philosophers find it obvious that if your parts were gradually replaced with inorganic prostheses that duplicated the function of the organic parts they replaced, so that the resulting being always continued to think as you did, you would gradually come to have more and more inorganic parts and fewer and fewer organic ones until you were entirely inorganic (Baker 2000: 109; Unger 1990: 122). But it seems unlikely that any *brain* could become entirely inorganic. An organ that is now made up of living cells—that very thing—could not come to be made up entirely of metal and silicon.

[3] Burke 2003 gives further reasons, which I find equally unpersuasive. Logical behaviorists might argue that brains don't think because they have no observable behavior; but I doubt whether there are any logical behaviorists nowadays.

Our brains also appear to have histories different from our own. Physiologists tell us that our brains come into being early in our gestation, before arms and legs appear, and long before we are capable of having any mental properties. If they are right, then according to the brain view that is when we begin. That is, we begin well after conception but before we acquire any mental capacities.

Or consider Einstein's brain. A well-documented urban legend has it that Einstein's brain is kept in a jar in Kansas, in the possession of the pathologist who did the autopsy after his death. Suppose the legend is true. It says that Einstein's brain is now in a jar in Kansas. And the phrase 'Einstein's brain' as it occurs in the legend appears to refer to the thing that was once the brain in Einstein's head. If so, and if Einstein *is* the thing that was once (as we say) the brain in Einstein's head, it follows that the thing in the jar in Kansas is Einstein himself.

No one is going to be happy with all of this. The persistence of my brain does not appear to be either necessary or sufficient for *me* to persist. Now in deriving these unwelcome consequences of the brain view, I assumed a number of things about what it takes for a brain to persist. I assumed that you cannot move a brain from one place to another merely by transmitting information, that a brain cannot become wholly inorganic, and that a brain may continue to exist after the death of the organism of which it was once a part. And natural though these assumptions may be, they are not beyond question.

Perhaps a brain *could* become wholly inorganic. Perhaps it might one day be possible to point to a gadget made entirely of metal and silicon and say truly, "That machine was once made entirely of living tissue," or "That machine developed from a single cell."

Or maybe the thing in the jar in Kansas isn't really Einstein's brain, and was never in Einstein's head. Strictly speaking, it is may be only a sort of fossil relic of the organ that filled the great man's cranium: it is made of much of the same matter as that organ was when Einstein died, and has inherited many of its properties, much as a mineralized skeleton has many of the properties that a certain animal had when it died. It may be correct to describe this situation loosely by saying, as the legend does, that the thing is the jar "is Einstein's brain," just as the museum curator might call a fossil skeleton a tyrannosaurus. But for all that, it may be no more strictly accurate to say that the thing in the jar was once in Einstein's head than it would be to say that the skeleton in the museum was a fearsome predator 100 million years ago.

Someone might even propose that the brain-state transfer machine doesn't merely copy the psychological information from one brain onto another brain, but somehow moves a *brain* from one brain to another.

Perhaps, despite appearances, there are really *three* brains in the transfer story: the brain that the machine moves across the room, the brain left behind after the machine has done its work, and the brain onto which the first brain's mental contents get copied. We might call them the traveling brain, the donor brain, and the recipient brain, respectively. The transfer procedure would presumably bring the donor brain into being (otherwise there would have been two brains in the same place before the transfer, the traveling brain and the donor brain—leaving us wondering why the machine moved one of them but not the other). No brain would first have and later lack the donor's mental states. And the recipient brain, onto which the traveling brain's mental contents are copied, would presumably cease thereby to exist, else there would be two brains in the same place after the transfer, the traveling brain and the recipient brain.

These suggestions seem to me more interesting than plausible. No sort of psychological continuity *appears* to be necessary and sufficient for a brain to persist, for the same reason as no sort of psychological continuity appears to be necessary and sufficient for an organism to persist (§2.8). If brains really did persist by virtue of psychological continuity, however, it would be unsurprising if the same were true of human animals, thus rebutting one of the main objections to animalism.

A better response to these worries about identity over time (or at least to some of them) may be to say that the relation between a person and her brain is something more subtle than numerical identity. Some say that each of us is not strictly a brain, but rather a *functioning* brain, or a brain *insofar as it is in certain states*—states of the sort that make someone capable of thought and consciousness.[4] Because we are functioning brains—brains in the right states—we could not come to be nonfunctioning brains, brains in the wrong states. So the brain in the jar in Kansas is not Einstein. It is Einstein's brain, but not his functioning brain. And you and I were never rudimentary embryonic brains incapable of consciousness, even though our brains were. The suggestion has to be that a functioning brain is something numerically different from a brain, so that when a brain stops functioning in the relevant way it may persist in a nonfunctional state, but the functioning brain goes out of existence altogether. If your functioning brain *were* your brain, or if 'functioning brain' were simply what we call

[4] Tye says that we are "brains insofar as those brains are in the appropriate physical states (states sufficient for psychological states making up a single psychological framework)" (2003: 143). McMahan (2002: 88, 92) makes similar remarks—though he suggests a few pages later (94) that we have mental states as parts. In the same way, someone might try to avoid animalism's consequences about our identity over time by saying that we are "functioning animals" rather than animals.

a brain when it is functioning, then the view that we are functioning brains would be no different from the view that we are brains, and would have the same consequences about our persistence.

But what sort of thing is a functioning brain? How do functioning brains relate to brains—plain, ordinary brains that may or may not be functioning? (What sort of thing is a sleeping dog, and how does it relate to an ordinary dog that may or may not be asleep?) You might suggest that the functioning brain is something the brain *constitutes*, in the sense of §3.1, just when it functions in the appropriate way. Or perhaps a functioning brain is a temporal part of a brain: a part composed of those temporal parts of a brain that function appropriately. It is hard to see what else the claim that we are functioning brains could amount to, if it is to block the brain view's unwelcome consequences about our identity over time. Someone who took this line might also say that in special circumstances one of us might be constituted by different brains at different times, or by a brain at one time and by an inorganic gadget at another time. Or the view might be that one of us could be composed of temporal parts of two different brains, or of earlier temporal parts of a brain and later temporal parts of something inorganic.

But the view that we are things constituted by brains, or temporal parts of brains, is not the view that we are brains. It is not the brain view—though of course it resembles the brain view in obvious ways. These views may have an advantage over the brain view in that they agree better than the brain view does with what most of us are inclined to believe about our identity over time. But they also inherit the disadvantages of constitutionalism or the ontology of temporal parts. Moreover, they appear to face the same thinking-brain problem that arises for any other view according to which we are not brains: they make it hard to see how we can know that we are not the brains thinking our thoughts. They have no clear advantage over the view that we are constituted by or are temporal parts of whole organisms.

Those who say that we are brains will have to say some surprising things about our identity over time—though perhaps no more surprising than what they have to say about our size.

4.4 Thinking-Subject Minimalism

To my mind, the most serious problem for the brain view has nothing to do with its implications about our size or our identity over time. The real trouble is that it is unprincipled and that there is no good reason to believe it.

If we are brains, it can only be because the brain is our organ of thought and therefore is the thing—the only thing—that thinks our thoughts in the strictest sense. (We could hardly be *un*thinking brains.) The reason why no one ever supposed that we might be livers or stomachs is that no one ever took the liver or the stomach to be our organ of thought. But what makes the brain our organ of thought? That is, why should the things that think our thoughts in the strictest sense be brains and not, say, entire organisms?

Presumably the reason is that the parts of a thinker must all be in some sense directly involved in its thinking. Things larger than brains cannot think, except in the derivative sense of having a thinking part, because they have parts not directly involved in thinking. Yet not just any object, all the parts of which are directly involved in a being's thinking, is a genuine thinker. No individual brain cell thinks, even if all its parts are directly involved in thinking. That's because it doesn't produce thought on its own: for any cell that is directly involved in my mental activity, many other cells are involved in it in an equally direct way.

So the brain view appears to be based on the principle is that something is a part of a thinker—a genuine thinker, something that thinks in the strictest sense—if and only if it is directly involved in that thinker's thought, or mental life generally:

> If x thinks in the strictest sense at a time t, then y is a part, at t, of x if and only if y is directly involved in x's thinking at t.

Call this *thinking-subject minimalism*. It is hard to see how the brain view could be true unless something like this is right. Otherwise it would be completely arbitrary to say that we are brains.

Thinking-subject minimalism is not very plausible. We *seem* to have parts not directly involved in our thinking: fingers, for instance. Suppose a certain part of your brain became inactive, so that it was no longer directly involved in your mental goings-on. Minimalism implies that this would make you a bit smaller and lighter—but losing a finger wouldn't.

Still, it might have theoretical virtues. Consider the fact that there appear to be many candidates, of varying sizes, for being me: beings that seem to have all the equipment they need to think, and within which my mental activity takes place. There is my brain and various parts of it, such as my cerebral hemispheres. There are also many candidates larger than my brain: my head, my upper half, this entire human organism, and so on. For that matter, we might ask why I am not something bigger still, which has this organism as a proper part. If there really are all these beings, what could prevent them *all* from thinking my thoughts? And if they do all think my thoughts, how could I ever know which one I am? How could I ever know how big I am—whether I am the size of half a brain or the size of a planet? Thinking-subject minimalism might seem to solve this problem, by ruling out most of the candidates for being me on the grounds that they are either too big or too small to be genuine subjects of my thinking: too big because they have parts not directly involved in my thinking, or too small because not all the things directly involved in my thinking are parts of them. Then I could work out what I am by discovering which things are directly involved in my mental states and activities.[5]

So minimalism might tell us which of the many things that look like thinkers of our thoughts really do think them, thereby telling us which things we are. It would also appear to tell us what determines our boundaries and what makes things parts of us—something we wanted an account of what we are to provide. Animalism tells us that we extend as far as our biological lives extend, because that is what determines the boundaries of a living organism (§2.2). Minimalism seems to tell us that we extend as far as our mental states and processes extend, because that is what determines the boundaries of a thinking being. Not every view about what we are tells us what fixes our boundaries; we noted in §3.6 that the constitution view doesn't.

I have serious doubts about this story, however. Thinking-subject minimalism does not in fact tell us what beings think our thoughts. Nor does it tell us how big we are or what determines our boundaries—even supposing that we know which particles are directly involved in which thoughts. Suppose for the sake of argument that all and only the parts of my brain are directly involved in my mental states and activities. Or rather, to avoid assuming the point at issue, suppose that all and only the parts of my brain are directly involved in those mental states and activities I think of as mine, or those that any part of this organism is directly involved in. Suppose further that every mental state must have a subject. Would minimalism imply, in that case, that my brain (or at any rate something the size of my brain) is the subject of my thoughts, and therefore what I am?

No. Minimalism would not even imply that *any* thinking being is the size of my brain, let alone that I am. Suppose that one part of my brain is directly involved in some of those mental states and activities I think of as mine while another part, perhaps overlapping the first, is directly involved in the rest of them. Call them part one and part two, and call the mental states and activities they are directly involved in the part-one thoughts and the part-two thoughts, respectively. And suppose that every part of my brain overlaps part one or part two. (This story is not meant to be fanciful:

[5] Hudson makes this claim (2001: chap. 4). Because he believes that brains have temporal parts, some of which are not directly involved in producing thought, he takes thinking-subject minimalism to imply that we are certain temporal parts of brains rather than "whole" brains. We will return to the problem of how I can know how big I am in §9.3.

it doesn't require me to suffer from any sort of mental disunity.) Now it may be that both part one and part two are parts of me, in which case both the part-one thoughts and the part-two thoughts will be my thoughts, just as we should expect. But minimalism is also consistent with the view that the part-one thoughts belong to part one, the part-two thoughts belong to part two, and *no* being is the subject of both the part-one and the part-two thoughts. For all minimalism says, there may be just one thinker here—my entire brain—or there may be two—part one and part two. Nor does it rule out the possibility that the thoughts I think of as mine are divided among more than two thinkers. Minimalism will tell us the boundaries of a thinker only if we already know which thoughts belong to that thinker (as well as which particles are directly involved in those thoughts). But it doesn't tell us which thinkers there are or what thoughts belong to a given thinker. And so it doesn't tell us what our boundaries are. It doesn't tell me whether I am my brain, or part one, or part two, or something else.

Now we could rectify this by combining thinking-subject minimalism with a principle that assigns thoughts to thinkers: a principle that would tell us, for instance, whether the part-one thoughts and the part-two thoughts all belong to the same thinker or whether the part-one thoughts belong to one thinker and the part-two thoughts belong to another. That is, we need an account of when mental states or properties belong to the same thinker and when they belong to different ones.

The only such account I know of that is any use here is the psychological individuation principle of §2.9. This was the idea that mental states belong to the same thinker if and only if they are causally unified in the right way: if and only if they are disposed to interact with one another, and with no other mental states, in the way that is characteristic of mental states. Your desires tend to interact with your beliefs to produce action; roughly, your desire for something tends to cause you to act in ways that you believe will satisfy that desire, unless you have stronger competing desires. Your desires don't interact in that way with *my* beliefs. With any luck, it will turn out that all and only the mental states realized in your brain are unified in this way. The psychological individuation principle will then imply that the mental states realized there, but no proper subset of them, are the thoughts of a single thinker, and that thinker will of course be you (who else?). It will rule out the possibility that some of the mental states realized in your brain might belong to one thinker, whereas others belong to another thinker. Putting this together with thinking-subject minimalism and our assumption that all and only parts of your brain are directly involved in the mental states realized in your animal body, we get the conclusion that you are your brain (or something the size of your brain). We will see in §6.3, however, that the psychological individuation principle fits badly with the brain view; it seems to imply that we are bundles of mental states and not material things at all.

4.5 Direct Involvement

Whether or not thinking-subject minimalism can tell us where our boundaries lie, there are grounds for suspicion about the principle itself. One worry is whether the principle has any real content. The very idea of "direct involvement in a being's thinking" is suspiciously elusive.

One way to see this is to try applying the principle. What should we expect the true thinkers of our thoughts to be, according to minimalism? What thing is it that is composed of all the things directly involved in my thinking? (Let us assume that all the mental states I think of as mine really are mine and are not divided among several thinkers.) The brain view takes for granted that it is nothing larger than my brain: nothing outside my brain is directly involved in my thinking. This is questionable (Clark and Chalmers 1998; Schechtman 1997). Take visual experience. Aren't your eyes directly involved in your visual experience? You can't have visual experience without eyes, or at least something like eyes. But if your eyes are directly involved in your visual experience, then according to minimalism they are parts of you, and you are larger than your brain.

Even if nothing outside the brain is directly involved in my thinking, I am unlikely to be my brain. According to thinking-subject minimalism, brains will be too big to be genuine thinkers for the same reason as whole organisms are too big. The thing anatomy books call 'the brain' has many parts that appear to be no more directly involved in producing thought than the heart is. Blood vessels, for instance. If the thing that pumps the blood to the brain isn't directly involved in thinking, how can the vessels that distribute the blood within the brain be any different? Minimalism appears to provide no reason at all to suppose that we are brains. If we are anything smaller than whole organisms, we must be parts of brains.

But which parts? What parts of my brain are directly involved in my thinking? Its nerve cells, surely? Yet even that looks doubtful. No one knows exactly how nerve cells produce thought and experience, but it appears to have something to do with electrical and chemical signals that they store and communicate to other nerve cells. And a good deal of what goes on within a nerve cell appears to be no more directly involved in this storage and transmission of information than the activities of the heart and other vital organs are. Many parts of a nerve cell are involved in acquiring nutrients, or in expelling waste, or in maintenance and repair, or in maintaining the cell's boundary. They don't seem to be *directly* involved in whatever it is that gives rise to thought. Minimalism seems to imply that not even the whole of any nerve cell could be a part of a thinker.

This ought to make minimalists uneasy. If neither the whole of the brain nor even the whole of any nerve cell within the brain is directly involved in thinking, what *is* directly involved? This unease can only grow if we think about how to distinguish in a principled way between direct involvement in a being's thinking and indirect involvement. The point has nothing to do with thinking in particular. Imagine a factory that makes knives—an old-fashioned factory where the work is done mainly by hand, with no robots. All the factory workers are involved in some way in the manufacture of knives. Some deliver the steel; others beat it with hammers, sharpen the blades, stoke the fires, repair the tools, sweep the floors, run the canteen, keep the accounts, and so on. Which workers are *directly* involved in making knives, and which only indirectly? I don't think we can say. There may be some sense in the idea that those who actually work the steel are *more* directly involved in the making of knives than those who sweep the floors. But is there really an absolute distinction—even an imprecise one—between those who are directly involved in making knives and those who are only indirectly involved? We could of course draw such a distinction for legal purposes—to work out insurance costs, say. But wouldn't any such distinction be artificial?

Or think of walking. Which parts of a human being—which atoms—are directly involved in his walking? Those in his legs, surely. But are *all* the atoms in his legs directly involved in his walking? Suppose he has excess water in his legs owing to poor circulation, which hinders his walking. Are the atoms making up the excess water directly involved in his walking? (And what could determine which molecules are "excess" and which belong there?) What about his arms, or spinal cord, or heart? Is their involvement in his walking direct or indirect? Again, although we may, perhaps, be able to say which parts of a human being are more directly involved in his walking than others, there seems to be no principled way of saying which are directly involved and which are not. This is not because of any ignorance of the mechanics of walking: we should be just as baffled if we knew all that. Nor is the problem that the boundary between the parts of a human being that are directly involved in his walking and those only indirectly involved or not involved at all is indefinite, so that there are borderline cases that we cannot confidently classify either as "directly involved" or as "not directly involved." Asking which parts are directly involved and which aren't is like asking which rivers are long and which are not long. I see no reason to suppose that direct involvement in a being's thinking is any different from direct involvement in someone's walking or from direct involvement in making knives. Any decision about which are directly involved in its thinking is bound to be arbitrary.

I don't mean to say that there is no truth at all in the claim that the brain, and not the liver or the stomach, is the organ of thought. Many parts of the brain are probably more directly involved in thinking than any other parts of the organism, just as those who beat the metal are more directly involved in making knives than those who sweep the factory floor. And anatomists distinguish an organ called the brain from the rest of the organism because what they call the brain contrasts noticeably with its surroundings (though its boundaries are not so neat as the anatomy books suggest). That is why we call the brain the organ of thought. But this is only a loose description. A great deal goes on within the brain besides thinking, and a great deal that goes on outside the brain contributes vitally to thinking. To say that the brain, or some part of the brain, is what does our thinking is no more strictly accurate than saying that the people who beat the metal are the ones who make the knives.

If this is right, thinking-subject minimalism has very little meaning. Saying that all the parts of a genuine thinker must be directly involved in its thinking is like saying that all the parts of a genuine walker must be directly involved in its walking. Because there is no saying, even roughly, which things are directly involved in thinking, there is no saying even roughly which things, according to minimalism, are the parts of a thinker. Or if there is a nonarbitrary way of saying which things are involved in a human being's thinking, it is likely to be that they are all and only the parts of the organism. The organism has a nonarbitrary boundary, and it would appear to be the largest thing whose behavior we can explain in terms of its thinking. Though there may be a real sense in which thinking is something an organism does, there seems to be no real sense in which thinking is something a brain does.[6]

[6] Clark and Chalmers (1998) suggest that some of us are not parts of animals, but rather have animals as parts. We extend beyond our skin and are made up of all the matter that makes up our animal bodies and then some. That is because our mental processes might extend beyond the skin. Suppose I am forgetful and must constantly consult my diary. The information in my diary figures in explaining my behavior in much the same way as the information encoded in my brain does. In that case, Clark and Chalmers say, my intentions are located as much in my diary as in my brain. They infer from this that my diary is a part of me. This inference is presumably based on the principle that something is a part of a genuine thinker if it is directly involved in that being's mental processes—a close relative of thinking-subject minimalism. For this reason, "the extended self," as they call this proposal, appears to share the most serious problems of the brain view.

4.6 Homunculism

The view that we are brains is based on the idea that the parts of a genuine thinker are just those that are directly involved in its mental activity: thinking-subject minimalism. I have argued that there is no principled way of saying, even approximately, which things are directly involved in a being's thinking and which are not. This leaves minimalism with no content, and the brain view without support.

I have another worry about minimalism. It arises even if we can say which things are directly involved in mental activity and which are not. Imagine that we know what direct involvement in mental activity is. Now why suppose that the parts of a thinking being must be just those things that are directly involved in its mental activity? Why can't a thinker—something that thinks in the strictest sense—have parts that *aren't* directly involved in its thinking? In other words, why accept thinking-subject minimalism?

Minimalism is unsatisfying in isolation. If it is true, it ought to be true because it is an instance of some more general principle about the relation between a thing's activities and its parts. It ought to be true because any being engaged in *any* activity of a certain sort (in the strictest sense, not merely in the sense of having a part that engages in that activity) is composed entirely of things directly involved in that activity. We shouldn't expect this to apply only to mental activity. Thinking-subject minimalism ought to be true because it follows from something like this:

> If x engages (in the strictest sense) in states or activities of kind K at time t, then y is a part, at t, of x if and only if y is directly involved in x's K states or activities at t,

where K is the sort of activity that forces those things engaging in it to be made up entirely of things directly involved in it. We might call this *general activity minimalism.*

What general activity minimalism means depends on what K is—that is, on what kind of activity is special in this way. If mental activity in general belongs to that kind, then general activity minimalism entails thinking-subject minimalism: it entails that whatever engages in mental activity generally is composed of things directly involved in that activity. That would support the brain view. On the other hand, it may be that specific types of mental activity, such as seeing or remembering or philosophizing, are of kind K. The principle might entail that whatever sees must be made up entirely of things directly involved in its seeing. That is, general activity minimalism might entail not the "general" thinking-subject minimalism we have been discussing up to now, but what we might call *specific thinking-subject minimalism*:

> If x engages in mental activity of any specific kind at t, then y is a part, at t, of x if and only if y is directly involved in x's mental activity of that kind at t.

General activity minimalism cannot entail *both* thinking-subject minimalism and specific thinking-subject minimalism, for they are inconsistent. (Or at least it cannot entail both unless it is itself inconsistent.)

If thinking-subject minimalism supports the brain view, *specific* thinking-subject minimalism has implications that make the brain view look tame. If the brain and nothing outside it is directly involved in our mental activity, then different parts of the brain are directly involved in different sorts of mental activity. One part of the brain is directly involved in your visual perception; another part is directly involved when you try to remember someone's name; and so on. Specific minimalism appears to imply that the true subject of your current visual perception is the largest part of your brain that is now directly involved in your seeing: your current vision module, we might call it. And the true subject of your current philosophical thinking would be the largest part of your brain that is now directly involved in your philosophical thinking: your philosophy module. (Here we have to pretend that it is possible to say what part of your brain is directly involved in your seeing or your philosophizing. But if we could say what part of a human organism is directly involved in mental activity generally, this ought to be possible.)

If all of this makes sense, it is probably a safe bet that your vision module is not the same as your philosophy module. They may overlap, but they won't coincide exactly. It follows that no genuine philosopher—no being that does philosophy in the strictest sense—is a genuine "seer." One being now sees the book before you. Another being understands it. The one that sees the book does not understand a word of it, and the one that understands it sees nothing. Nothing both sees and does philosophy—not in the strictest sense, anyway. All true philosophers are blind. Reading, which involves both seeing and understanding, is an activity that nothing does, except in the derivative sense of having one part that sees and another part that understands. It is always a cooperative activity, like playing a duet.

More generally, given what we know about the division of labor in the brain, specific minimalism would make it unlikely that any being ever engages in more than one type of psychological task. Some see, some hear, some remember, some reason; but nothing does all these things, or even any two of them. For that matter, no one being is likely to engage in both short-term and long-term memory, or to reason about both geography and history. What we take to be one person with general mental abilities is in reality a vast colony of numerically different specialists, each of which performs only a single sort of mental task. Call this view *homunculism*.

It is hard to see how homunculism could be true. Suppose I run a finger over the arm of my chair. I feel its rough texture and hear the scratchy sound it makes. In order to do this, I must both feel and hear. But homunculism implies that nothing both feels and hears. I should have thought it was utterly obvious that I do both feel and hear. For that matter, homunculism implies that nothing both hears and is reflectively aware that it hears, for the atoms directly involved in hearing are unlikely to be exactly those that are directly involved in being aware that one is hearing. Homunculism looks incompatible with the most basic sort of self-knowledge (Chisholm 1981: 87–88).

You might suggest that the being that thinks, "I both feel and hear," needn't itself feel or hear but could be aware of another being's feeling and a third being's hearing as if they were his own. Then it might appear to me that I feel and hear even if I neither feel nor hear in reality. This would mean that a sensation or other mental state might appear to me for all the world to be mine even though it wasn't. I could be aware of a searing pain down my left side that seemed to be mine, even though it was not mine but someone else's. I might be aware of both a searing pain down my left side and a searing pain down my right side. The pains might be indistinguishable to me. For all I could ever know "from the inside," the pain in my left side might be mine, and the pain in my right side someone else's. Or it could be the other way round. Or it could be that neither was mine. I could never know, by introspection, which mental states were mine and which belonged to other beings. That, surely, is absurd.

Or consider what sorts of beings you and I might be if homunculism were true. There would be many candidates, so to speak, for being me. There would be the being that does my philosophical thinking, or at any rate the philosophical thinking I take to be mine. (Or maybe different beings would do different kinds of philosophical thinking.) There would be the being that composes my written sentences, and the being that tastes my food. For every sort of mental activity that I engage in, there would be a different being—the genuine subject of that activity—that is a candidate for being me. But what thing should *I* be?

I might be one of the candidates. Which one? Perhaps the one asking the question: If I know anything, do I not know that I am now wondering what I am? It would follow, given homunculism, that I am not the author of this book, for the atoms now directly involved in my wondering what I am are unlikely to be precisely the atoms directly involved in my writing. Now according to homunculism, this book is unlikely to have any *one* author; it is almost certainly a collaborative effort. But if I am now wondering what I am, then I am probably not any of this book's authors. It is doubtful even whether I wrote this book in the sense of having one of its authors as a part. Who's to say whether any of the authors within my brain is a part of the being now wondering what I am? More generally, few of the mental states I think of as mine would really be mine. Most of them would belong to beings that are not even parts of me.

Or perhaps I am not definitely any of the candidates. Rather, when I say 'I' or 'Olson' I refer ambiguously to each of them. In that case, it is presumably neither definitely true nor definitely false that I am the author (or an author) of this book, for although some of the referents of my 'I' were involved in writing it, many more were not. Nor will it ever be definitely true that I am feeling hungry, or thinking about Vienna, or in any other mental state.

Or I might be the thing composed of all the candidates. In that case it might be definitely true that I wrote this book, at least in the sense that all its authors are parts of me. But it would follow from this that I am probably not the true subject of any of my mental states or activities: I should reason, perceive, and remember only in the sense of having a part that reasons, a part that perceives, and a part that remembers. This would deprive the brain view of any attraction it may have had. There is no point in supposing that we are *brains* that think only in the sense of having thinking parts. If we have to accept that we think only in a derivative sense, we may as well say that we are whole organisms.

Homunculism is a hard view to like. Suppose it is false. Where does that leave the brain view? Well, the brain view assumes that whatever engages in mental activity generally is composed of just those things that are directly involved in its mental activity. But again, why suppose that? Why not suppose instead that whatever engages in some specific sort of mental activity, such as seeing, is composed of just those things directly involved in that specific activity? That leads to homunculism. Does anything support the brain view that does not equally support homunculism? (The other arguments for the brain view that we considered in §4.1 would support homunculism as much as they support the brain view.) In other words, is there any reason to suppose that thinking-subject minimalism is true rather than specific thinking-subject minimalism?

Call an activity such that whatever engages in it in the strictest sense must be composed of just those things directly involved in its engaging in that activity a *minimalistic* activity. Thinking-subject minimalism says that thinking or mentality in general is minimalistic. Specific minimalism says that specific types of thinking, such as remembering, are minimalistic. (Given how the brain works, thinking in general and remembering will not both be minimalistic.) Which is it? Is thinking in general minimalistic, or are specific types of thinking minimalistic? Or neither? What determines which activities are minimalistic and which are not? I have never seen an answer to these questions. Without such an answer, though, it is hard to see how anyone could be warranted in taking thinking in general to be minimalistic. And because the brain view depends on that claim, it too is unwarranted.

Someone might use the psychological individuation principle (§2.9) to argue that thinking in general is minimalistic whereas specific types of thinking are not. The principle says that particular mental states belong to the same subject if and only if they are causally unified with each other, and with no other states, in a certain way. Your seeing and your philosophizing are clearly unified in that way; so according to the principle they must belong to the same thinker. But there couldn't be a being that was the subject of your seeing alone—a being that none of the other mental states we attribute to you belonged to—for although its mental states would be unified with each other in the right way, they would be unified in that way with many other states as well. That would be an argument against specific thinking-subject minimalism and homunculism, but not against general thinking-subject minimalism and the brain view. However, for reasons we will come to in §6.3, the psychological individuation principle appears to be incompatible with our being brains.

To sum up: The main reason to suppose that we are brains is the idea that our brains are the true thinkers of our thoughts. That in turn is based on the claim that every part of a genuine thinker must be somehow directly involved in its thinking. But there appears to be no such thing as direct involvement in a being's thinking. And even if there is, there is no evident reason to stop at thinking. Why suppose that every part of a genuine thinker must be directly involved in its thinking, and not that every part of a genuine seer must be directly involved in its seeing? Whatever supports the brain view appears equally to support the absurd idea that genuine thinkers are specialists capable of performing only a single mental task. The brain view is unprincipled as well as implausible.

5

Temporal Parts

5.1 Four-Dimensional Hunks of Matter

Having considered the idea that we are spatial parts of human animals, I turn now to the view that we are temporal parts of them. The idea of a temporal part is notoriously confusing, and even professional philosophers often get it wrong. It is foreign to our ordinary ways of thinking in a number of ways. Learning to convert ordinary thoughts about persisting things into the ontology of temporal parts is a bit like learning a foreign language. I will try to explain in nontechnical terms what it means to say that we are temporal parts of animals. Despite my best efforts, however, I fear that some of what I am going to say will sound like Greek.[1]

You and I are extended in space. (We appear to be, anyway, though a few philosophers disagree. Suppose we are.) We seem to be extended in space by having different parts—spatial parts—located in different places. For instance, you are now both above and below the seat of your chair: partly above it and partly below. That is because you have a part, or several parts, that are above the seat of your chair—wholly above it—and another part, or several parts, that are entirely below it.

[1] The most comprehensive exposition of the ontology of temporal parts is Sider 2001b. Also recommended are Heller 1990: chap. 1; and Hawley 2001.

We also persist through time. (We appear to, anyway. Suppose we do.) Some philosophers think that we relate to time in much the same way as we relate to space. You have a location in time, just as you have a location in space. And just as you are extended in space, you are also extended in time: most of us extend for a bit less than six feet in space and for something less than a century in time. You are extended in time by having temporal parts spread out across time. Just as you are present in different places by having different spatial parts located entirely in those places, the idea goes, you are present at different times by having different temporal parts entirely located at those times. If you exist both in 2000 and in 2010, that is because you are partly in 2000 and partly in 2010. In other words, you have a temporal part located in 2000—located wholly during that year—and another temporal part entirely located in 2010. More generally, every part of you shares a part with one or more of your temporal parts: you are *composed* of temporal parts.

We all know what spatial parts are. They are just ordinary parts of spatial objects. If we know what 'part' means, we know that hands (if there are such things as hands) are parts—spatial parts—of human beings. But what are temporal parts? A temporal part of a thing is supposed to be a part of it that incorporates "all of that thing" for as long as the part exists. A temporal part of you is spatially just as big as you are, and located just where you are, while it exists. More precisely, a temporal part of you is a part of you that overlaps all of your parts that exist when that part exists (where 'overlapping' means sharing a part). If something is a temporal part of you, then any part of you that *doesn't* overlap that thing will exist only at times when that thing doesn't exist. So:

> x is a temporal part of $y =_{df} x$ is a part of y, and every part of y that does not overlap x exists only at times when x does not exist.

Your nose may be a part of you, but it is not a temporal part, for it doesn't overlap all of your parts that exist when it does. You have parts that exist when your nose does without overlapping it: your feet, for instance. Your nose doesn't incorporate all of you while it exists: it's too small to be a temporal part of you. But suppose there is such a thing as your first half. It would be just like you, apart from lasting half as long. It would walk and talk and study philosophy. It would take up all of you for as long as it existed. Any part of you that didn't overlap it—your final hour, say, or a certain wisp of gray hair—would exist only at times when your first half didn't exist. Suppose, if you can, that this thing would be a part of you. Then it would be a temporal part of you.[2]

[2] I say more about what a temporal part is in Olson 2006c.

We ordinarily think of events, such as games—particular matches that occur at particular times and places—as being made up of briefer events or phases, and these seem to be temporal parts of those longer events. A baseball game takes up time by having different parts located at different times. It starts at six and is still going on at ten past seven insofar as one part of it—the first inning, say—starts at six, and another part of it—the third inning—is going on at ten past seven. And each inning takes up "all of the game" while it is going on: any part of the game that doesn't overlap its third inning exists, or occurs, only when the third inning is not going on.

It also seems that any temporary property we attribute to the game at a particular time is a property that some temporal part of the game occurring at that time has without temporal qualification: the game is dull between six and twenty past because the first inning is dull—not dull at that time, but just plain dull—and exciting at ten past seven because the third inning is exciting. I will return to this important point in the next section.

Perhaps there is a long-running event consisting of everything you ever do and all that ever happens within your boundaries: call it your "history." Its temporal parts or phases include your birth, your first day at school, your adolescence, and your reading of this book. The view I want to consider is that *you* have temporal parts just as your history does. Most of those who take this view say that there is a temporal part of you coinciding with every portion of your history: a part for every time, instantaneous or extended, continuous or discrete, when you exist. So you have an infant-sized temporal part that extends from your birth until your first birthday, a part that extends from the midpoint of your history until your demise, a part that exists throughout June and August 2010 and at no other times, and many more. In fact you and your history may be so similar, on this view, as to be the same thing: you might *be* your history (Quine 1960: 171).

This view is often put by saying that we are "four-dimensional objects," because it says that we are extended in one dimension of time as well as the three dimensions of space (if that is how many spatial dimensions there are). Others put it by saying that we are "space-time worms," because space-time diagrams are typically drawn in a way that makes a person's spatial extent small compared with her temporal extent: six feet looks small on most diagrams compared with 80 years. These descriptions can be misleading. The view that we are space-time worms does not imply that units of time can be converted into units of space—so many seconds to the meter—so that we are literally longer in time than we are in space. We're not *really* worm-shaped. And the claim that we are "four-dimensional" by being extended in time is not strictly the same as the view that we are composed of temporal parts, for it may be that we are extended in time and yet lack temporal parts (Mellor 1998: 86). More generally, the name 'four-dimensionalism' has been given to a wide variety of views that have nothing to do with temporal parts. It might be better to call the view that all persisting objects are composed of many temporal parts simply "the ontology of temporal parts." However, I will sometimes follow custom and call it four-dimensionalism. I will call the view that we in particular are composed of many temporal parts the *temporal-parts view*.

Supposing that we exist and are located in time, there are two broad alternatives to the temporal-parts view. One is that we don't persist at all: what we think of as a single persisting person is really just one momentary person followed immediately by a similar but numerically different momentary person, followed by another, and so on. If we follow the jargon and call momentary temporal parts of things *stages*, the view is that we are stages rather than worms. We will return to it in §5.8. The other alternative is that we persist through time but have no temporal parts. (Or at least no *proper* temporal parts—no temporal parts other than ourselves. The definition of 'temporal part' appears to make everything located in time a temporal part of itself.) We don't fill up time by having temporal parts spread out across it. There is no such thing as your first half.

By itself, the temporal-parts view says little about what we are: only that we are persisting concrete objects composed of temporal parts. It leaves entirely open what *sort* of four-dimensional objects we are. For instance, it is compatible with our being bundles of mental states, or even immaterial substances. But most advocates of the temporal-parts view say that we are material objects—"four-dimensional hunks of matter," as Heller (1990) puts it. We might be animals, or brains, but the more common view is that we are proper temporal parts of animals (see §5.6). Most of what I will say about the temporal-parts view applies equally to all of these variants.

Those who think that we have temporal parts usually accept four-dimensionalism generally: they think that all persisting things are composed of temporal parts. Most say that nothing *could* persist without having temporal parts: for a thing to exist at different times *is* for it to have different temporal parts located at those times. A number of important arguments support the ontology of temporal parts (usefully surveyed in Sider 2001b). Two of them are of particular interest for the question of what we are, and they are the subjects of the next two sections.

5.2 Temporary Intrinsics

The most common argument for four-dimensionalism is that it offers the best solution to something called the *problem of temporary intrinsics*, or *problem of change* (Lewis 1986: 202–204; Sider 2001b: 92–98). Intrinsic properties are roughly those properties that a thing has by virtue of the way it is in itself: those it would share with any duplicate of itself. (This is not a satisfactory definition. Intrinsicness is notoriously hard to define. But it will do for present purposes.) Extrinsic properties—those that are not intrinsic—are those a thing has by virtue of the way it relates to things outside itself. Shape is an intrinsic property; being an uncle and being north of the equator are extrinsic. The argument is highly abstract, but it is essential to understanding the ontology of temporal parts (Olson 2006c).

I am now sitting down: I have a bent shape. An hour ago I was standing: I was straight and not bent. So I am bent, and yet not bent: somehow I both have and lack the intrinsic property of being bent. The same goes whenever something has any intrinsic property temporarily. For that matter, it goes for temporary *ex*trinsic properties. I am now an uncle, yet five years ago I wasn't; somehow I both am and am not an uncle. Now it is plain enough that nothing can literally be both bent and not bent. Logic ensures that nothing can both have and lack the same property, or have both that property and its complement. Yet I clearly relate in *some* way to both the property of being bent and the property of being not bent. What way is it? The problem of temporary intrinsics is to answer this question.

The answer might seem obvious. I am bent *now* and was not bent an hour ago. (Or, if you like, I am bent at noon and not bent at eleven.) For a thing to be bent is for it to be bent at some particular time. If someone is bent, we can always ask *when* he is bent; and there will always be an answer, even if it is that he always was and always will be bent. A persisting thing has its properties at particular times, and if something has incompatible properties such as bentness and straightness, it must have them each at a different time. That, we might say, is what time is *for*. The obviousness of this reply might even lead us to wonder whether there is really any problem of temporary intrinsics to be solved. Temporary properties seem problematic, the idea would go, only if we infer from my being bent at some particular time that I am just plain bent, without any temporal qualification at all, and if we likewise infer from my not being bent at some time that I am just plain not bent. But why should that follow? No one ever thought that deleting temporal qualifications was a valid mode of inference, like deleting double negations. And if we don't commit that fallacy, where is the problem of change?

But four-dimensionalists are not satisfied with this reply. Even if it is right that to be bent is to be bent at a particular time, they say, we need to explain what it is for something to be bent at a time, as opposed to being just plain bent. How does the temporal qualification—my being bent *now*, or at noon—block the inference to my being bent *simpliciter*? If my relation to the properties of bentness and straightness is not simply *having*, how do I relate to them?

The earlier thought that things don't just *have* temporary properties like bentness but have them at times might suggest that the temporal qualification is built into the having relation. So *having* or *instantiating* is a three-place relation involving an object, a property, and a time. Some things may have some properties without temporal qualification—maybe the number 7 is odd *simpliciter*—but that is another story.

Four-dimensionalists object that this makes intrinsic properties extrinsic. The proposal is that to be bent is to relate not only to a property, but also to a time. For a thing to be bent, it says, is for it to relate in a certain way to something outside it—a time. Whether a thing is bent or straight depends on how it relates to times, just as whether someone is an uncle depends on how he relates to other people. It follows, the complaint goes, that nothing could be bent in itself: "In itself, considered apart from its relations to other things," Lewis complains, a thing would have "no shape at all" (1986: 204; see also 2002: 4–5). Having a bent shape would therefore not be an intrinsic property. More generally, *no* property could be both temporary and intrinsic, for a property could be had temporarily only if that having were relative to a time in a way that would make it extrinsic. But we know that being bent is both temporary and intrinsic.

Whatever the merits of this reasoning may be, it has an important consequence: things must have their intrinsic properties timelessly, not relative to times. Whatever has bentness must be just plain bent, without temporal qualification; otherwise its being bent would be its bearing the having-at relation to bentness and a time, and being bent would not be intrinsic. That, the idea goes, is part of the nature of intrinsicness.

Four-dimensionalists solve the problem of temporary intrinsics in a way that respects this consequence. They say that things have different properties at different times by having different temporal parts, located at those times, that have the properties without temporal qualification. I am bent now insofar as the temporal part of me located at this moment is just plain bent. That part is not temporarily bent, or bent now, or even bent at every time when it exists. It is bent *simpliciter*, timelessly bent, just as 7 is timelessly odd. Its being bent involves no relation to a time whatever. That allows being bent to be intrinsic, as we always knew it was. Likewise, I am straight, and not bent, at some other time insofar as a temporal part of me located at that other time is timelessly straight. Moreover, I have those parts without temporal qualification. I don't have a straight temporal part at one time and lack one at another, for having a straight temporal part and not having one are no more compatible than being bent and being straight, and just as intrinsic. (My straight temporal part and my bent temporal part are *located* at different times, but they are not parts of me at different times.)

This means that I don't simply *have* either the property of being bent or the property of being straight. How then do I relate to those properties? Am I bent, or am I straight? The answer is neither: I simply have a bent temporal part and a straight temporal part. (Compare the spatial analog: Am I hand-shaped, or am I foot-shaped? Neither: I simply have a hand-shaped part and a foot-shaped part.) My relation to the property of bentness is that of having a part that has that property *simpliciter*. My relation to the property of straightness is that of having another part that has *that* property *simpliciter*.

So according to four-dimensionalism, when we say that a thing has different intrinsic properties at different times, we are speaking loosely. The strict truth of the matter is that the thing has different temporal parts, located at those times, that have those properties without temporal qualification. In the strictest sense, I don't have the properties of bentness or straightness at all. My properties are not *being bent* or *being straight*, but rather *having a bent part* and *having a straight part*. If I had bentness and straightness (or *being bent* and *not being bent*), I should have to have them relative to times, which four-dimensionalists say would make my shape objectionably extrinsic. Nothing can strictly have both bentness and straightness, since they are incompatible, and nothing can have either property relative to a time, since they are intrinsic; thus, whatever has bentness must be bent and not straight *simpliciter*. So the things that are bent or straight are brief temporal parts of me, rather than I myself. I *can* have the intrinsic properties *having a bent part* and *having a straight part*, though, for unlike bentness and straightness they are compatible. I can have them without temporal qualification.

The argument for four-dimensionalism, then, is this: There are intrinsic properties, such as bentness and straightness, that each of us in some sense has. Because these properties are intrinsic, we cannot have them relative to times, but must relate to them in some timeless way. But we cannot simply *have* them timelessly, for they are incompatible: nothing can be both bent and not bent. Therefore I am bent now only in the sense of having (timelessly) a temporal part located now that is bent *simpliciter*, and I was straight an hour ago insofar as I have another temporal part located then that is straight *simpliciter*. It follows that I have at least two temporal parts. Moreover, the fact that my intrinsic properties are continuously changing—the way my atoms are arranged, for instance, is changing continuously, owing to their constant motion—implies that I have a different temporal part for every moment I exist. And what goes for me goes for concrete objects generally.

Ironically, this argument has the very consequence it accuses the opposing view of having, namely that no property could be both temporary and intrinsic. If, *per impossibile*, something did first have and then lack an intrinsic property such as bentness, then according to the argument that thing would both have and lack it, for bentness, being intrinsic, can only be had or lacked without temporal qualification. According to four-dimensionalism, no intrinsic properties are temporary. Our momentary temporal parts have properties such as bentness, and we have properties such as having bent parts; but nothing has those properties temporarily. (This presumably goes for extrinsic properties as well: I am an uncle now insofar as I have a temporal part located now that is an uncle without temporal qualification. No one will suppose that I bear a timeless, two-place instantiation relation to intrinsic properties and a three-place instantiation relation involving a time to extrinsic properties.)

For this reason and others, four-dimensionalists disagree about the persuasive force of the argument from temporary intrinsics. That is, they disagree about how much better their own solution to the problem of change is than the alternative view that things have temporary properties relative to times.[3] Even so, they nearly all agree that their solution is *true*: that persisting, changing objects don't strictly have temporary intrinsic properties, but instead have short-lived temporal parts that have intrinsic properties timelessly. This seems to belong to the very idea of a temporal part. We will see the importance of this in §5.7.

5.3 Lumps and Statues

Four-dimensionalism has important theoretical virtues. One of them is its capacity to solve problems about the identities of material objects in a different way from constitutionalism (see Sider 2001b: chap. 5, for a detailed discussion).

Recall the clay-modeling puzzle (§3.2). A shapeless lump of clay is modeled first into a statue and then into a cube. We want to say that the same lump of clay is first shapeless, then statue-shaped, then cubical, but that the statue is never shapeless or cubical. If this is so, then the statue and the lump must be two different things. Constitutionalists say that the statue and the lump are numerically different even though they coincide materially, making the statue physically indistinguishable from the lump

[3] There is more than one alternative to the four-dimensionalist's account of change, but the one I have sketched here seems the most plausible. Haslanger 2003 is a useful guide to this messy debate.

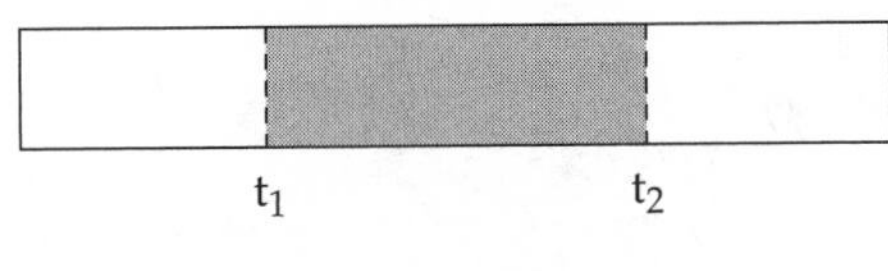

FIGURE 5.1

at every time when the statue exists. But we expect physically indistinguishable material things to be indistinguishable in all their intrinsic properties. So their view makes it a mystery how the two objects could differ in their qualitative properties (§3.4). For instance, what could give them different persistence conditions?

Four-dimensionalists say that the statue is a temporal part of the lump: the largest such part that is statue-shaped. (Suppose the lump is made into a statue only once.) We can illustrate this with a space-time diagram, where the vertical axis represents space and the horizontal axis time (Figure 5.1).

The statue is made at t_1 and squashed at t_2. The whole "worm" is the lump, and the shaded part in the middle is the statue. The lump is composed of earlier temporal parts that have a nondescript shape, later temporal parts that are cubical, and intermediate temporal parts shaped like Thatcher (as it may be); it is these last that compose the statue. So the lump and the statue don't coincide materially, in the sense of there being things that compose both of them: the lump has temporal parts—timelessly has them—that are not parts of the statue and do not even overlap any parts of the statue. That is what makes the two objects qualitatively different. We can explain the qualitative differences between the statue and the lump in terms of the differences in their parts: the lump is different from the statue because it, but not the statue, has temporal parts that are not statue-shaped. The lump and the statue are no more alike than a baseball game and its third inning are alike.

In the replacement puzzle (§3.3), we burn a clay statue's arm to ashes and replace it with a new arm made of different clay (where this is the only change of parts in the statue's history). We want to say that the statue persists through this change, whereas the lump of clay is destroyed and replaced by a new lump. Constitutionalists say that the statue coincides materially first with one lump and then with another. Four-dimensionalists say that the statue is (timelessly) composed of spatiotemporal parts of two different lumps.

In Figure 5.2, the first lump, L1, occupies the forward-slashed space-time region; the second lump, L2, occupies the back-slashed region. If we suppose again that the statue is made at t_1 and squashed at t_2, it occupies

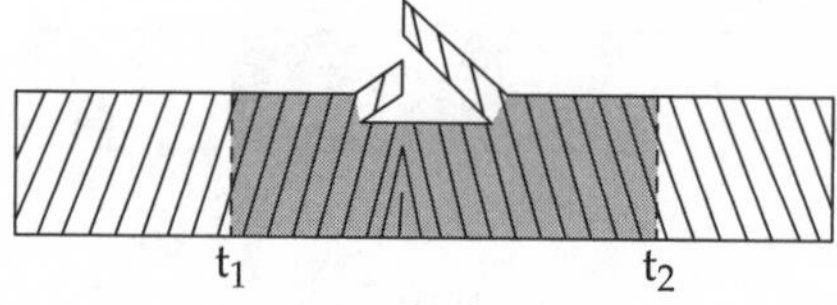

FIGURE 5.2

the shaded region between those times. The earlier part of the statue, on this view, is a temporal part of L1; the later part of the statue is a temporal part of L2. The statue is not identical with either lump; but neither is it composed of the same parts as either lump. Neither lump coincides materially with the statue. Again, the qualitative difference between the statue and the two lumps is explained by their having qualitatively different temporal parts. (The four-dimensionalist's solution to the amputation puzzle is similar; we will come to it in §7.4.)

5.4 The Problem of Modal Incompatibility

The four-dimensionalist's story about lumps and statues may sound agreeable, particularly in comparison with constitutionalism. So it may seem to support the claim that persisting objects, including ourselves, are composed of temporal parts. There is, however, something about this story that we might find deeply puzzling.

Suppose we ask *why* the statue ceases to exist when we squash it, but the lump doesn't. According to the story, there is no physical difference between the statue and the lump when we squash them, for they share all their temporal parts while they both exist. How, then, can objects that are physically identical at a time and treated in the same way behave so differently at that time? Wasn't this our objection to constitutionalism? Four-dimensionalists say that we are to explain the qualitative difference between statue and lump in terms of their having qualitatively different temporal parts. That seems to imply that the statue perishes and the lump carries on in the clay-modeling story because the lump has certain temporal parts located after the squashing and the lump hasn't. But that is no explanation at all. It is like saying that Descartes ceased to exist in 1650 because his history doesn't extend beyond that year.

If squashing a clay statue really does, necessarily, destroy the statue without destroying the lump it is made of, we expect the reason to be that lumps have something statues lack, namely a power or capacity to survive squashing. Otherwise it would be a mystery why clay statues always perish when squashed, yet lumps of clay never do. If lumps and statues didn't differ in this way, we should expect them to behave more or less alike when squashed, and we should be unable to say confidently of any statue that if it *were* squashed it would perish. But such a difference in capacities appears to be incompatible with the ontology of temporal parts.

We can make the problem more vivid by imagining a case where a lump and a statue *always* coincide. Imagine a lump of clay that comes into being shaped like Thatcher and retains that shape throughout its history without losing any parts. In that case, the lump and the statue will share all their parts, temporal and otherwise (at any rate, there will be things that compose both the statue and the lump). They will coincide materially. Four-dimensionalists say that in this case the lump *is* the statue; otherwise they would face the troubles of constitutionalism. Yet the lore of lumps and statues tells us that any lump of clay *could* survive being squashed, even if it never is. Otherwise their differing behavior under pressure would be a mystery. If this is right, then four-dimensionalism is committed to these three claims:

1. The lump (in our story) could survive squashing.
2. The statue could not survive squashing.
3. The lump = the statue.

And these claims look inconsistent. If the lump *is* the statue, how could it—that one thing—be able to survive squashing, yet also unable to survive it?

The same problem arises in the case of people and animals. Most philosophers, including four-dimensionalists, want to say that if your cerebrum were removed from your head and kept "alive" and functioning in a vat, and the rest of you were destroyed, you would survive as a detached cerebrum. (This seems to follow from the conviction that you would go along with your cerebrum if that organ were transplanted.) But no human animal could survive if its cerebrum were preserved and the rest of it destroyed. That seems to give human people and human animals different modal properties: different persistence conditions.

This may not look like a problem if your cerebrum actually is removed and kept alive. In that case you are not an animal; you are, rather (according to the temporal-parts view), composed of the preoperative temporal parts of an animal and the postoperative temporal parts of a cerebrum. But of course that isn't going to happen. Your history will coincide exactly with that of an animal, so that every proper temporal part of that animal is a part of you and vice versa. You and the animal coincide materially. In that case, four-dimensionalists will say that you *are* that animal. How, then, could it be the case that you, but not the animal, could survive as a detached cerebrum? Friends of the temporal-parts view will want to say things like these:

4. You could survive as a detached cerebrum.
5. No animal could survive as a detached cerebrum.
6. You are an animal.

And these claims are no more consistent than the others.

Now many four-dimensionalists say that we are not animals, even though there are no cerebrum transplants. Suppose that having certain mental properties is necessary for being a person; and call a more-or-less momentary temporal part of an organism that has those properties a *person-stage*.[4] Then it may be natural to suppose that a person must be something made up entirely of person-stages. (We will come to the question of which person-stages would go to make up a person in a moment.) Because every human animal starts out as an embryo with no mental properties at all, no human animal is composed entirely of person-stages. Alternatively, you might think that the stages of a person must all be in some way psychologically continuous with one another, whereas the embryonic stages of a human animal are not psychologically continuous with anything. Either way, it follows that human people, and therefore we ourselves, are not animals. We are, at best, proper temporal parts of animals—parts that include no unthinking embryonic stages.

But it makes no difference here whether we are animals or temporal parts of animals, for if the persistence conditions of animals have nothing to do with psychology, neither do those of their temporal parts. So the view that we are temporal parts of animals appears to imply this:

4. You could survive as a detached cerebrum.
7. No temporal part of an animal could survive as a detached cerebrum.
8. You are a temporal part of an animal.

And these too look inconsistent.

The general problem these cases illustrate is that things the temporal-parts view says are identical appear to have incompatible modal or dispositional properties—properties that appear to figure in the explanation of why those things cease to exist when they do. Because you are a person,

[4] This assumes that a more-or-less momentary object can have the sorts of mental properties characteristic of people: thinking, for instance. And that may be doubtful. Four-dimensionalists generally say that a momentary thing can have mental properties if it has the right causal antecedents (Sider 2001b: 197–198). What something does for a moment might count as thinking in part because of what other beings do at earlier (and perhaps later) times, in something like the way that an event counts as the turning point in a war because of what happens earlier and later. Given what we said earlier about temporary intrinsics, four-dimensionalism appears to require this. It implies that thinking is an extrinsic property. The subject of momentary thinkers will come up again at the end of §7.4.

you could survive as a detached cerebrum; but because you are an animal or a temporal part of an animal, you couldn't. Call this the *problem of modal incompatibility*.

Some four-dimensionalists take a tough line here: Quine, for instance, denies that there are any modal properties at all (1960: 199), and Heller says that all material objects have their spatiotemporal boundaries essentially (1990: 53). Either view would make at least one proposition of each triad false, or at any rate not true.

But most four-dimensionalists want to accept the modal convictions that feature in the first two claims of each triad. They try to solve the problem by saying that the appearance of inconsistency is an illusion. You could survive as a detached cerebrum, they say, and the animal or animal part that you are could not survive it, yet these claims are consistent. The reason is that the modal predicate 'could survive as a detached cerebrum' expresses one property in 5 and 7 and a different property in 4. When we say that you could survive as a detached cerebrum, we mean that you *qua person* could survive it. When we say that no animal could survive as a detached cerebrum, we mean that no animal *qua animal* could survive it. So it would be more perspicuous to write 4 and 5 like this:

4*. You, qua person, could survive as a detached cerebrum.
5*. No animal, qua animal, could survive as a detached cerebrum.

This does not express a modal difference between you and your animal body. Both you and that animal have the property of possibly surviving as a detached cerebrum qua person, and you both lack the property of possibly surviving as a detached cerebrum qua animal. Thus 4* and 5* are consistent with the claim that you are an animal. The same holds, mutatis mutandis, for the other cases.

This means that that there are no absolute, unqualified modal properties of the form *being possibly F* or *being necessarily G*, but only qualified or kind-relative modal properties of the form *being possibly F qua person* and *being necessarily G qua animal*. If there were such a property as *possibly surviving as a detached cerebrum*—not possibly surviving it qua this or qua that, but just plain possibly surviving it—then we should want to say that you have that property, and that no animal or temporal part of an animal has it, thus raising the problem of modal incompatibility all over again.

So what are these qualified modal properties? What do the qualifications 'qua person' and 'qua animal' *mean*? Many views are possible, but the most familiar is counterpart theory (Gibbard 1975; Lewis 1968, 1971, 1986: 248–263). The ordinary view of modal properties is that for a thing to be possibly *F* is for it to be *F* at some possible world. Counterpart theory says that for a thing to be possibly *F* is not for *it* to be *F* at a world, but for a "counterpart" of it at a world to be *F* at that world.[5] A counterpart of you at a world is a thing at that world that is at least as much like you as anything else at that world, and is enough like you that we are willing to treat it as a modal stand-in for you. (The thing most like you at a certain world might be a chimpanzee. If we are not willing to consider how things would be if you were a chimpanzee—if our response to your question, "What if I were a chimpanzee?" were always, "You couldn't be a chimpanzee"—then there would be no counterpart of you in that world.)

So far this is no help. If you have a counterpart at a world that survives as a detached cerebrum, and no animal (or temporal part of an animal) has such a counterpart, then you cannot be an animal (or a temporal part of an animal). But things can be similar in different ways: something might resemble you in origin and physical composition, say, but not in psychology and behavior. And because the counterpart relation is based on similarity, whether a thing is a counterpart of you may depend on what respects of similarity are relevant in the context. So there appear to be as many different potential counterpart relations as there are respects of similarity. If we say that you are possibly *F*—that is, that some world has a counterpart of you that is *F*—we don't say anything determinate until we specify a particular counterpart relation—that is, a particular respect of similarity. And it needn't be the same one each time: a modal predicate can express different counterpart relations in different contexts.

So when we say that *you* could survive as a detached cerebrum, we might mean that you have a *personal* counterpart at some world—someone who resembles you in "personal" respects—who survives as a detached cerebrum at that world. Now whatever else a personal counterpart of something might be, it ought to be a person. Suppose a person is by definition a being composed of person-stages, each of which is psychologically continuous, in some appropriate way that is open to debate, with every other and with nothing else: a *maximal psychological continuer* for short.[6] Then any being that fails to go along with its transplanted cerebrum is not a maximal psychological continuer, and therefore not a person, and so not a personal counterpart of you or of anyone else. Thus, every

[5] For the sake of simplicity I am here indulging in the fiction that there *are* things that exist only in other possible worlds: things that don't actually exist but might have existed. Although Lewis believes that this fiction is true, counterpart theory can be formulated in a way that does not require it (Stalnaker 1986).

[6] This has the interesting implication that personhood is an extrinsic property: whether a thing made up of appropriately connected person-stages is a person depends on whether it connects in that way to any other person-stages. If personhood were intrinsic, the temporal-parts view would have the absurd consequence that every connected temporal part of a person is a person.

personal counterpart of you whose cerebrum is removed and kept alive will go along with that organ. Presumably there *are,* at some possible worlds, personal counterparts of you whose cerebrums are removed and who go along with those organs. (At least this is so according to the ontology of temporal parts: see note 8 on page 120.) And the personal pronoun 'you' in the sentence 'You could survive as a detached cerebrum' makes the personal counterpart relation the relevant one. That makes it true to say that you could survive as a detached cerebrum.

When we say that no *animal* could survive as a detached cerebrum, on the other hand, we might mean that no animal has an *animal* counterpart at any world—something that resembles it in "animal" respects—that survives as a detached cerebrum at that world. An animal counterpart of something must presumably be an animal itself. An animal, according to four-dimensionalism, is a thing composed of animal stages related to one another and to nothing else in a certain biological way that I won't attempt to specify. And because a detached-cerebrum stage is not an animal stage, nothing made up partly of detached-cerebrum stages is an animal. Thus, no animal, and no animal counterpart of anything, survives as a detached cerebrum at any possible world. So nothing has an animal counterpart that survives as a detached cerebrum. The word 'animal' in the original sentence makes the animal counterpart relation the relevant one. That is why it is true to say that no animal could survive as a detached cerebrum.

So the claim that you could survive as a detached cerebrum but that no animal (or temporal part of an animal) could survive it, understood in terms of counterpart theory, is compatible with your being an animal (or a temporal part of an animal). Similar remarks apply in other cases: the claim that any lump could survive crushing but no statue could, understood in terms of counterpart theory, is compatible with the claim that some statues are lumps.

Whether counterpart theory is the right account of modal properties is disputed, and I will not enter into this dispute here. The point is that friends of the temporal-parts view must either reject the modal claims about people and animals that we have discussed or else endorse counterpart theory (or some other view according to which modal predicates express different properties depending on their context). Some philosophers find this a sufficient reason to reject the ontology of temporal parts (van Inwagen 1990a).

Even if we accept counterpart theory, however—or, for that matter, if we follow Quine in denying that there are any modal properties at all—the question remains: Why do statues but not lumps always cease to exist when squashed? Four-dimensionalists deny that there is any modal or dispositional difference between a statue and its coincident lump: the lump, they say, hasn't got any capacity to survive that the statue lacks. Statues and lumps are modally indistinguishable. So their modal properties play no role in explaining why they cease to exist when they do. What does it explain it, then? What accounts for the striking difference in the actual behavior of lumps and statues when we squash them?

Four-dimensionalists reply that there is no explanation: the question is based on a misunderstanding of the nature of persisting objects. For every period of time when a lump of clay exists, they say, there is a temporal part of the lump located exactly then. It follows from this that there is a temporal part of our imaginary lump that extends from the time when it is made Thatcher-shaped to the time when it gets squashed. That is the thing we call the statue of Thatcher. Why does that object cease to exist when it gets squashed? What stops it from carrying on for a bit longer and simply changing its shape? The four-dimensionalist's answer is that nothing stops it. That is simply where its temporal boundary lies. To ask why it comes to an end when it does is like asking why a given period of time comes to an end when it does. Why does the 20th century come to an end at the end of 1999? What stops it from going on for a bit longer? The question is based on a misunderstanding of the nature of periods of time. The only answer we can give is that we wouldn't call a period of time that extended beyond 1999 the 20th century. But that is an answer to a different question, one not about why a particular thing ceases to exist when it does but about why we talk the way we do. It is the same with the lump and the statue. There are temporal parts of the lump that extend beyond the time when we squash it, but for one reason or another we don't call them statues. And that is all the answer we can give to the question of why the statue doesn't continue to exist after we squash it. (That does not mean, however, that nothing could have lasted longer than it did. Our statue could have lasted longer, for there are "statue" counterparts of it that do last longer.)

This is one of the aspects of the temporal-parts ontology that is most foreign to our ordinary thinking. Foreign or not, however, four-dimensionalism is a powerful theory of persisting objects.

5.5 Puzzles of Personal Identity

We have seen that the ontology of temporal parts offers an important solution to metaphysical puzzles about the persistence of material things, including ourselves. And we saw that this solution comes at the cost of requiring modal predicates to be inconstant: it implies that in a sense you could survive as a detached cerebrum, but in another perfectly good sense you couldn't possibly exist in that state. Here are some further implications of the temporal-parts view.

The "brain-state transfer" machine of §1.7 was supposed to record the psychological information encoded in your brain (thereby erasing that organ) and copy it onto another brain (thereby erasing that organ's previous contents). Some say that this process would literally move you from one human organism to another. But we may wonder what sort of thing *could* move from one animal to another in this way. What sort of thing could be sent as a message by telegraph? Not a material thing, surely?

The ontology of temporal parts implies that a material thing *can* move, in a sense, from one human animal to another via brain-state transfer. Perhaps no material thing would move from one place to another in the sense of passing through all the points in between, but there would be a material thing that was first in the one place and later in the other. There would be a material thing made up of the temporal parts of the "donor" animal located before the adventure and those of the "recipient" animal located afterward. That thing would be rational and intelligent in the same way as you are (supposing that you are material), for it would share your rational, intelligent stages. So the machine would bring it about that a rational, intelligent being is first in one place, associated with one human organism, and later in another place, associated with another organism. Those who believe that we can move from one animal to another via brain-state transfer will say that this being would be you. Thus, the temporal-parts view is compatible with the claim that you could swap animal bodies via brain-state transfer.

But the temporal-parts view is also compatible with the claim that you could not swap bodies via brain-state transfer. The animal that ends up with your mental contents in the story does not inherit them from you in anything like the usual way. If you did swap bodies, your mental capacities would not be continuously physically realized. This suggests that you would have a gap in your history: you would cease to exist while the machine does its work, then come into being once more when the work is finished. (Suppose the machine records the psychological information from the first brain, then prints it on sheets of paper. Much later, the information is entered by hand into a second machine, which then reconfigures the second brain to match the first one. In what form could you exist after the first brain is erased but before the second brain is reconfigured? What sort of thing could you be then?) And we might deny that any material thing could exist intermittently. The temporal-parts view can accommodate this conviction.

The ontology of temporal parts provides three salient candidates for being you in this case. First there is the one that stays behind: the human animal whose mental contents are erased when the machine does its work and then lives on as a sort of human vegetable. Second, there is the one that ceases to exist: the temporal part of the first animal that extends from its beginning (or from the point where it first acquires mental capacities of the right sort) until its mental contents are erased. Finally, there is the one that gets transferred: the thing composed of the pretransfer stages of the first animal and the posttransfer stages of the second (or at least those stages of them that have the right mental properties). On the usual ontology of temporal parts, these three beings all exist. The question of what happens to you in the brain-state-transfer cases is the question of which of them is you.

Friends of the temporal-parts view say that this depends on which of them counts as a person, for you are the only person in the story. Now all three candidates are rational, intelligent, and self-conscious, at least for a time, and the ordinary view is that being rational, intelligent, and self-conscious suffices for being a person. (Don't we call a rational, intelligent, self-conscious being a some*one* and not a mere some*thing*?) But friends of the temporal-parts view deny this. They have to, or else there would be far too many people in the world: not only would all three candidates in the brain-state-transfer story count as people, but so would most of your temporal parts. (Remember that on the ontology of temporal parts, a being is intelligent at a time by virtue of having a temporal part located then that is intelligent without temporal qualification.) A person, they say, must consist of stages that are not only rational, intelligent, and self-conscious, but that also relate to one another in the right way.

There is room for disagreement about what this way is: whether it is continuously physically realized psychological continuity, psychological continuity of any sort, some wholly nonpsychological relation, or what have you. This is the old debate about personal identity over time—the persistence question of §1.6—transposed into the ontology of temporal parts. Those who say that personal identity over time consists in continuously physically realized psychological continuity will call the candidate that ceases to exist when the machine does its work the person. Those who say that any sort of psychological continuity suffices will call the one that gets transferred the person, whereas those who think it is something wholly nonpsychological will probably say that the candidate that stays behind is the person.

Who is right? They might all be right. According to four-dimensionalism, all three candidates exist, and all three satisfy some reasonable definition of the word 'person'. Those who appear to disagree about which candidate is the person may only be using the word 'person' in different senses. More generally, those who appear to disagree about what it takes for a person to persist through time may all be right. They may not disagree at all. They may only be talking about different beings—about "people" in different senses of the word. There are people in the sense of beings composed of person-stages related to one another, and to nothing else, by continuously physically realized psychological continuity—"conservative people," we might call them. There are people in the sense of beings composed of person-stages related to one another by psychological continuity of any sort—"liberal people." And so on. Different accounts of personal identity over time are accounts of the identity over time of different sorts of people. Friends of the conservative psychological-continuity view have given the right account of the persistence of conservative people; those who prefer the liberal psychological-continuity view have given the right account of the persistence of liberal people. For that matter, those who say that our identity is animal identity have given the right account of the persistence of "animal people." *Any* proposed account of what it takes for us to persist through time will presumably be the right account of the persistence of beings of some sort that are plausible candidates for being people. (Or almost any account. The view that you persist if and only if your immaterial soul continues to exist will not be the right account of the persistence of anything unless there are immaterial souls, and four-dimensionalism in no way implies that there are.)

This would vindicate the common view that the facts about personal identity over time are in some sense up to us to decide. According to four-dimensionalism, the facts are up to us to decide insofar as it is up to us which sorts of "people" to talk about (Olson 1997b; Sider 2001a). No other view of what we are (with the possible exception of the bundle view, some versions of which incorporate the ontology of temporal parts) has this consequence. Whether this speaks in favor of the temporal-parts view or against it will be a matter for debate.

Here is one more point about our identity over time. The temporal-parts view is the only account of what we are that is consistent with the attractive idea that some sort of psychological continuity suffices for us to persist. It seems possible for a person to be psychologically continuous, by any standard, with two future people. Let each of your cerebral hemispheres be transplanted into a different head. It is easy to believe that you could survive if one hemisphere were destroyed and the other were transplanted, so that the operation produced only one being psychologically continuous with you. But it seems impossible for both offshoots to be you, for there are two of them and only one of you, and two things cannot be numerically identical with one thing. (Suppose one of the offshoots had a beard, and the other didn't. If both were you, you would both have a beard and not have a beard at the same time, which most of us regard as a contradiction.) And the claim that just one of the two offshoots would be you would make it a mystery which one it was, and why. This leads many philosophers to say that you could survive a single transplant but not a double transplant: if two beings each got half your brain, that would be the end of you. It follows that psychological continuity is not sufficient for you to persist: you may perish even though a later person is psychologically continuous with you. Only "nonbranching" psychological continuity suffices. But it is hard to believe that you could fail to survive the transplant merely because it produced two beings, rather than one, that were psychologically continuous with you.

Friends of the temporal-parts view are able to say that you *can* survive the double transplant (Lewis 1976). You survive, so to speak, as both offshoots. That is because in fission cases there are, in effect, two of you all along, who share their preoperative temporal parts but not their postoperative parts. One of them starts when you do and then goes along with your left cerebral hemisphere in the operation; the other has the same beginning but goes along with your right hemisphere. But they do not coincide materially; they merely overlap, like two railway lines that diverge after having a section of track in common. Thus, as long as someone is psychologically continuous with you in the right way, you survive. It doesn't matter if more than one is.

This has the surprising consequence that if there is fission in your future, there are two people sitting there and thinking your thoughts even now—though they look for all the world, even to themselves, like one. To know whether they are two or one—or, more generally, to know how many people there are at any one time—we need to know what the future holds. (This is not a case of backwards causation, however. The fission operation doesn't *cause* it to be the case that there are two people there earlier. It simply makes it the case, in a noncausal way, that the pre-fission stages are parts of two people rather than one.)

The story the temporal-parts view tells about fission is surprising in other ways too. You might want to know which person *you* are. Suppose the one who gets your left hemisphere—"Lefty"—will be in pain after the operation, whereas the one who gets your right hemisphere, "Righty," will be comfortable. Will *you* be in pain? The temporal-parts view suggests that when we say 'you', we refer to that person whose stage we are addressing. If that stage is a part of more than one person, as the preoperative stages in the fission story are, we refer ambiguously to both. So if there is fission in your future, we refer at once to two different people when we say 'you' (supposing we refer at all, anyway). Our sentence 'You will be in pain' says two things at once, one true and one false. It is like saying that the planet between the earth and the sun is cloudy. One of you will be in pain, the other not. But we cannot say that either of those people is you. To say that you are Lefty is, at most, half right, because only one of you, as it were, is Lefty; and the same goes for the claim that you are Righty. Nor can we say that either person is not you. So we can know what happens to all the people in the story, and yet not know what will happen to you. The question we so urgently want answered—will you be in pain?—is unanswerable, based as it is on the false presupposition that the pronoun 'you' refers to only one being, or at any rate that all of the beings it refers to share the same fate.[7]

Friends of the temporal-parts view will point out that we say similar things about analogous spatial cases, such as railway lines that share their tracks at one place and diverge at another. How many lines there are here depends on what is the case elsewhere. And simple questions such as whether this line goes to Tulsa may have no straightforward answer because the expression 'this line' refers ambiguously to two lines, one of which goes to Tulsa and one of which doesn't. The logic, we might say, is impeccable. But that may not make the story any easier to believe. It may only be a reason to deny that fission is like spatial branching—that is, to deny that we have temporal parts.

And although the proposed view implies that psychological continuity is sufficient for our identity over time in the sense that you persist if someone in the future is psychologically continuous with you, it implies that psychological continuity is *not* sufficient for our identity over time in another sense: not every future being who is psychologically continuous with you is you (Parfit 1976; see also Lewis 1983). Lefty is not psychologically continuous, before the operation, with Righty as he is afterward. A person can be psychologically continuous with someone other than himself.

5.6 Thinking Animals and Other Worries

We saw that the constitution view faces a problem about those human animals that think our thoughts and perform our actions but which, according to that view, are not ourselves. A similar problem arises for the temporal-parts view. Most four-dimensionalists say that we are not animals, but maximal psychological continuers: beings composed of person-stages, each of which is in some way psychologically continuous with each of the others and with no other stages (§5.4). Since all human animals have embryonic stages that are in no way psychologically continuous with anything (and some have senile stages not psychologically continuous

[7] Blackburn (1997: 181) makes a similar complaint. The semantic theory developed in Perry 1972 is intended to avoid this consequence.

with anything), this means that we are, at best, temporal parts of animals. Yet four-dimensionalists cannot deny that the animals we are parts of think. They say that for a persisting thing to think at a time is for it to have a temporal part located at that time that thinks; and since your thinking stages are all temporal parts of a human animal, the animal thinks just as you do. So according to the temporal-parts view, you share your thoughts with an animal numerically different from yourself. And you ought to wonder, it seems, how you could ever know that you are not the animal.

Four-dimensionalists could avoid the consequence that our bodies are thinking animals other than ourselves by saying that we *are* animals. That would mean giving up the idea that any sort of psychological continuity is necessary for us to persist. (They could still say that it is sufficient for us to persist by appealing to counterpart theory.) But it wouldn't help, for on their view your current stage is a temporal part of a thinking maximal psychological continuer as well as a temporal part of a thinking animal. So you would still face the problem of how you could know whether you are the animal or the maximal psychological continuer. That is why most animalists deny the existence of maximal psychological continuers and thus reject four-dimensionalism generally.

In fact four-dimensionalism implies that there are all sorts of beings now thinking your thoughts. Your current stage is a temporal part not only of a maximal psychological continuer and an animal, but also of the first or second half of that animal. And it is a part of a vast number of gerrymandered and badly behaved objects: the thing made up of the temporal parts of your animal body located before midnight tomorrow and the temporal parts of Kilimanjaro located thereafter, for instance, and the thing made up of the temporal parts of the moon located before last Friday, the temporal parts of my left ear located after tomorrow, and the temporal parts of your animal body located in between. All of these objects, by virtue of sharing your current thinking stage, now think in the same sense as you do. So there are far more beings sitting in your chair and thinking about philosophy than we thought.[8]

How could you ever know which of these beings you are? It is bad enough not knowing whether you are the animal or the maximal

[8] At any rate, all four-dimensionalists that I know of believe in these objects. They accept universal composition for momentary stages: for any momentary temporal parts of any objects whatever, there is an object that those things compose. One might be able to accept an ontology of temporal parts without holding this: perhaps one could say that only some momentary stages compose something. But that would prevent one from saying many of the things four-dimensionalists want to say; see, for instance, §5.3 and Sider 2001: 120–139.

psychological continuer. Now it seems you ought to wonder whether you are the first or second half of the animal or one of the countless gerrymandered objects that share your current stage. What grounds could you possibly have for accepting any of these alternatives? If you really had no idea which thinker you are, you would have no idea what your future holds. The fact that there will be a human person tomorrow who is psychologically continuous with you as you are today would be no reason at all for you to believe that *you* will be a human person tomorrow. As far as your evidence in the matter would go, you could just as well be an enormous volcano tomorrow.

Faced with this absurd prospect, friends of the temporal-parts view appear to have no option but to embrace personal-pronoun revisionism, the linguistic hypothesis discussed in §2.7. The idea is that your current temporal part is a part of only one *person*. There is room for disagreement about just what counts as a person, but any reasonable definition of 'person' will imply that there is just one being of that sort now thinking your thoughts: just one maximal psychological continuer, for instance.

Or at least this is nearly true. The usual temporal-parts ontology implies that for every person (in any ordinary sense of the term), there is another being just like it but a nanosecond longer or shorter—a being entirely indiscernible from the first by any practical means, and just as good a candidate for being a person. So in reality there is not one person there, but a large class of more or less indiscernible and mostly overlapping people. This is a version of what Unger (1980) calls the *problem of the many*. It suggests that it is indeterminate which of those beings *you* are. This is of course not very attractive. Four-dimensionalists point out that we would "count those people as one" for ordinary purposes: when all the people in a certain situation overlap and differ from one another only trivially, those of us who are not engaged in metaphysics describe this by saying that there is just one person there (Lewis 1976, 1993). And perhaps it shouldn't worry us too much if we cannot know which of *these* beings you are, or if all ordinary ways of referring to you are ways of referring to all of them ambiguously, since we can't tell them apart anyway. For that matter, the problem of the many is not obviously unique to the temporal-parts view: anyone who thinks that we are material things will have to say something about those beings, if there are such, that are just like us but larger or smaller by a single particle.

But the important point here has nothing to do with the problem of the many. It has to do not with the surplus of good candidates for being you, but with the surplus of bad candidates: the human animal (if you are a maximal psychological continuer), the animal's first or second half, and all the arbitrary and gerrymandered objects that share your current stage but diverge wildly at other times. Pronoun revisionism says, first, that these beings are not people. Second, personal pronouns, first-person thoughts, and other "personal" referring devices denote only people. Third, as a competent speaker of English, you know that your first-person thoughts and utterances must refer to a person if they refer at all. So if you know what it is to be a person, you can work out (subject to the caveat about "the many") which of the beings that share your current stage you are.

This proposal has the repugnant consequence that the vast majority of rational, intelligent speakers are not people. Nor can they refer to themselves in the first person—not, anyway, in the language they actually speak. Their language also prevents them from having first-person thoughts about themselves. That is a strange sort of disability. If the ontology of temporal parts is true, however, and if most of what we say in ordinary life about ourselves and others is right—if it really is true to say that you will be a human person tomorrow and that you were never a satellite of the earth—then it seems that some such linguistic hypothesis must be correct. We may not like it much. But the alternatives might not be very nice either.

5.7 Thinking Stages

I come now to what is perhaps the most serious objection to the temporal-parts view. Recall the problem of temporary intrinsics (§5.2): How can a persisting thing have incompatible properties, such as sitting and standing? Four-dimensionalists say that for a thing to sit at a time is for it to have a temporal part located at that time that has the property of sitting without temporal qualification. I sit now only insofar as my current stage sits. Assuming that I persist, I don't strictly have the property of sitting at all, but rather the property of having a sitting part. And what goes for sitting goes for temporary properties generally.[9] Given that persisting things change continuously, it seems that the things that strictly have ordinary properties must literally be momentary: only a momentary being could

[9] The property of being 43 years old might seem to be an exception: I don't have it now by having a temporal part located now that is 43 years old. Four-dimensionalists will deny that there is any such property. Otherwise things would have to have it relative to times, and four-dimensionalists hold that all things have all their properties without temporal qualification. They will say that the sentence 'Olson is 43 years old', uttered at a time t, expresses a true proposition if and only if Olson is born 43 years before t. So I don't temporarily have the property *being 43 years old*; I timelessly have the property *being born 43 years before t*.

have a shape without temporal qualification, and any material thing with ordinary properties has a shape.

This means that although certain momentary temporal parts of me have such familiar properties as sitting, sleeping, writing, weighing 150 pounds, and being conscious, I myself have none of those properties. I don't have the property of sitting, or of sleeping, or of writing. Strictly speaking, I have no shape or weight. I have no mental properties, or at least none such as being conscious or thinking about Vienna. I have no temporary properties of any sort. If I did, I should have them relative to times, and four-dimensionalists agree that things do not have properties relative to times. I am not even perceived, except perhaps by Berkeley's God. My stages may be perceived, but if I had the property of being perceived I should also have the property of not being perceived, for being perceived is a temporary property. This is all rather troubling. The temporal-parts view implies that the familiar objects that think and act and are seen and heard are our stages, not ourselves. We ourselves are unobservable theoretical entities.

Four-dimensionalists will reply that we still have these familiar properties in a certain sense. We often attribute to an object the properties of its parts: we say that someone is sunburned when only a part of her nose is sunburned, or that the day was wet when only most of the afternoon was. And these descriptions are perfectly correct. So even though I don't bear a property such as sitting in the strict sense in which my current stage bears it, I nonetheless relate to that property in a way that makes it true to say that I am sitting. I have that property in what Butler (1975) in another context called "a loose and popular sense." The temporal-parts view does not deny that I sit or think in *any* sense. It is compatible with the way we ascribe ordinary properties to ourselves in ordinary situations.

Of course, more needs to be said, for it isn't generally right to attribute to an object the properties of its parts. My left foot is a part of me. It weighs about three pounds and is entirely unconscious. Yet it would be absurd to describe this fact by saying that *I* am foot-shaped, weigh three pounds, and am unconscious. Why is it right to say that I sit by virtue of having a sitting temporal part but wrong to say that I am foot-shaped by virtue of having a foot-shaped spatial part?

Four-dimensionalists will presumably concede that I have the properties of being foot-shaped and being unconscious in the same way as I have the properties of sitting and thinking: my relation to all those properties is the same. They will explain why we say that I am sitting but not that I am foot-shaped by appealing to our interests and expectations. Those interests and expectations make it useful, in ordinary circumstances, to describe me as sitting or thinking when my current temporal part has the property of sitting or thinking, whereas it would not be useful—in fact it would be positively misleading—to describe me as foot-shaped or unconscious, even though I have parts with those properties too. There may be possible circumstances in which it *would* be right to attribute to me the shape or the mental properties of my left foot, but, as things are, it isn't. Just why this should be so is a nice question, but I don't doubt that it has an answer.

This is all fine and good, but it misses the point. Let us grant that nothing the temporal-parts view says conflicts with the way we ascribe ordinary properties to ourselves in ordinary situations. Suppose it is true to say, when we are not doing metaphysics, that we sit and think and are conscious, even if the real bearers of those properties are not ourselves but brief temporal parts of us. Still, don't we have a deep conviction that *we* are among the real bearers of such properties as thinking and being conscious? Doesn't it seem evident not only that you and I think and are conscious in some sense or other, but that we think and are conscious in the strictest possible sense? Of all the things we know about ourselves, isn't this the most certain? Surely we cannot suppose that we think only in virtue of the fact that some *other* thing thinks for us. As Chisholm said, if there are two beings thinking these thoughts, one thinking them on its own and the other having its thinking done for it by the first, then I am the first thing and not the second.

Someone is bound to reply that this "thinking-stage problem" is no different in principle from the thinking-brain problem. Nearly everyone believes that we are animals, or at any rate material things the size of animals (things constituted by animals, perhaps). And it follows from this belief (the reply goes) that we think only in the sense of having spatial parts—brains—that think in the strictest sense. So if there is a problem here, it has nothing to do with the temporal-parts view in particular. It is one that nearly everyone shares. Moreover, no one worries about the thinking-brain problem. So why worry about the thinking-stage problem?

Now I think we ought to worry about the thinking-brain problem. I worried about it at some length in the previous chapter. If it really were true that only our brains think in the strictest sense, then in my view we ought to conclude that we are brains.

In fact the thinking-stage problem is more serious than the thinking-brain problem. There are three possible ways of solving the thinking-brain problem. (I don't regard saying that we "think" only in the sense of having thinking brains as parts to be a solution.) One is to deny that there are such things as brains. An analogous solution to the thinking-stage problem would say that there are no such things as person-stages, which is incompatible with the temporal-parts view. The second and most popular is to deny that only our brains think in the strictest sense. An analogous solution to the thinking-stage problem would be to deny that our stages think in the strictest sense. That too is incompatible with the temporal-parts view. So two of the three possible solutions to the thinking-brain problem are unavailable in the case of the thinking-stage problem. The third is to say that we are brains. Four-dimensionalists *could* say, analogously, that we are stages. That would solve the problem, though at a considerable cost: that we are momentary stages is no easier to believe than that we are brains. It is, however, an important variant of the temporal-parts view and deserves a section of its own.

5.8 The Stage View

According to the temporal-parts view, it is stages that think and act, strictly speaking; yet we are not stages. That is hard to believe. It is also hard to believe that the things that bark and wag their tails and chase postmen are not dogs but mere parts of dogs, dog-stages. One way to avoid this is to reject the ontology of temporal parts altogether. But another is to say that people and dogs are stages. Call this the *stage view*.

If there is any reason to suppose that we are momentary things that don't strictly persist, this is it. There are powerful arguments in support of the ontology of temporal parts, and anyone who holds that view must either say that we are stages or deny that we think or talk or have any other temporary property in the strictest sense. The stage view has other virtues too. It avoids the thinking-animal problem by implying that our animal bodies don't strictly think. The only true thinker of my current thoughts, it says, is my current stage, which is me. It also gives us the right number of objects existing at any one time (setting aside the problem of the many): it implies that there is just one person sitting here now, even if there is fission in my future, just as we thought—whereas on the temporal-parts view there are at least two (Sider 2001: 188–190).

But although the stage view has important advantages over the temporal-parts view, it is rather hard to believe. Most obviously, it implies that we don't persist through time. This means that you are not the person who began reading this sentence. That was someone else—someone very similar to you, of course, and strongly causally connected to you, but a numerically different being all the same. We are all far younger than we thought. We were never children. We have no past and no future. For that matter, we can't move or change. What appears to be a persisting, changing person (or dog or what have you) is in reality only a series of static momentary beings.

Defenders of the stage view—and it has its defenders (Hawley 2001; Sider 1996, 2001: 188–208)—are surprisingly easy about this. They respond, following a pattern that will now be familiar, by insisting that their view is compatible with everything we ordinarily say and believe and care about. Even if the stage view is true, they say, certain past and future stages relate to me in ways that lead us, for reasons to do with our interests, to call them by my name. Sider calls such stages "temporal counterparts" of me ("personal temporal counterparts," to be more precise). He says that the ordinary belief that I was once a boy is true because I—the current momentary bearer of my name—have as a personal temporal counterpart an earlier boy-stage.

This means that when we say that I was once a boy, we are not asserting or implying that anything persists through time. We are not asserting the numerical identity of any earlier thing with any later thing. When we say such things we are only speaking *as if* something persisted because that is a convenient way to talk. (You can imagine how inconvenient it would be if we had to call every new momentary object by a different name.) We are doing what Hume called "feigning a continu'd being" (1978: 208). Saying that I was once a boy is rather like saying that the prime minister is a man today but was a woman twenty years ago. When we say this we don't ordinarily mean to imply that anyone has changed sex. We're not saying that something that is a man today and something that was a woman twenty years ago are one and the same. Rather, we are saying that a man who exists today and a woman who existed twenty years ago relate in some other way: that the woman then held, and that the man now holds, the office of prime minister. If we are using the language of identity over time here, we are using it loosely.

When a currently existing stage relates to earlier stages in a way that leads us to speak of them as if they were one—that is, when they are temporal counterparts—we might describe this by saying that the current stage has persisted in the same sort of loose sense. Although the stage view denies that people and dogs *really* persist—that they persist "in the strict philosophical sense of the word," as Butler would say—it is compatible with their "persisting" in the loose and popular sense in which the prime minister has persisted for some two centuries. Stage theorists claim that this "loose and popular persistence" is the only sort of persistence that most of us think or care about. Our ordinary, nonmetaphysical thought and talk about identity over time is concerned only with the having of earlier and later temporal counterparts. It is facts about temporal counterparts, not facts about ourselves at other times, that make our ordinary statements and beliefs about our persistence true or false. Our practical attitudes are likewise based not on strict identity but on the personal temporal-counterpart relation: we hold people responsible for the actions of their earlier temporal counterparts, and each of us has a special, selfish concern for the well-being of her later temporal counterparts (we encountered a view like this in §2.8). So according to the stage view, we *do* persist, in the only sense that matters. Whether things persist in the strict philosophical sense, stage theorists say, is of interest only to metaphysicians. Thus, only a metaphysician will object to the stage view on the grounds that it rules out our persisting through time. To anyone else this is a mere technical detail.

This story is not easy to believe. When we say, in ordinary contexts, that I was once a boy, we *seem* to be asserting that I myself once had the property of being a boy, and not that I relate in a certain way to some *other* being that had that property. Even if the story were true, though, it would not entirely silence the complaint. The fact that most of us find the stage view more or less incredible shows that it contradicts *something* that most of us believe. I, for one, believe that I persist in the strict philosophical sense, and not merely that certain past beings are temporal counterparts of me, even if the existence of such beings makes it correct for ordinary, nonmetaphysical purposes to describe me loosely as having existed in the past. I don't believe that this conviction of mine is eccentric, or that it came about only as a result of my philosophical training. It may be that it is a metaphysical conviction and that our ordinary, nonphilosophical beliefs do not imply it. But it is no less widely or deeply held for all that.

In any case, the stage view has further troubling consequences. For one, it is incompatible with any plausible view of personal identity over time. It conflicts, for instance, with the view that our identity over time consists in some sort of psychological continuity. In fact it implies that no sort of continuity at all, psychological or otherwise, suffices for us to persist. Of course, it may still suffice for us to persist in a loose and popular sense: the fact that some future person inherits her mental and physical properties from you in some appropriate way might make her a personal temporal counterpart of you. But it does not suffice for her to be *you*.

Someone might find this consequence not merely implausible but incoherent. No momentary being, you might think, could count as a person: anyone who believes, or seems to believe, that people never persist through time has just not got the concept of a person, just as someone who believed, or seemed to believe, that cats are inanimate fuzzy toys would not have the concept of a cat. If it belongs to the concept of a person that people ordinarily persist in the strict philosophical sense, then people cannot be stages. If it also belongs to the concept of a person that people have the property of thinking, then the ontology of temporal parts in general is inconsistent with the existence of people, as it implies that persisting and thinking are incompatible.

If the stage view *is* compatible with the existence of people, it gives us far too many of them. You might have thought that this book has only one author. (That's what it says on the cover.) Not so, according to the stage view: even if only one philosopher was at work on it at any one time, a vast number of momentary philosophers successively took over the job—though none stayed at it long enough to write even a single word.

Finally, the stage view implies that none of the people who exist are the ones we know and love. Take Socrates. What stage is he? According to the stage view, plenty of stages successively bore the name 'Socrates'. But nothing could make it the case that just one of those stages, rather than another, was Socrates. We couldn't discover that Socrates—the teacher of Plato and the wisest man in Athens—existed for only an instant during the evening of August 6, 417 B.C. No stage could be Socrates. If Socrates can only be a stage, then there can be no such thing as Socrates. The same goes for the rest of us. What stage could I be? You might say that I am the current bearer of my name: the current "Olson-stage." (Set aside the inconvenient fact that we cannot refer uniquely to any one momentary stage.) But why should I be *that* stage? Choosing it would be just as arbitrary as choosing a moment during an August evening as the instant when Socrates existed.

There are many clever things that stage theorists can say in response to these complaints. They can say, for instance, that because all the authors of this book are personal temporal counterparts of one another, there is a perfectly good sense in which only one person wrote it. And they can say that because there are many successive bearers, of the right sort, of the name 'Socrates', it is true to say that Socrates existed, even if none of those things is Socrates. That is, they can reply to these complaints in much the same way as they reply to the objection that the stage theory violates our conviction that we persist through time. And the objections can be sharpened, as before, in a way that makes them immune to those replies, if perhaps less forceful.

Whatever the outcome of this debate may be, four-dimensionalists must choose between the temporal-parts view, according to which we persist but don't strictly think or act, and the stage view, according to which we think and act but don't strictly persist. It would be nice if we could avoid this dilemma.

6

Bundles

6.1 Bundle Theories

We have now considered a number of views according to which we are material things: organisms, things coinciding materially with organisms, and spatial and temporal parts of organisms. I cannot think of any other promising materialistic view of what we are. So let us turn to views according to which we are not material.

One such view is that we are composed of mental states or events: particular beliefs, desires, sensations, emotions, and so on. In particular, each of us is composed of his own mental states or events. Our parts may include both occurrent states or events—things actively going on within the mind, such as your current philosophical cogitations—and nonoccurrent states and dispositions lying dormant, such as your memories of last summer and your taste in furniture. Or our parts may be particular mental qualities or "tropes." But none of our parts are material things. We are not made of matter. Though our bodies may be made of matter, the parts of our bodies are not parts of us. Call this the *bundle view*.

We need to distinguish the bundle view from other claims that sound similar. One is that our parts include both mental states and a material body that is not itself composed of mental states. Because this suggestion has no obvious attraction over the bundle view, and most of what I will say about the bundle view applies equally to it, I won't discuss it separately.

A more urgent matter is that a number of claims very different from the one that concerns us have been called "bundle theories." First, there is supposed to be something called the bundle theory of the *mind*: the view that the mind is nothing but a bundle of mental states. What this means depends on the meaning of the word 'mind'. If 'mind' means 'thinking being', then *we* are minds (since we are thinking beings), and the view that our minds are bundles is the view that we are bundles. But those who assert that minds are bundles are sometimes merely making a claim about the nature of our mental lives, to the effect that they are not unified in the way that certain philosophers have thought. This is not a view about what we are. In fact it looks consistent with any view about we are.

Another bundle theory says that *all* concrete objects, and not just ourselves, are composed of particular states or qualities. This "global" bundle theory is not the same as the bundle view. Someone could hold either view without holding the other: someone could say that we are bundles but that unthinking objects such as trees are not; or someone might think that all concrete objects are bundles but deny that we exist. I will argue in §6.5, though, that friends of the bundle view are better off with a global bundle theory.

A third sort of bundle theory says that concrete objects are composed not of particular states or qualities but of universals. The view is roughly that Kilimanjaro (say) is composed of a certain height, a certain shape, a certain geological structure, and so on—not a particular height, shape, and geological structure that necessarily belong to that mountain alone, but the very same height, shape, and so on that other mountains might have. Applied to ourselves, the view would be that we are composed of psychological universals. I will consider this view in §6.6.

Then there is the view that we are "logical constructions" out of mental states. Ayer once wrote, "We know that a self, if it is not to be treated as a metaphysical entity, must be held to be a logical construction out of sense-experiences" (1946: 125). (By "a metaphysical entity," Ayer meant an immaterial substance, and he thought he had shown talk of immaterial substances to be meaningless.) What does it mean to say that we are logical constructions? The phrase 'logical construction' is a tricky one. To say that *F*s are logical constructions out of *G*s sometimes means that *F*s are sets, in the mathematical sense, built up out of *G*s. But Ayer did not think that you and I were sets. (The idea that we might literally be abstract objects that have their members essentially is hard to take seriously.) As Ayer used the term, a logical construction is not a kind of thing at all. We cannot say that, among the things that there are, some are logical constructions and some are not. That would be like saying that among the things that there are, some are real and some are unreal—no one thinks that *there are* leprechauns, and that they belong to a kind called "unreal objects." When Ayer said that we are logical constructions out of sense experiences, he meant that all statements that appear to be about ourselves, or about thinking beings generally, could be translated without loss of meaning into statements that make no reference to thinking beings, but only to sense experiences (1946: 63). When we say, "Paul heard a noise," what we are saying is equivalent to some more complicated statement that refers to or quantifies over nothing but mental states.

This is not the view that we are composed of experiences. (Ayer is explicit about this at 1946: 127–128; see also Pike 1967.) The logical-construction view does not say that we have experiences as parts. In fact it says nothing at all about our metaphysical nature. It is not a metaphysical claim at all, but rather a claim about meaning—specifically the meaning of "person talk." In fact it is unclear what it *could* mean, on the logical-construction view, to ask what we are. If *all* so-called talk of people is synonymous with talk of things other than people, what could it mean to ask what sort of things people are?

If the logical-construction view suggests any metaphysical claim, it is that there are really no people. There are only the mental states or what have you that figure in Ayer's translations of person talk and account for the appearance of there being people. If there *were* people—if our thoughts had subjects—then surely our talk of people would refer to or quantify over them, and thus would not be synonymous with talk that refers to or quantifies only over mental states. But this is to put a metaphysical gloss on an antimetaphysical view. On the logical-construction view, the statement "There are no people" can mean only that there are no mental states (or whatever it is out of which people are "logically constructed") of the appropriate sort—which of course logical constructivists deny. To ask about the metaphysical nature of people, they say, is to misunderstand the meaning of person-talk. It is like asking about the metaphysical nature of sakes: to wonder whether there is such a thing as Kolya's sake and, if so, what sort of entity it might be is to misunderstand the meaning of the word 'sake'. Those who understand the term correctly know that 'Kolya's sake' is not an expression that purports to refer to anything. Ayer is saying that 'Kolya' is not an expression that purports to refer to anything either. To use another analogy, asking what the logical-construction view says about the metaphysical nature of people is like asking what logical behaviorism says about the metaphysical nature of mental states, or what phenomenalism says about the metaphysical nature of physical objects.

Most of this book rests on the assumption that the logical-construction view is false. I could say a good deal about why I think it is false, but this is not the place for it. In any case, it is not an account of what we are. The bundle view I want to consider says that we are bundles of mental states and events.

Given that you and I think, it follows from the bundle view that bundles of mental states think: the subject of my thoughts is something composed of those very thoughts. Now it is hard to understand how a bundle of mental states could think (see §6.4). This might lead someone to suggest that we are bundles that don't think: an "unthinking-bundle view." I can see no attraction whatever in this proposal. No one who takes us to be unthinking bundles will suppose that other things think our thoughts. That is, no one will suppose that *we* don't think our thoughts, but other beings—things that are not even parts of us—do think them. The unthinking-bundle view could be true only if nothing thinks our thoughts: that is, if thoughts occur, but have no subjects or thinkers. But if nothing thinks our thoughts, does it not follow that we don't exist? First-person singular statements, such as that I am now awake, refer to their subject, the being that makes them and whose thoughts they express. If there is no such subject, they don't refer at all. And if the word 'I' never refers to anything, then there is no such thing as I, just as if the word 'Atlantis' never refers to anything there is no such thing as Atlantis. (Assuming, anyway, as the unthinking-bundle view does, that 'I' is a referring expression in the sense of §1.4.)

Even if someone were to suppose that we exist but don't think, and that our personal pronouns refer to unthinking beings, we should not expect her to suppose that those terms refer to bundles of thoughts. If personal pronouns and proper names refer to something, but never to thinking beings, what unthinking beings might they refer to? Maybe some things would be better candidates for their reference than others. Given that we say such things as "Thatcher is a human being" and "Thatcher is sitting down," it would be absurd to say that the name 'Thatcher' refers to a bicycle or a tree. If anything, we might expect it to refer to a human organism—one that, according to the unthinking-bundle view, is for some reason unable to think. That's the sort of thing it appears to refer to. But why suppose that it refers to a bundle of thoughts?

In any case, the unthinking-bundle view is not really an answer to our question. Although it answers the question, What do our personal pronouns and proper names refer to? it does not answer the question, What sorts of beings think our thoughts and perform our actions? Indeed, it assumes that these two questions have different answers. And I said in §1.4 that the second question was to have priority over the first should the two diverge. The interesting idea behind the unthinking-bundle view, as I see it, is that nothing thinks our thoughts. We will come to that suggestion in due course.

Let us return now to the bundle view that concerns us, the claim that we are composed of mental states. This is not a complete account of what we are. Though it implies that we are concrete particulars, that we are not substances, and that our parts are particular mental states, it does not say which or what sorts of mental states are parts of us and why, or which properties are essential to us, or whether we persist through time. We will come to these questions shortly. Still, the idea that we are made up entirely of thoughts tells us a good deal about what we are, enough to rule out many rival accounts. It stands in stark contrast with the other views we have considered. That is enough to work with.

The bundle view is counterintuitive for some of the same reasons as the brain view is. It implies that we are wholly invisible and intangible: you can no more touch a bundle of thoughts than you can touch a dream. So it is perhaps unsurprising that it has few defenders. Hume proposed that each of us is "nothing but a bundle or collection of different perceptions" (1978: 252), but even he found it hard to believe. Quinton says that each of us is "a series of mental states connected by continuity of character and memory" (1962: 398; see also 1973: 97–105), and I have already mentioned Rovane's claim that a person is "a set of intentional episodes" (1998: 172; see also S. Campbell 2006). I suspect, however, that the bundle view has a large underground following. I will argue that a number of popular views about personal identity support it. First, though, I will briefly review some traditional arguments for the bundle view.

6.2 Traditional Arguments for the Bundle View

The bundle view was once considered the obvious alternative to our being simple immaterial substances (by Hume and Quinton, for instance). Arguments against substance dualism were taken to support the bundle view. Nowadays we know better.

Others argued for the bundle view (and for the global bundle theory more generally) on the grounds that the very idea of a substance is incoherent. This reasoning usually began with a certain picture of what substances are supposed to be, something like this:

> To perceive an object is to perceive its qualities: shape, size, motion, and so on. Some philosophers suppose that there must

> be more to a thing than just its qualities: there must also be something that stands under and supports them. They posit something called a 'substance' to play this role. Their view is that an ordinary thing like a cat is made up not only of the furriness, the feline shape, and the sinuous movements that we perceive, but also of a substance in which those qualities inhere. Yet even those who say this admit that we never perceive the substance itself. How could we? The substance is by definition something apart from its qualities, and therefore incapable of characterization. *It* is not furry or feline or moving. It has no qualities at all; it only supports the qualities we observe. And the mere fact that the substance supports certain qualities tells us no more about how it is in itself than the fact that something supports certain books tells us how it is in itself. It is a mere "something, we know not what." A substance is therefore a mysterious theoretical entity: a metaphysical abstraction of the most dubious sort.

We might call this the Lockean picture of substance (K. Campbell 1990: 4–11 is a recent example). If this is what substances are, sensible philosophers will have nothing to do with them. The idea of a thing uncharacterized by any qualities makes no sense at all. What could we be, then, if not substances? Bundles of qualities, presumably. There is little else that we *could* be, on the Lockean picture. We needn't be bundles of mental qualities only: we might be made up partly of brute physical qualities as well. But some sort of bundle view will be all but inevitable.

The core of the Lockean picture is the idea that what is furry or shaped or moving in the strictest sense is not a substance but a particular quality or trope. That leaves the substance with nothing to do but fix the qualities in place: it stands to them much as a lump of soft clay stands to colored feathers stuck into it. So the qualities the substance supports do not characterize it, but merely clothe it. If there is anything the cat's qualities characterize, it is the bundle of those qualities.

But we are not forced to accept the Lockean picture. In fact I see no reason at all to accept it. Why suppose that the thing the qualities characterize—the thing that is furry or moving—is a quality, or a bundle of qualities? The idea of a bare particular clothed in qualities is an absurd caricature of what *I* take a substance to be. As I see it, a substance is not a metaphysical abstraction, but an ordinary thing. A cat—a thing that moves and purrs and is furry—is a substance. A cat is not a compound made up of qualities and the substratum that supports them. Nor is it made up of qualities alone. It is made up of other substances: cells and particles. What makes it a substance is not that it is "something apart from its qualities" (a dark phrase if ever there was one), but that it is not itself a state or a quality of something else. A substance is not "incapable of characterization": to characterize something is precisely to say what qualities it has. It is not qualities that we perceive, but the substances they characterize.

Of course, this alternative picture provides nothing like a complete theory of substances. It leaves plenty of hard questions unanswered. But as far as I can see, nothing in the Lockean reasoning shows that there is anything wrong with it. So I set little store by the argument that we must be bundles because the idea of a substance is not in good order.

6.3 Personal Identity and the Bundle View

To my mind, the best arguments for the bundle view (the bundle view of ourselves, not the global bundle theory) have to do with personal identity. Since the time of Locke, philosophical orthodoxy has assumed that personal identity is grounded in psychological facts. No account of what we are fits better with this assumption than the bundle view.

Consider the view that you could move from one human animal to another via Shoemaker's brain-state transfer procedure. No substance, material or otherwise, thereby moves from one animal to another (the ontology of temporal parts aside, anyway). What does move? Well, according to Shoemaker's description, the process moves the particular mental states realized in the first animal's brain to the second animal's brain. And if it is possible to move you by moving nothing but mental states, the natural conclusion is that you are composed of mental states.

More generally, many philosophers think that our identity through time consists entirely in facts about mental states or events. What is necessary and sufficient for a person x existing at one time to be identical with something y existing at another time, they say, is for the mental states that x is in at the first time to stand in certain relations—causal ones, perhaps—to the mental states that y is in at the second time. In fact the very question of personal identity over time is sometimes stated as what is necessary and sufficient for mental states or events occurring at different times to belong to the history of a single person (Grice 1941; see also Perry 1975c: 7–12). What sort of thing could have its persistence determined entirely by facts about relations among mental states? Well, something composed of mental states could. It is doubtful whether any concrete object made up entirely of things *other* than mental states could survive or perish just by virtue of relations among mental states. The obvious conclusion is the bundle view. (Or perhaps the view that we are made up partly of mental states and partly of something else. Again, I take this to be an uninteresting variant of the bundle view.)

Or one could argue for the bundle view from considerations about what determines how many of us there are at any one time. We might wonder whether there could be several people "inhabiting" a single human organism at once in commissurotomy cases—where the main neural connections between the cerebral hemispheres are cut—or in an extreme case of multiple personality. A deeper question is what sorts of facts would settle the matter. What would make it the case that there were two people sharing a single human animal? Or is it possible at all? For that matter, what makes it the case that there is just one person associated with an ordinary human animal, and not more? Many philosophers say that the answer lies in psychological facts: just as (they say) facts about psychological continuity over time determine whether we have one person or two in "diachronic" cases, facts about psychological unity at any one time determine how many of us there are in "synchronic" cases. They say that simultaneous mental states belong to the same subject just when they are in some sense unified. The reason why the mental states of an ordinary human animal are all the thoughts of a single person is that they are unified in the right way. But if they were sufficiently disunified, they might be the thoughts of two different people.

There are different accounts of what this unity amounts to. Kant thought that what made something a mental state of a particular being, and hence a mental state at all, was that being's ability to combine or synthesize it with its other mental states—to unite those states, as he put it, "in one self-consciousness" (1929: B134). More recent accounts exploit the fact that many mental states are disposed to interact in special ways with other mental states. It is characteristic of desires, for instance, to interact with beliefs to produce action: roughly, your desire for something tends to cause you to act in ways that you believe will satisfy it, unless you have stronger competing desires. That seems to be part of what it is to be a desire—and also part of the nature of belief. The claim that the *entire* nature of *all* mental states consists in such facts about their causal dispositions is the core of the functionalist theory of mind. That theory is controversial. But few would dispute that these causal roles are at least part of the nature of many mental states.

It appears to follow from this that many mental states necessarily come in packages. For something to be a desire, for instance—as opposed to a memory or a visual sensation or something nonmental—it has to occur as part of a network of beliefs and other states with which it is disposed to interact, directly or indirectly, in characteristic ways. Call such packages *mental systems*. (Let us not confuse matters by calling them *minds*. You and

I are minds in the sense of thinking beings; but we don't want to conflate this platitude with the contentious idea that we are mental systems. For what it's worth, I find the word 'mind' as a count noun dangerous in thinking about personal identity.) Mental states belong to the same mental system if and only if they relate causally to one another and to actions (or are disposed so to relate) in the right way. A mental system is something composed of mental states related to one another and to certain actions, but not to anything else, in this manner.

Now mental systems match up pretty well with people, or with thinking beings generally. If I want an orange and believe that there is an orange in the bag and that it is within my power to get it out of the bag, this will ordinarily result in my attempting to do so, unless I take that to be incompatible with some other goal of mine. My desire for an orange will not combine in this way with anyone else's beliefs to cause action. Ordinarily all and only the mental states of a given thinker will be parts of a single mental system. Where there is more than one independent mental system, there is ordinarily more than one thinker. So it is tempting to suppose that being parts of the same mental system is *what it is* for mental states to belong to the same thinking being. This is Shoemaker's view:

> It is only when the belief that it is raining and the desire to keep dry are copersonal that they tend (in conjunction with other mental states) to lead to such effects as the taking of an umbrella; if the belief is mine and the desire is yours, they will not directly produce any joint effects. And it seems that if a belief and desire do produce (in conjunction with other mental states) just those effects which the functional characterizations of them say they ought to produce if copersonal, then in virtue of this they are copersonal.... Whether mental states... should count as belonging to the same person, or mind, would seem to turn precisely on whether they are so related that they will jointly have the functionally appropriate sorts of effects. (1984: 94; see also 1997: 294)

The claim is that, necessarily, for every person or thinking being ("mind"), there is exactly one mental system, all and only the elements of which are the mental states of that being ; and that for every mental system, there is exactly one thinking being whose mental states are the elements of that system. Mental systems and thinkers must match up one to one. This is the *psychological individuation principle* of §2.9.

This principle may sound attractive, and Shoemaker is not alone in advocating it. It is also closely connected with his explanation of why organisms are unable to think (see §2.5), giving opponents of animalism another reason to look favorably on it. And those who accept the orthodox view that psychological facts determine our identity over time may find it natural to suppose that psychological facts also determine how many of us there are at any one time.

The psychological individuation principle suggests that thinking beings are themselves mental systems. How could the number of mental systems necessarily fix the number of anything but mental systems? Remember: the number of mental systems is determined entirely by causal relations among mental states and actions. And it is hard to see how causal relations among mental states and actions could entail both the existence and the precise number of things that are not made up even partly of mental states or actions. But if thinking beings have mental states among their parts, then you and I have mental states among our parts, which is a version of the bundle view.

It is especially hard to see how the psychological individuation principle could be compatible with our being material things. (I assume that no material thing has mental states as parts.) Any material thing that could have mental properties at all, it seems, could be mentally *dis*unified. Nothing could guarantee that the mental states of any material thing must be psychologically unified in the way that Kant and Shoemaker demand of a mental subject. Think of an extreme case of multiple personality, in which many of the usual interactions among mental states break down. This would be a being whose beliefs, desires, perceptual states, and so on don't interact in the usual way to produce actions, any more than your mental states interact with mine to produce actions. They would not form a unified mental system. Even if there is enough interaction among the mental states of a human organism in any actual case of multiple personality for them to form a mental system, this doesn't seem to be a necessary truth.

Suppose there really were such psychological disunity within a human being. If every mental state must belong to a mental system, these disunified states would have to belong to different mental systems. In that case, two or more unified mental systems would be associated with one human organism at once. According to the psychological individuation principle, there would therefore be two or more thinking beings—two or more *people*—"sharing" that animal. Could those people be material things? Well, what sorts of material things could they be? They would have to be physically different, else there would be nothing to explain their mental differences. (No materialist would suppose that two people could be physically identical, with the same surroundings and history, yet differ radically in their mental properties.) It seems that each would have to be a different part of the animal's brain. But that presupposes thinking-subject minimalism, and as we saw in chapter 4, minimalism faces no end of trouble.[1]

So the psychological individuation principle looks incompatible with our being material things. It appears to rule out any account of what we are apart from the bundle view. This has dramatic implications. It is not only an argument for the bundle view, but also an argument against materialism generally. It means that materialists cannot accept many of the things we are inclined to say about personal identity. In particular, they cannot accept the psychological individuation principle. This is especially inconvenient for those materialists—usually advocates of the constitution view—who argue against animalism on the grounds that it is incompatible with our convictions about personal identity. It now turns out that their own view is incompatible with those convictions. Being a materialist is harder than it looks.

6.4 Can Thoughts Think?

I hope I have shown that there is something to be said for the bundle view. Let us now examine it more critically.

To my mind, the most forceful objection to the bundle view is expressed in this quotation from Reid:

> I am therefore [according to Hume's bundle view] that succession of related ideas and impressions of which I have the intimate memory and consciousness. But who is the *I* that has this memory and consciousness of a succession of ideas and impressions? Why, it is nothing but that succession itself. Hence, I learn that this succession of ideas and impressions intimately remembers and is conscious of itself. I would wish to be further instructed whether the impressions remember and are conscious of the ideas, or the ideas remember and are conscious of the impressions, or if both remember and are conscious of both.... This, however, is clear, that the succession of ideas and impressions not only remembers and is conscious, but that it judges, reasons, affirms, denies—nay, that it eats and drinks and is sometimes merry and sometimes sad. If these things can be ascribed to a succession of ideas and

[1] Some of those troubles might be mitigated somewhat by combining minimalism with the psychological individuation principle. Such a combination might be worth exploring, though I doubt whether the end result would hold much attraction. I argue at greater length in Olson 2003b for the claim that the psychological unity principle rules out our being material things.

> impressions, in a consistency with common sense, I should be very glad to know what is nonsense. (1940: 378)

As I understand him, Reid is objecting to the idea that a bundle or "succession" of thoughts should think or act. There may *be* such things as bundles of thoughts, but it is a metaphysical or logical blunder to suppose that such things are the *subjects* of the thoughts that compose them. Reid doesn't say why it is a blunder: he takes the claim to be patently absurd once we set it out clearly. That seems right to me. (Even philosophers sympathetic to the bundle view have agreed: see, for instance, Pike 1967: 163.) But can we say more to help those not yet convinced?

Well, consider the idea that a particular thought might think that very thought. Might your belief that it's cloudy believe that it's cloudy? Does your dream of white horses dream of white horses? Surely not. Even hardened bundle theorists will accept that. Nor can your dream of white horses believe that it's cloudy, or have any other thought. If we know anything, we know that thoughts don't think—any more than games play or dances dance. A particular thought is one thing; the being that has or thinks it, if anything does, is another.

Now, could it be that a thing composed of *many* thoughts might think, even though no individual thought can? Again, it seems not. That would be like saying that a thing composed of many games might play, or that a thing composed of many dances might dance, even though no individual game plays or dance dances. No matter how many games or dances you combine, they will never add up to a player or a dancer. More generally, combining many acts will never get them to compose an actor. And no matter how many acts of thinking you put together, you will never get them to add up to a thinking subject. If anything thinks, it is the object—the substance—of which acts of thought are states or aspects or modes. A thinker is something that stands to acts of thought as a player stands to a game or as a dancer stands to a dance (a solo game or dance, that is, not one involving a group).

As far as I can see, the only way to resist this reasoning is to deny that there is any real distinction between states and events, on the one hand, and the things that are in those states or that participate in those events, on the other—between thoughts and thinkers, or dances and dancers, or games and players.[2] If there is no distinction between physical objects and events or between actors and acts, then there is no obvious absurdity

[2] "Physical objects," wrote Quine, "conceived thus four-dimensionally in space-time, are not to be distinguished from events or, in the concrete sense of the term, processes" (1960: 171). It is not clear whether the ontology of temporal parts leads inevitably to this conclusion, but Quine's opinion is by no means eccentric.

in the claim that bundles of thoughts think. For that matter, there is nothing wrong with the idea that individual thoughts think: that beliefs believe, or that dreams dream. But the idea that a thought thinks is perfectly absurd. The proposal also appears to have the awkward implication that every thought has at least two thinkers, namely the thought itself and the bundle it is a part of. That would leave me wondering which thing I am: a bundle, or an individual thought. If I believe that I am a bundle of thoughts, then that belief itself would seem to believe, mistakenly, that it is a bundle of thoughts. Why couldn't I be the one making that mistake?

Now from the fact that a bundle of thoughts thinks, it does not follow that any individual thought does so. Why should bundlers suppose that the thoughts making up a thinking bundle think individually, any more than materialists suppose that the atoms making up a thinking material object think individually? Well, materialists can explain why no individual atom thinks by pointing out that the activities of an individual atom are too crude to be acts of thought. Thought comes about only when the activities of vast numbers of individual atoms come together. What an individual atom does is insufficient for thought to occur. Bundlers, however, cannot say anything like this. An individual thought is perfectly sufficient for thought to occur. If a thing composed of many thoughts can think, it will be hard to explain why something composed of just one thought cannot think. (You might suggest that a thought could not think unless it were a part of a complete mental system. But if that is so, it is presumably because nothing could be a thought at all unless it were a part of a mental system. In any case, this does nothing to explain why a suitably situated individual thought could not think.)

Anyone who believes that a bundle of thoughts could think ought to believe that an individual thought might think. So much the worse, it seems to me, for the bundle view. Nor is this the only worry it faces.

6.5 Thinking Animals Once More

Suppose for the sake of argument that a bundle of thoughts really could think. What about the thinking-animal problem—the problem of how we can know that we are not those human animals that appear to think our thoughts?

To answer this question, we need to know what sort of thing animals would be if the bundle view were true. Would they too be bundles of states or events or qualities? Or would they be something else—substances, perhaps? Friends of the bundle view will want to say that animals are bundles. If your animal body were a substance, we should expect your mental states to be states of it (or perhaps states of your brain; in any case they would be states of some substance or other). If there are substances, then some states, anyway, will be states *of* those substances. That's what substances are *for*. But if your thoughts are states of an animal, that animal ought to be a subject of those thoughts. It ought to *have* them. It ought to think. What could be the difference between being in a state of belief and believing, or between being in a state of hunger and being hungry? And if animals think our thoughts, yet are nonbundles different from ourselves, the thinking-animal problem arises once more.

Here is another argument against a "mixed" bundle view. Anyone who says that we are bundles but that organisms are substances will want to deny that organisms and other substances think. Why wouldn't substances think? Presumably because it is impossible for them to think: substances could have nonmental properties but never mental properties. Something about mental properties would prevent substances from having them. That would open a deep metaphysical gulf between the mental and the nonmental. It would not be substance dualism, the view that some substances have mental properties and others have physical (or nonmental) properties and nothing could have both. It would be an even more profound sort of mind-body dualism: not only could no substance with physical properties have mental properties, but no substance of *any* sort could have mental properties. The boundary between the physical and the mental would be the boundary between substances and nonsubstances.

Bundle theorists are unlikely to find this attractive. Nor does their view provide any support for it: the claim that thinking things are bundles rather than substances in no way suggests that material things should be substances rather than bundles. If the subjects of mental states are bundles, we should expect the subjects of nonmental states to be bundles as well. Let us suppose, then, that not only we ourselves, but human animals too are bundles of states or events or qualities. More generally, all ordinary concrete objects are bundles: there are no substances as traditionally conceived.

But this would not yet solve the thinking-animal problem. If animals are bundles of states, which states make up your animal body? We should expect them to include those physical states and activities we attribute to you: your height, your mass, the activities of your digestive system, and so on. But wouldn't they also include your mental states? If the nonmental activities going on within the animal are parts of the animal, why shouldn't the mental activities going on within it be parts of it too? And if the animal has thoughts as parts, how can it fail to think? *You* think, according to the bundle view, by having thoughts as parts. Why shouldn't the animal also think by having thoughts as parts? If the animal digested in virtue of having digestive activities as parts but didn't think in virtue of having mental activities as parts, that would again be a metaphysical dualism of the mental and the nonmental. We should want to know the explanation for it, and the bundle view suggests none.

One could get round this problem by saying that we *are* those animal bundles: we are not bundles of mental states only, but bundles composed of both mental and nonmental states. That would mean that we are animals. This would solve the thinking-animal problem, all right. However, it would raise the problem of how we know we are not thinking bundles of mental states. And anyway, wasn't the whole point of the bundle view to offer an alternative to our being animals? Bundle-theoretic animalism would have no obvious advantage over the usual "substance animalism."

6.6 Bundles of Universals

I will say no more about the view that we are bundles of mental particulars. What about the view that we are bundles of mental universals? The idea is that I am composed of such properties as *believing that it's cloudy* and *feeling hungry*—properties that I might share with others. In particular, I am composed of those psychological universals that I have or instantiate. Now I have a hard time understanding this. I have enough trouble thinking about universals by themselves. The idea that I myself might be made up of nothing but universals—abstract objects not strictly located in space and time—sounds to me like the sort of thing that comes to one in a dream after eating too many oysters. But I will venture a few brief remarks.

It is not obvious what advantages the "universal bundle view" has over the particular bundle view. If it is hard to see how a bundle of mental particulars could think, it is even harder to see how a bundle of mental universals could think. And if a bundle of mental particulars would have no grounds for believing that it was not an animal, a bundle of mental universals would seem to face the same difficulty.

The universal bundle view also has troubles of its own. Start with the "problem of distinct discernibles." There could be someone else psychologically just like me. It is of course enormously unlikely that anyone else has a mental life *exactly* like mine, right down to the smallest detail—so unlikely that we can be confident that it isn't the case. But it doesn't seem absolutely impossible. It would be like winning the lottery a million times in a row without cheating, rather than like winning the lottery without having a ticket. It would not be possible, however, if I were a bundle of psychological universals. For then my doppelgänger and I should be composed of the very same universals. Our parts would be not merely exactly alike but numerically the same. And surely the same universals cannot compose two different objects. At least it looks impossible to me—though my lights are dim in these regions.[3]

Another problem is that I have different mental properties at different times. I once believed that I was 20 years old. I used to like bubble gum. There was a time when I had never heard of George W. Bush. Not any longer. But a collection of universals cannot be composed of different universals at different times. The collection composed of universals *A*, *B*, and *C* cannot come to be the collection of *B*, *C*, and *D*, let alone the collection of *D*, *E*, and *F*. These can only be three different collections. So it seems, anyway. Which collection of universals might *I* be, then? If I am the collection of *A*, *B*, and *C*, I must always be that collection. I cannot come to be a numerically different collection, for the simple reason that one thing cannot come to be another, numerically different thing. But if I must always be the collection of *A*, *B*, and *C*, then presumably I must always instantiate those universals: I must always remain just the same and can never change. Yet if I know anything, I know that I do change.

Universal bundlers may reply that I am composed of temporal parts (O'Leary-Hawthorne and Cover 1998: 208). If I first instantiate the psychological universals *A*, *B*, and *C* (and only those), then later instantiate *B*, *C*, and *D*, and still later *C*, *D*, and *E*, then these three bundles—*A-B-C*, *B-C-D*, and *C-D-E*—are each temporal parts of me. Every bundle, all and only the elements of which I instantiate at some time, is one of my temporal parts. I am a bundle of bundles of universals.

But this looks wrong. Imagine that *A-B-C*, *B-C-D*, and *C-D-E* are my only temporal parts. And suppose that *C-D-E* is a later part of me than *B-C-D*, and that *B-C-D* is later than *A-B-C*. (It belongs to the idea of temporal parts that one can be later than another—though what could make one bundle of universals earlier or later than another is not obvious.) Now it seems possible for someone to instantiate the same psychological universals as I do but in a different order. For instance, someone could start by instantiating *C*, *D*, and *E*, then instantiate *B*, *C*, and *D*, and finally instantiate *A*, *B*, and *C* before ceasing to exist. His history would be just like mine only in reverse. Someone's history could also be just like mine but rearranged in some other way. The universal bundle view appears unable to account for this possibility. It implies that such a person would have the very same parts as I have, making us both qualitatively and numerically identical. But surely we should be both qualitatively and numerically different.

[3] Zimmerman 1998 is a useful discussion of some of these matters.

Technically minded philosophers can no doubt think of solutions to these problems, but they are unlikely to hold much attraction. Those drawn to the idea that particulars are composed of universals are probably better off with the logical-construction view of §6.1. They could say that statements about people and other particulars are true if and only if certain universals relate in such and such a way, without saying that particular things are actually composed of universals—much as phenomenalists say that statements about physical objects are true if and only if certain facts about sense experiences hold, without saying that physical objects are composed of sense experiences. Whatever its merits, though, this is not a view about what we are.

6.7 The Program View

One final thought that has some affinity with the bundle view is that we are something like computer programs. We stand to our bodies or our brains as computer programs stand to the physical machines they run on. We are not made of matter or of particular states or qualities. We're not made of anything particular at all. Call this the *program view.*

The word 'program', like many expressions, has a type-token ambiguity. For instance, the English language has some 300,000 words—that is, word types. If you have to submit an essay of not more than 5,000 words, however, this means word tokens: if the word 'and' occurs ten times on page two it counts as ten words, not one. Just as we distinguish word tokens from word types, we need to distinguish the particular copy of the word-processing program *Mariner Write 3.6.2* now running on my Macintosh from the type or universal of which it is an instance. The copy I use to write these words, if there is such a thing, is presumably some sort of concrete electronic event or state. It has a fairly definite location, changes over time, and will cease to exist when I erase it from the hard drive. But when we speak of *the* word processor *Write 3.6.2*, as when we speak of *the* word 'and', we don't seem to be referring to any particular, changeable thing located at a particular time and place, but rather to the universal of which the particular copies are instances. In any case, it is computer programs as universals that interests us here. The idea that we are computer program tokens would be a version of the bundle view. I want to consider the view that we are universals.

Let us not confuse the view that we are computer programs with the so-called computational theory of mind. This is roughly the claim that human cognition is a computational process: a matter of manipulating symbols according to mechanical rules. The program view may entail the computational theory of mind, but the computational theory does not entail that we are programs; in fact it has no obvious implications at all about what we are.

It is hard to find an explicit endorsement of the program view in the philosophical literature. This quotation from Dennett comes close:

> If [as Dennett urges] you think of yourself as a center of narrative gravity..., your existence depends on the persistence of that narrative..., which could theoretically survive indefinitely many switches of medium, be teleported as readily (in principle) as the evening news, and stored indefinitely as sheer information. If what you are is that organization of information that has structured your body's control system (or, to put it in its more usual provocative form, if what you are is the program that runs on your brain's computer), then you could in principle survive the death of your body as intact as a program can survive the destruction of the computer on which it was created and first run. (1991: 430)

The program view is also a common theme in science fiction, and I have found philosophers attracted to it when pressed in conversation.

Here are some considerations that look like arguments for the program view. In his story "Where Am I?" (1978), Dennett invites us to suppose that we could survive the complete destruction of our brains if the information encoded there were "downloaded" into an electronic computer. What sort of thing could literally be transferred by wire from a human being to a computer? It is tempting to say that no concrete object literally moves from brain to machine; all that really happens is that the machine comes to instantiate or realize the informational state that the brain first instantiated. All that is first "in" the brain and then "in" the computer is some sort of universal. And the universals that computers are designed to instantiate or realize are programs. So the view that you could be downloaded into a computer suggests that you are a program. Those who accept the possibility of resurrection or reincarnation but hesitate to accept Cartesian dualism may find themselves drawn to the program view for a similar reason.

Or consider fission cases. We don't want to say that transplanting each of your cerebral hemispheres into a different head would necessarily destroy you. We want to say that both resulting people would be you. Yet there are two of them and only one of you, and two things cannot be one thing. And we don't want to say, as the temporal-parts view does, that there were really two of you all along. Friends of the program view can say that both offshoots are you even though there was only one of you to begin with. They cannot, of course, say that each offshoot is numerically identical with you, but they can say that each is you in the sense of being a concrete instance or token of you: both could be you in the way that the tattered paperback on my shelf and the leather-bound volume on yours are both *Moby-Dick*. Where there was previously only one instance of you, there are now two. What if one of the offshoots has a beard and the other doesn't? Do you have a beard, or don't you? Well, if you are a universal, you can't strictly have any physical feature—beard, nose, sunburn, or what have you—but, speaking more loosely, we can say that you have a beard insofar as one instance of you has a beard, and that you have no beard insofar as another instance of you has none. Asking whether you have a beard would be like asking whether *Moby-Dick* has a torn cover. No account of what happens in the fission story is very attractive, and someone might prefer this one to the alternatives.

Finally, consider artificial intelligence. Many people think that it is possible in theory to build and program an electronic computer in such a way that it would produce thought as genuine as our own. It is no accident that this is commonly described by saying that *computer programs* may one day be intelligent. There is something odd about saying that *computers*—material objects made of metal and plastic—may one day be intelligent. If we were to produce an intelligent being by programming a computer, it would seem wrong to say that we had made the computer itself intelligent—that what was previously an ordinary desktop workstation had now acquired the ability to think. When the machine on which the crucial program was first run finally lands in the dustbin, no one would point to it and say that for a few exciting hours *that piece of hardware* was once intelligent. Nor would the intelligent thing seem to be a concrete electronic state or event going on within the computer at some particular time or, for that matter, a material object that the computer temporarily constitutes. It seems wrong to say that erasing the program from the computer's data-storage devices would destroy an intelligent being. If anything there is intelligent, it might be more natural to say that it continues to exist as long as the relevant information is still stored somewhere or other. And it would be tempting to say that the intelligent thing we had created could be stored on CDs and run on different machines, just like the word processor *Write 3.6.2*. That is, the subject of artificial intelligence—the artificially intelligent being—would be a program.

But if artificially intelligent beings would be computer programs, we should expect naturally intelligent beings such as ourselves to be something like programs too. If an electronic computer of the right sort (the right hardware, the right programming, the right surroundings, and so on) could "realize" an intelligent universal, then a biological organism of the right sort ought to be able to realize an intelligent universal too. How could the fact that the underlying physical processes are electronic and artificial in the one case and neurochemical and natural in the other make any difference to the metaphysical category of the resulting intelligent being? And if each normal human organism is the home of a thinking universal, it is hard to avoid the conclusion that *we* are those universals.

Despite these arguments, however, there are grave problems with the program view. For one, it is very hard to say *which* program, or which universal more generally, you or I might be. This human organism—my body—now instantiates all sorts of universals. If it instantiates any program, it probably instantiates a vast number of them. And it is hard to see what could make just one of those programs intelligent and sentient. But if there are many intelligent, sentient programs "running on my biological hardware," what could make it the case that just one of them was me?

Even if there is a computer program, the running of which is uniquely responsible for my current mental life, it would be doubtful whether it has *always* run on my brain. Was the very program responsible for my current mental life responsible for it in my infancy? It is more likely that my brain ran a different program then. If brains run programs at all, they are constantly being *re*programmed. But I cannot be numerically identical with different programs at different times. So if I were the intelligent program now running on my brain, I should not be the program that ran on my brain when I was a child, or for that matter the program that will be running on my brain in a year's time. My existence would be brief. Or perhaps I should be eternal and timeless, and my life as an embodied human person would be brief. Neither view is attractive.

Most obviously, universals don't *do* anything. They don't act. They don't change. It isn't the program type *Write 3.6.2*—the program that you too can use on your own Macintosh—that converts my keystrokes into text, but rather a particular, local instance of it. Nor does *Write* change when I install it on my machine or when I start it up or shut it down. Only the concrete instance of it running on my machine changes. Or rather, the program changes only in the way in which the number twelve changed by ceasing to be the number of apostles when Judas hanged himself: it undergoes only "Cambridge change." It doesn't undergo any real, intrinsic change. Computer programs as universals are inert and immutable.

But *I* am not inert or immutable. If I know anything, I know that I am writing these words—words that would not be written but for my actions. (Or if Descartes' evil genius is deceiving me and I am not really writing, I am still doing *something*.) I know that I sometimes feel tired, sometimes hear the sound of the wind, sometimes wish I were somewhere else—and sometimes don't. It couldn't be the case that what seems to be real, intrinsic change in me is really only Cambridge change. It couldn't be that when I seem to grow tired, all that really happens is that something else—a particular human organism that instantiates me—grows tired, whereas I myself remain ever the same. If I am a universal, I don't think or act—not really. The thinker of these thoughts and the author of these words is not a universal. But am *I* not the thinker of these thoughts and the author of these words? If there is a concrete thing that thinks my thoughts and performs my actions, and an immutable universal that can be said to think and act only in the loose sense of having a concrete instance that think and acts, isn't it clear that I am the concrete thing?

7

Souls

7.1 Immaterialism

We might be immaterial substances: *souls* for short. Or we might each be composed of an immaterial soul and a material body. I will consider this variant in §7.6.

What is an immaterial substance? Not a sort of immaterial matter or stuff. A soul is a substance in the sense of something that exists in its own right and is not a mere state or aspect of something else. What it is for a substance to be immaterial is not easy to say. It may suffice to say that souls are immaterial in that they are not made up, even partly, of matter—the stuff that makes up sticks and stones—or that they lack mass, energy, temperature, electric charge, and other paradigmatically physical properties. This characterization has the disadvantage of being entirely negative: it tells us what souls are only by telling us what they're not. Descartes and Leibniz tried to characterize souls positively by saying that their essence is thinking. By this they meant that souls are mental through and through: their only intrinsic properties are mental ones. However that may be, souls as immaterial substances are clearly supposed to *have* mental properties, even if they have intrinsic nonmental properties as well: they are supposed to be *thinking* substances.

Most philosophers who believe in souls take them to be mereologically simple—that is, to lack proper parts. They deny that souls are made up of "smaller" parts, things that may belong to different souls at different times or exist without being parts of any soul at all. Likewise, souls are usually taken not to be made up of some sort of immaterial stuff that could exist without being formed into souls. It is certainly hard to imagine what the parts or the stuff of an immaterial soul might be like—more difficult even than to think about souls generally. And many of the arguments for the view that we are souls imply that souls are simple.

Call the view that we are immaterial substances *immaterialism*. It is not the same as substance dualism: the view that substances come in two exclusive kinds, thinking immaterial substances and unthinking material ones. Immaterialism does not imply that there are any material substances (Berkeley was an immaterialist). Another difference is that according to substance dualism *all* thinkers are immaterial, whereas immaterialism says only that we are. For all immaterialism says, there may be material thinkers other than ourselves. It would of course be very strange to suppose that some thinkers are material but that *we* are immaterial. Still, it is a possible view. Despite their differences, however, substance dualism and immaterialism are close cousins: most immaterialists are dualists, and most discussions of immaterialism, whether critical or supportive, assume the reality of material things and are thus discussions of substance dualism.

It would be an understatement to say that immaterialism is out of favor nowadays. Most philosophers of mind treat it as little more than a historical curiosity. Introductory textbooks dispense with it briefly in their opening pages, often citing objections that would be considered flimsy if they were directed against a more fashionable view. In the current intellectual climate, the interesting question about immaterialism is not whether it might be true, but how the likes of Plato, Descartes, and Leibniz could ever have believed it.

I will try not to be so dismissive. Immaterialism has its problems—plenty of them. But it also has hidden virtues. Its strength is the weakness of materialism. As I see it, that weakness is not the traditional problem of how a material thing could think or be conscious, but rather the problem of what material things we thinkers could plausibly be said to be. It is the ontology of material objects, not the nature of the mental, that makes trouble for materialism. One way to avoid that trouble is to say that we are immaterial.

7.2 Traditional Arguments for Immaterialism

There are many traditional arguments for the claim that we are immaterial substances. These three are perhaps the most common:[1]

[1] The divisibility argument appears in Descartes' Sixth Meditation. For an interesting variant, see Swinburne 1984: 14–21. For the argument from disembodied survival, see

1. The *divisibility argument* says that any material thing, or at least any that is a candidate for being a thinker, is divisible into parts. But no thinking thing could be divided into parts: the very idea of half a thinker—half a mind—is absurd. Thinkers, ourselves included, must therefore be simple, and hence immaterial.
2. The *argument from disembodied survival* says that it is possible for me to survive in a disembodied state. But no wholly material thing could survive in a disembodied state. Not only could no material thing become disembodied and remain a material thing, in the way that no white thing could become blue while remaining a white thing. More strongly, nothing can start out as a material thing and then stop being material and carry on existing in an entirely immaterial state. Anything that *could* become disembodied must be at least partly immaterial already. It follows that I am not a material thing. (It doesn't follow that I am a wholly immaterial thing: I might have both material and immaterial parts. But for reasons we will come to presently, immaterialism is the most likely conclusion.)
3. The *inadequacy-of-physicalism argument* says that thinkers must be immaterial because we cannot account for the nature of certain mental phenomena in physical terms. One version goes like this: if we try to conceive of thought or consciousness arising out of the interactions of physical particles, we draw a blank. No matter how carefully we examine the workings of even the most complex physical object, we shall never see anything that could account for thinking or consciousness. This is not merely because we don't fully understand the physical workings of the brain. It doesn't matter what those workings are: as long as they are physical, it will be inconceivable how they could produce thought or consciousness. Hence, mental phenomena cannot arise out of the interactions of physical particles. But if any material thing *could* think, its thinking would have to arise out of the interactions of its physical particles. (What else could explain why only material things with a very special physical structure—things with brains—show evidence of thinking?) Therefore no material thing could think: we thinkers must be immaterial.

If there is anything that the critics of immaterialism have got right, it is that these arguments are unconvincing.

Swinburne 1984: 29–30, and 1997: 322–332. The classic statement of the inadequacy-of-physicalism argument is §17 of Leibniz's *Monadology*. A good contemporary defense of it is Foster 2001: 25–28. §8.4 considers two further traditional arguments for immaterialism.

The main premise of the first argument is that no thinking thing could be divided into parts. But how can we know that without already knowing whether a thinking thing could be material? Suppose there *were* a material thinker: a biological organism, say. In that case, we should understand well enough how a thinker could be divided into parts. So unless we can rule out this possibility on other grounds, there is no evident reason to agree that thinkers must be indivisible.

The second argument asserts that it is possible for us, but not for any material thing, to survive in a disembodied state. But why suppose that we can survive in a disembodied state? If we already knew that we were at least partly immaterial, that might give us a reason to suppose that we could survive disembodied. But suppose that for all we know, we are entirely material. Then for all we know, we can't survive disembodied. If there *were* material thinkers, they would have the same grounds for supposing that they could survive in a disembodied state as we have for supposing that we could; yet they would be mistaken. How can we be sure that we're not mistaken in this way? Only by ruling out the possibility of our being material ourselves. But that is what we were trying to establish in the first place.

As for the third argument: it may well be that we cannot conceive how a material thing could produce thought or consciousness. But then we can no more conceive how an *im*material thing could produce thought or consciousness: no matter how carefully we reflect on the notion of an immaterial substance, we shall never find anything that could account for thought or consciousness. It is no easier to explain a thing's ability to think on the assumption that it is immaterial than it is on the assumption that it is material (Taylor 1963: 25). And if an immaterial thing could produce thought in a mysterious and inexplicable way, why couldn't a material thing produce thought in a mysterious and inexplicable way?

There is of course more to be said about these arguments, both on the part of the prosecution and on the part of the defense. But not here. Let us turn to an altogether different sort of case for immaterialism.

7.3 The Paradox of Increase

One obvious advantage of immaterialism is that it can solve the thinking-animal problem. It could hardly be the case that *both* immaterial human souls and human organisms think. If we thinkers are immaterial, human animals will lack any mental properties at all. At any rate, they will be unable to think as we do. So if we were souls, we could know that we are not thinking animals. For that matter, we could know that we are not thinking brains. Only one being would think your thoughts. Whether any other account of

FIGURE 7.1

what we are has this advantage is contentious (see chapter 9). Of course, immaterialists will still need to explain *why* human animals cannot think. But they will have resources for doing so that are unavailable to materialists. It is easier to explain why human animals cannot think on the hypothesis that no material thing could think than it is to explain why they can't think even though other material things *can* think.

Here is something different: a problem for almost any account of what we are save immaterialism.[2] If we were anything other than simple immaterial substances—if we were animals, or material things constituted by animals, or parts of animals, or bundles of mental states, for example—then we should have different parts at different times. We should sometimes grow by acquiring parts, and sometimes shrink by losing them. But there is a metaphysical obstacle in the way of a thing's acquiring new parts.

Suppose we have an object, *A*—anything at all—and we want to make it bigger by adding a part, *B*. That is, we want to bring it about that *A* first lacks and then has *B* as a part. Let us therefore conjoin *B* and *A* in some appropriate way. Never mind what this amounts to; let us do whatever it would take to make *B* a part of *A* if it can ever be. Have we thereby made *B* a part of *A*?

It seems not. We seem only to have brought it about that *B* is attached to *A*, as in Figure 7.1. It appears that we have rearranged *A*'s surroundings by giving it a new neighbor, but we haven't given it a new part. If we have made *B* a part of anything, we have made it a part of the thing made up of *A* and *B* after our conjoining. But that thing didn't gain any new parts either. It didn't exist at all when we began. Our conjoining *B* and *A* brought it into existence. Or if it did exist at the outset, it already had *B* as a part then, and we didn't make it any bigger, but merely changed it from a disconnected object (like an archipelago) to a connected one. It seems that nothing we can do would ever give *A* a new part. And because this reasoning makes no assumptions about the nature of *A* or *B* or the manner in which they are conjoined, it entails that nothing, including you or I, can grow by gaining new parts. This is the *paradox of increase* or growing argument.

[2] The argument below is derived from Chisholm (1976: 89–113, 145–158; see also van Inwagen 1981). Zimmerman (2003) offers a complex argument a bit like this one for the same conclusion. Another important argument for immaterialism is in Unger 2006: chap. 7. This section and the next are based on Olson 2006b.

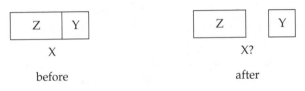

FIGURE 7.2

A similar argument appears to rule out a thing's shrinking by losing parts. Suppose we want to make an object *X* smaller by removing a part, *Y*. That is, we want to bring it about that *X* first does and then doesn't have *Y* as a part. Let us therefore detach *Y* from *X* in some appropriate way: let us do whatever would bring it about that *Y* ceases to be a part of *X* if *X* can ever lose *Y* as a part and carry on without it. Have we thereby made it the case that *X* no longer has *Y* as a part? Have we made *X* smaller? It seems not. *X* starts out made up of *Y* and the rest of *X*—call the rest of *X* '*Z*'—as in Figure 7.2. What happens to *X* when we detach *Y*? Apparently it ceases to exist. Or if it does still exist, it still has *Y* as a part, and we have merely changed it from a connected object to a scattered one. Either way, it doesn't shrink by losing a part. And of course *Y* and *Z* don't lose any parts either. It seems that nothing we can do would make anything smaller by removing one of its parts. Alert readers will recognize this as the amputation puzzle of §3.3. Like the growing argument, it assumes nothing about the nature of *X* or *Y* or the manner in which *Y* is detached. So it threatens to show that nothing could ever lose a part: the very idea of shrinking by losing parts is incoherent.

If these arguments are sound, it is equally hard to see how anything could exchange an old part for a new one without shrinking or growing. So they suggest the more general conclusion that nothing can have different parts at different times: it is absolutely impossible for anything to have a certain part at one time and exist without that part at another time. This is the *doctrine of mereological constancy*. (It is not the same as mereological essentialism, the claim that nothing could exist without having just the parts it actually has. Mereological constancy does not entail mereological essentialism: the impossibility of my having a certain thing as a part at one time and lacking it at another would not rule out my existing without ever having it as a part. It might be possible for me to have had different parts all along, even if I cannot *change* my parts.)

The doctrine of mereological constancy is plainly trouble for anyone who takes us to be material things. If you are a material thing, your atoms are constantly coming and going. Mereological constancy implies that the atoms you assimilate do not become parts of you, and the atoms you expel do not cease to be parts of you. It follows that you are not the being who bore your name a moment ago, for you now have parts that were not then parts of that being. Nor are you the being who will answer to your name a moment hence, for that being will have parts then that are not now parts of you. What appears to be a persisting human being is in reality a series of numerically different beings, succeeding one another at a rate of trillions per second. You retain your human form for only a moment.

What happens to you when your metabolism assimilates or expels an atom—supposing that you are a material thing? Mereological constancy by itself does not answer this question. It says only that you don't gain or lose any parts. That doesn't tell us what happens to you because it doesn't say what it would *be* for you to gain or lose parts. Specifically, it doesn't tell us whether the atoms you shed thereby stop being parts of you, or whether the atoms your metabolism assimilates are parts of you before it assimilates them. And what happens to you when you expel an atom depends, among other things, on whether that atom continues to be a part of you when it no longer coheres with the rest of your atoms.

Suppose that it doesn't. Then according to mereological constancy, you—or perhaps we ought to say 'the being we now call you'—exist only as long as all your current atoms stick together: not long at all. As soon as you shed an atom, you cease to exist and are instantly replaced by something new: something very like the human being who existed a moment earlier, but numerically different because it has different parts. You are what we might call a *momentary mass of matter*.

Now suppose the opposite: that your atoms do remain parts of you when they disperse. In that case, you presumably continue to exist for as long as your atoms exist, no matter how they come to be arranged. (If your atoms remain parts of you even when they are scattered to the four winds, it is hard to see what *could* cause them to cease to be parts of you, save destroying them.) So the being we now call you survives the expulsion of an atom and merely changes thereby from a connected object to a disconnected one. Part of you remains in one piece; the rest of you disperses. In a few years' time, when all your current atoms have been expelled, you will be scattered thinly across the biosphere. You were similarly scattered in the past. You have existed for billions of years, and will continue to exist until one of your atoms is destroyed. Most of your history up to now has been as a nondescript and widely scattered cloud of cosmic dust. More recently you became confined to the earth, and a short time ago you began to coalesce into human form. But the moment you become fully human you immediately begin to disperse once more. In all likelihood, your future holds nothing but eons of unremitting tedium. As in the first story (where you perish when you shed an atom), you are instantly replaced, when you cease to be human, by another human being. The difference is that in the second story, the beings that successively bear your name exist before and after they take on human form, whereas in the first story, they exist only for the brief moment when they are human. On this account, you are what we might call a *persisting mass of matter*.

Now these are, I suppose, possible views about what we are. The *momentary-mass view* would be that each of us is a momentary mass of matter: a material thing that exists only as long as the atoms composing it remain stuck together. The *persisting-mass view* would be that each of us is a persisting mass of matter: a material thing that exists if and only if the atoms that compose it at some time exist. Either view would make it impossible to say *which* mass of matter you are. Presumably you would be a mass the size of a human being, rather than something larger or smaller. But a different mass would bear your name at every moment, and it would be entirely arbitrary to say that any one of them, rather than another, was you. In this respect both proposals resemble the stage view (§5.8).

The view that we are masses of matter, whether momentary or persisting, can only be described as dreary. If that is what materialism comes to, so much the worse for it. It would be no help to suppose that we are bundles of mental states, for mental states come and go nearly as rapidly as atoms do. Given mereological constancy, the only account of what we are that is compatible with our having anything like the sorts of lives we think we have—with our persisting as human thinkers for dozens of years—would seem to be immaterialism. So here is an argument for immaterialism: Nothing can have different parts at different times; but the only sensible account of what we are that is compatible with this is immaterialism; therefore we are immaterial substances.

There are two broad ways of resisting this argument. One is to argue that we needn't accept the doctrine of mereological constancy. That is, we might try to solve the paradox of increase and the amputation puzzle. The other is to propose a materialist account of what we are that is compatible with mereological constancy. The momentary- and persisting-mass views are examples of this, and in §7.8 we will consider two more. But let us first see what it would take to avoid mereological constancy.

7.4 The Cost of Materialism

What would it take to solve the paradox of increase? Let us examine it more closely.

The paradox purported to show that an object, *A*, can never acquire a new part, *B*. Well, suppose for the sake of argument that attaching *B* to *A* in some appropriate way *does* make it a part of *A*. Suppose, that is, that *A* and

FIGURE 7.3

B don't come to make up some new thing, as Figure 7.1 invites us to think, but rather that *A* comes to be made up of *B* and something else. That something else may appear to be *A* itself: it is made of the same matter as *A* was a moment earlier (supposing that *A* is a material thing), and that matter continues to be arranged in just the same way. It differs from *A* as it was before only in its surroundings. This fact—that the thing *B* ends up attached to appears to be *A*—is what supports the claim that *B* never comes to be a part of *A*, thereby generating the paradox. But let us try to resist this thought. To avoid assuming the point at issue, call the thing that looks like *A* and ends up attached to *B* '*C*'. Suppose, then, that when we conjoin *B* and *A* we make *B* a part of *A*, so that *A* comes to be made up of *B* and *C* (Figure 7.3).

Is there anything wrong with this? Well, where did *C* came from? Where was it before we attached *B*? Presumably it existed then: conjoining *B* and *A* didn't bring *C* into being. If conjoining two objects adds anything to the furniture of the earth, it ought to be something made up of those two objects. We don't expect conjoining *B* and *A* to create a new object that is just like *A* was before the conjoining. We can make this more vivid by imagining the process in reverse: suppose *A* is made up of *C* and *B*, and we want to make it smaller by removing *B* as a part. If attaching *B* to *A* brings *C* into being, then detaching *B* again ought to destroy *C*. But surely we can't cause an object to cease to exist just by detaching from it an object that was never a part of it. We can't destroy an object *merely* by changing its surroundings.

Suppose, then, that *C* existed before *B* was attached. Presumably *C* was the same size as *A* was then: attaching *B* didn't make *C* any bigger or smaller. *A* and *C* must have occupied exactly the same place before *B* was attached. So Figure 7.3 ought to show *A* and *C* superimposed on the left-hand side. But their relationship then is more intimate than mere co-location: they coincide materially. They are made of the same matter then, and share all their proper parts; or at least there are things that then compose *A*, and also compose *C*.

But it seems that two different things cannot coincide materially. The same parts cannot make up two different wholes at once. In that case, *C* really is *A*, and our story has fallen apart. *C* wasn't supposed to acquire *B* as a part: that was the whole point of bringing *C* into the story. But if *C is A*, then *A* didn't acquire *B* as a part either, contradicting our original assumption that *A* did acquire *B* as a part. That assumption has therefore been reduced to absurdity.

Let us make the argument's premises explicit. First we supposed, for reductio, that conjoining *B* and *A* makes *B* a part of *A*:

1. *A* acquires *B* as a part.

In that case, we reasoned, *A* comes to be composed of *B* and a third thing, "the rest of *A* apart from *B*," which we called *C*:

2. When *A* acquires *B* as a part, *A* comes to be composed of *B* and *C*.

Now obviously *B* doesn't come to be a part of *C* when we attach it:

3. *C* does not acquire *B* as a part.

And making *B* a part of *A* doesn't appear to bring *C* into being; rather, *C* existed before we attached *B* to it:

4. *C* exists before *B* is attached.

Nor did *C* get any bigger or smaller when we attached *B*: it had the same boundaries, before *B* was attached, as *A* had then. What's more, there were things that composed *A* and also composed *C* then:

5. *C* coincides materially with *A* before *B* is attached.

But

6. No two things can coincide materially at the same time.

And 5 and 6 imply that

7. $C = A$.

But if *C is A*, and *C* doesn't acquire *B* as a part (3), then neither does *A*:

8. *A* does not acquire *B* as a part,

contrary to 1. The assumption that *A* gets bigger by gaining a part leads to a contradiction and is therefore false. There are, as far as I can see, four possible ways of blocking this argument.[3] Each involves denying one of its premises.

The first substantial premise is 2, that if *A* acquires *B* as a part, it comes to be composed of *B* and "the rest of *A*," *C*. This assumption makes trouble

[3] In Olson 2006b I consider a fifth option, which involves relativizing identity to times.

FIGURE 7.4

because *C* appears to be identical with *A*, and since *C* doesn't acquire *B* as a part, it follows that *A* doesn't either. So we might deny that there is ever such a thing as *C*. Of course, there is *something* in the box labeled '*C*' in Figure 7.3. *B* is never *A*'s only part: there is another part of *A* that *B* ends up attached to. But there is no *one* such thing as "all of *A* apart from *B*." There is no one thing whose boundaries the box represents. There are only a lot of smaller things—*D*, *E*, and *F*, say—each of which partly fills that space. We can illustrate this by redrawing the picture as in Figure 7.4. *A* starts out composed of *D*, *E*, and *F*, and when it gains *B* as a part it comes to be composed of *D*, *E*, *F*, and *B*. But *D*, *E*, and *F* don't themselves compose anything after *B* is attached: there is nothing that has *D*, *E*, and *F* as parts then, and every part of which then shares a part with *D*, *E*, or *F*. The proposal is not merely that *D*, *E*, and *F* don't then compose anything interesting or don't compose a "genuine object" or the like. It has to be that they don't then compose anything at all. Call this the *way of sparse ontology*.

We can perhaps best see how surprising this proposal is by considering the corresponding solution to the amputation puzzle (Lowe 2002: 75–76; van Inwagen 1981). (If the way of sparse ontology is to provide a general solution to the paradox of increase, we should expect it to solve the amputation puzzle in a similar way.) That would be to deny that anything ever has a proper part that it could be pared down to. Assuming that you could survive the loss of your left hand, this implies that there is now no such thing as your left-hand complement—"all of you but your left hand." Nothing wrong with that, you might think: hand complements would be arbitrary, gerrymandered objects, and there is little reason to believe that they exist. But it has worrying implications. For one thing, if there are no hand complements, there are unlikely to be any hands. What principled reason could there be to suppose that there are hands but no hand complements? Hands don't seem to be ontologically special. More seriously, the way of sparse ontology implies that there is now no such thing as your *head*, either—assuming that it is possible for you to survive, even briefly, being pared down to a head. That would demolish the ontology of "parts of the body" that we learned at nursery school—hardly a comforting thought.

A second way of resisting the argument is to accept that *C* exists after *B* is attached but to deny that it exists beforehand (step 4). We could say, rather, that attaching *B* to *A* brings *C* into being. More generally, whenever any object gains a part, a new thing—something composed of the object's original parts—is thereby created. Suppose we have a house made of red Lego bricks, and we make it bigger by adding an extension made of blue Lego bricks. (If any material thing can grow by acquiring new parts, it ought to be possible for a house to do so.) When the original red house expands by acquiring blue parts, a *new* red house, composed of the original red bricks, immediately comes into being to take its place. Or perhaps we ought not to call the new object a *house*: maybe no proper part of a house can be a house itself. In any case, the building work creates a new material object very like a house.

Applied to the amputation puzzle, the claim is that whenever anything loses a part, the complement of that part—the thing composed of all the object's parts save those that overlap the lost part—ceases to exist. So there *is* now such a thing as your head, but cutting away the rest of you would necessarily destroy it: the head you would be in this radically maimed condition would not be the head you have now.

Call this the *way of funny persistence conditions* (Burke 1994, 1996; Rea 2000). It is no easier to believe than the way of sparse ontology. When we lay bricks, we may expect to create a new object made up of those bricks. But the way of funny persistence conditions has the baffling implication that laying only blue bricks can bring into being an object made up entirely of red bricks. Likewise, we can destroy an object made entirely of red bricks by moving only blue bricks. This is not merely implausible, but arbitrary and unprincipled: it implies that things come into being and pass away in an apparently capricious and inexplicable way.

The next questionable claim in the argument is 6, that no two things can coincide materially at once. As we saw in chapter 3, constitutionalists say that different things *can* coincide materially at once. They will say that *C* is not identical with *A*; it begins, rather, by coinciding materially with *A*, and ends up as a part of *A* when *A* grows by assimilating *B*. Likewise, when an object shrinks by losing a part, it comes to coincide materially with the complement of that part—the largest part of the object that didn't share a part, before the loss, with the lost part. Call this the *way of coincidence.*

This may sound like a neat solution: simply drop the dogmatic assumption that no two things can be in the same place and made of the same matter at once. In fact some philosophers use the amputation case as an argument for constitutionalism (Thomson 1983). But if this solves the puzzle, it creates another: If *A* got bigger, why didn't *C* get bigger too? If attaching *B* to *A* makes it a part of *A*, why doesn't attaching it in the same

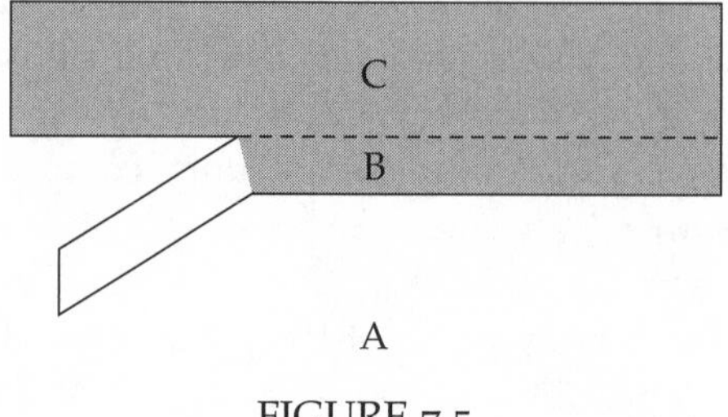

FIGURE 7.5

way to *C* make it a part of *C*? Presumably it is no accident, according to the way of coincidence, that *A* acquires *B* as a part and *C* doesn't: if we attached *B* a thousand times, it would come to be a part of *A* each time and would never become a part of *C*. *A*, but not *C*, has the *capacity* to grow by gaining *B* as a part. Presumably *C* cannot gain any parts at all. This is surprising. *A* and *C* are exactly alike before the attachment. They have the same parts then, arranged in the same way. They are physically identical. They have the same surroundings. They may even have the same past history. There is no difference between *A* and *C* that could account for their differing capacities to acquire parts. In any case, we saw earlier that constitutionalism faces all manner of problems.

Finally there is the *way of temporal parts* (Heller 1984; Sider 2001b: chap. 5). Suppose, to make things simple, that *A*'s acquiring *B* is the only change of parts it ever undergoes, and that *B* comes to an end when *A* does. Then *A* is composed of *C* and the largest temporal part of *B* located after it is attached. On this view, our "before" and "after" pictures are misleading; it is better to use a space-time diagram, where the vertical axis represents space, the horizontal axis represents time, and *A* is the shaded object (Figure 7.5).

The way of temporal parts is hard to compare with the alternatives because it holds that things have their parts without temporal qualification. In stating the paradox we spoke of the parts a thing has *at some time*, much as we speak of how tall something is at some time. But according to the way of temporal parts, things have their parts timelessly (§5.2). A thing may have parts that are located at different times, just as it may have parts located in different places, but those parts are parts of it *simpliciter*. Like the way of coincidence, the way of temporal parts rejects 6, the claim that no two things can coincide materially at a time. But because four-dimensionalists take parthood to be a timeless relation, their understanding of 6 is different from that of coincidentalists. On their view, for things to coincide at a time is simply for them to share those of their temporal parts that are located then. So as they see it, *A* coincides with *C* before *B* is attached only in the way that two roads may coincide for part of their length.

Four-dimensionalists accept the atemporal analog of 6: that no two things can coincide materially *simpliciter*. *A* differs from *C*, on their view, in that *A* but not *C* has the later temporal parts of *B* as parts. This gives the way of temporal parts an advantage over the way of coincidence: it is not committed to the mysterious view that things can differ in their kind and their capacity to gain parts without differing in their internal structure or surroundings. But as we saw in chapter 5, the way of temporal parts is no less controversial than any other way of solving the paradox.

To my mind, none of these four ways offers a satisfying solution to the paradox of increase. It is reasonable to ask whether any of them is better than the mereological ailment it is meant to cure. This might make the combination of mereological constancy and immaterialism look rather attractive.

Whether this is a strong argument for immaterialism, though, is uncertain. Even if the argument for mereological constancy is sound, there is peril in inferring from it that we are immaterial. Consider those material objects that, according to mereological constancy, take on human form for a moment before either ceasing to exist (if they are momentary masses of matter) or gradually dispersing (if they are persisting masses). Each of those beings has, for a moment at least, a working human brain and nervous system. It is surrounded by a community of thinkers and speakers. It has the same evolutionary history as we have. That ought to suffice for it to have mental properties. It ought to be conscious and intelligent, just as we are, for as long as it remains human. The material thing that is now human and sitting in your chair ought to be a subject of your current thoughts and sensations: it ought to think what you now think and feel what you now feel.

But if there are material beings thinking our thoughts, even if each one thinks for only a moment, there are unlikely to be *im*material beings thinking our thoughts as well. No one ever supposed that for each human person there is, at any moment, both an entirely material thing and an entirely immaterial thing, each bearing all the mental properties that person has then. And if there is no immaterial thing thinking your thoughts, then you are not an immaterial thing. (Surely you are not an *un*thinking immaterial thing.)

Those who say that you and I are immaterial will want to deny that any material things think our thoughts. But the argument from mereological constancy, by itself anyway, gives no grounds for such a denial. The claim that material things have histories very different from the ones we thought they have looks consistent with their being able to think as we do while they are human. Put it this way: the argument from mereological constancy implies that we are either immaterial things or material things with alien histories. But it gives no reason for choosing the first alternative over the second. For that, we should need a reason to suppose that the material things we should be if we were material at all would lack the mental properties that we have. But we appear to have no such reason.

You might argue that nothing could think for only a trillionth of a second. That just isn't long enough. Since no material thing would have more than a trillionth of a second to think if mereological constancy were true, it would follow that no material thing could think. This is certainly an argument worth considering. On the other hand, even if no *isolated* being that existed for only a trillionth of a second could think, maybe a thing could have a mental property for any length of time—even for an instant—if it has the right causal antecedents.[4] (The ontology of temporal parts appears to be founded on this claim.) What it is right to say here, it seems to me, is anyone's guess.

The paradox of increase may not be a strong argument for immaterialism. But even if it isn't, it looks like a powerful argument for *some* surprising claim. If nothing else, it shows how hard it is to be a materialist. Materialists will need to say something about it. We will return to this theme in chapter 9.

7.5 Objections to Immaterialism

Objections to immaterialism are all too familiar. Now I complained earlier that many common objections were overhasty, owing to the perceived weakness of their target. But here are three serious worries. They are not strictly objections to immaterialism per se but to substance dualism; but because few immaterialists want to accept idealism, we can see them as objections to most versions of immaterialism as well. (Nor is idealism entirely immune to them.) All have to do with the way the mental relates to the physical.

If you step on a tack and cry out in pain, it seems plain enough that the damage to your foot causes your pain and that your pain causes your cry. If you are a soul, your pain is a state of that soul. One of the overhasty objections to substance dualism denies that any nonphysical state of an

[4] See note 4 on page 110. Shoemaker's argument for the claim that no organism could think (§2.5) would also entail that no mass of matter could think, and his case against thinking masses might be stronger than his case against thinking animals. I doubt, though, whether it is compatible with our being immaterial substances (Olson 2002c; see also Shoemaker 2004). Immaterialists could also explain why there are no thinking material things by denying the existence of composite objects, thus combining mereological constancy with an extreme version of the way of sparse ontology.

immaterial thing could possibly bring about, or be brought about by, physical events in a material thing. I find this objection dogmatic. We cannot predict a priori what can cause what, and no experience tells us that nothing nonphysical can cause something physical. But we can sharpen the objection. We can ask, for instance, what it is about a given soul that enables it to interact in this way with a given organism. According to immaterialism, damage to my animal body causes pain in my soul, and mental events in my soul cause my body to move. It is a striking fact that no other soul interacts with my body in this way, and that my soul never interacts in this way with any other organism. Why should this be? Kim (2001) calls this the *pairing problem*: What "pairs up" souls with bodies?

We are unlikely to find an answer to this question in the intrinsic features of souls and bodies. It seems evident that I should not interact in this way with a duplicate of my body; nor would a duplicate of my soul interact in this way with my body. The same goes for material things. Why is it that turning this key opens that lock? It isn't just the way the two objects are in themselves. Turning a key in Tasmania, no matter what its size or shape, will never open a lock in Japan. For a key to open a lock, the key and the lock need to be in the same place. Perhaps that is how it is with souls and bodies: for a given soul to move a given body, they have to be in the same place. What prevents my soul from moving other bodies and other souls from moving my body might be that they are in different places.[5]

But this suggestion is problematic. For one thing, if the soul interacts with the body, it interacts with different parts of the body, specifically different parts of the brain, at the same time: for instance, it receives visual information from the occipital lobe at the same time as it receives auditory information from the temporal lobe. (Descartes was wrong about the pineal gland.) If this interaction requires spatial co-location, then the soul needs to be as big as the brain, threatening the claim that it is simple and immaterial. More seriously, we should have to wonder what *keeps* my soul and my body in the same place. Substances that don't share any parts ordinarily move independently. But if my ability to move and perceive requires my soul to be located where my body is, then wherever my body goes, my soul goes too: I never find myself suddenly unable to move or perceive because my body and my soul have become separated. What sort of psychophysical glue averts this calamity?

A second problem to do with soul-body interaction is what van Inwagen (2002a: 196–98) calls the *remote-control argument*. If it is souls that think, then they relate to their bodies in something like the way

[5] Foster (1991: 163–172) proposes a different solution, too complex to summarize here. Another important discussion of these matters is Shoemaker 1977.

someone relates to a device she is operating by remote control—a robot, say, that not only moves according to her commands but also sends her sensory information about itself and its surroundings via headphones and a video screen. We should expect damage to such a robot to interfere with this exchange of information, so that the robot stops acting on the operator's commands and stops sending her sensory information. That is, damage to the robot would affect the operator's ability to interact with it. But it wouldn't affect the operator directly in any other way. If this analogy is correct, then substance dualism leads us to expect a violent blow to the head to affect the soul's ability to interact with the body, perhaps rendering one unable to move or perceive anything—but it shouldn't affect the soul directly in any other way. We should expect someone who is knocked out to remain conscious, and to be able to tell us afterward what she was thinking while she was unable to move or perceive. Yet we know that this is not the case: a hard knock on the head causes complete unconsciousness. As long as we remain embodied, anyway, we cannot think or be conscious unless our brains are working. This is an awkward fact for the immaterialist. Why should damage to a material thing prevent something entirely immaterial from functioning?

One might answer by denying that souls think. Rather, the soul might do something necessary but insufficient for thought: for thought to occur, the soul's contribution must combine with some sort of activity on the part of the brain. All mental activity would consist of an immaterial ingredient in the soul and a material ingredient provided by the body. In that case, damage to the brain could stop thought by removing the material ingredient. Whatever merits this proposal may have, however, it rules out immaterialism, for if souls don't think our thoughts but something else does, then we are not souls. It suggests that we are things made up of both souls and bodies (or souls and brains)—a view I will take up in the next section.[6]

Then there is the *duplication problem* (van Inwagen 2002a: 198–201). Imagine a machine capable of making a perfect physical duplicate of anything: an object indistinguishable from the original, right down to the subatomic level. What would happen if we put a human being into this machine—you, for instance? Well, we should get a perfect physical duplicate of you. What would it be like? Unless modern biochemistry is badly mistaken, it would be *alive* in the biological sense. But what mental properties would it have? Immaterialism suggests that it would have none at all. (Let us suppose that there is no miraculous divine intervention.) Because it

[6] This will be even more worrying for idealistic immaterialists than it is for dualistic immaterialists. For a different proposed solution to the remote-control argument, see Robinson 1989: 49.

would lack a soul, it would be a sort of human vegetable. At any rate, it would lack those mental properties that only things with souls can have, and anyone who believes in souls will take there to be many such properties.

Of course, we shall never be able to test this prediction experimentally. But it doesn't *sound* right—not to most of us, anyway. It certainly isn't what medical science leads us to expect. As far as we know—and neurologists have studied the matter extensively—every actual case in which a human animal has a serious cognitive deficiency over a long period is a case in which there is a physical defect in its brain. It would be astonishing if the animal produced by duplication, which would have a physically normal brain, had anything but normal mental capacities. If our expectations are correct and the duplicate *would* have normal mental capacities, though—if reproducing your physical states suffices to reproduce your mental states—then we don't think by virtue of having immaterial souls, contrary to immaterialism.

Someone might try to solve this problem by saying that a brain brings a soul into existence when it is in the right state, much as a piece of iron in the right state produces a magnetic field (Hasker 1999: 190; 2001). Since your physical duplicate would have a brain just like yours, its brain would cause a soul to exist, just as your own brain causes your soul to exist. Given that like causes tend to have like effects, we should expect the new soul to resemble yours. This might help answer other hard questions too: for instance, the question of when in the course of its development a human organism acquires a soul (and why then, rather than earlier or later). It may even help with the remote-control problem: perhaps a hard knock on the head causes the soul to go out of existence, much as heating a magnet and thus realigning its particles destroys its magnetic field. If the brain recovers sufficiently, it then generates a new soul (or perhaps the original soul comes back into being), and mental activity resumes. Advocates of this sort of view call it *emergent dualism*.

Emergent dualism seems to me to face an awkward dilemma. We have been supposing that souls are immaterial substances. But it is hard to see how the physical activities of a biological organ could bring an immaterial substance into being. That would be creation ex nihilo (the soul wouldn't be forged out of previously existing materials). Of course, the mere fact that it is hard for us to see how one thing could bring about another may be a poor reason to suppose that it couldn't happen. But it doesn't help matters that there are no other uncontroversial cases in which a substance is created ex nihilo. The idea that brains produce immaterial substances also does nothing to solve the pairing problem.

The emergence of souls out of brains would be less mysterious if souls were not substances but rather states or aspects of the brain—like your fist or your lap, rather than like your hand. That is what the analogy of the magnetic field suggests: though the metaphysics of fields is poorly understood, they sound more like states—either of the objects generating them or of space (or space-time) itself—than like substances. This would also help with the pairing problem: your soul could no more leave your brain behind than your lap could wander off without you. But the view that souls are states rather than substances is incompatible with our being immaterial substances—that is, with immaterialism. What are we, then, if we think by virtue of having immaterial but insubstantial souls? If we *are* those souls, then we are something like collections of mental states: a version of the bundle view. If we are not souls but rather the substances of which they are states, then we might be organisms, or brains, or material things constituted by organisms or brains.

These worries would cause me a good deal of unease if I were an immaterialist.

7.6 Compound Dualism

That concludes my discussion of immaterialism. I turn now to some views that resemble it. One is not that we *are* souls, but that we have them as proper parts. We are only partly immaterial: each of us is made up of both a simple immaterial substance and a material organism. Call this *compound dualism*. We can call the view that we are souls and that we have bodies that are not parts of us *pure dualism*. (Pure dualism differs from immaterialism by implying the existence of material things.)

Those who speak of substance dualism more often state it as compound dualism than as pure dualism, and a least one prominent dualist is a compound dualist (Swinburne 1984: 27; 1997: 145). The attraction of compound dualism over pure dualism is presumably that it would give us the physical properties we ordinarily take ourselves to have. Pure dualism, like the bundle view, implies that we are not really visible or tangible. We don't literally grow larger in our youth or gray and wrinkly in old age. We are not even men or women: a man or a woman must surely be at least partly material. Only our bodies are visible or wrinkly or male or female, and they are not parts of us. Compound dualism, by contrast, implies that parts of us really are visible and tangible; and having a visible part seems to be a way of being visible. Despite this virtue, however, compound dualism has troubles that have nothing to do with worries about dualism generally, and which pure dualism avoids.

First, compound dualism inherits the problems facing materialist accounts of what we are. Consider, for example, the paradox of increase.

Pure dualists can give a neat solution: simply accept that nothing can change its parts and point out that this doesn't affect *us* because we are simple. Compound dualists will have to choose from the messy solutions available to materialists, thus forfeiting what is to my mind the best reason for accepting dualism in the first place.

Second, there is what we might call the *thinking-soul problem.* If our souls think, yet we are not our souls, then we are not the beings that think our thoughts. We merely have thinking parts. That might make it true to say, in the right context, that we think, just as it might be true to say in the right context that my house is made of glass owing to the fact that it has glass windows. But we are not thinkers in the strictest sense. And the idea that *we* don't strictly think, whereas things other than us think our thoughts, is hard to warm to. For that matter, if I believe that I am the compound, doesn't my soul believe that *it* is the compound? How do I know that I'm not making that mistake? What justifies my belief that I am the compound and not the soul? Compound dualists will also need to explain why intelligent, self-conscious souls don't count as people.

Of course, this sort of trouble is not unique to compound dualism. We saw in §5.7 that according to the temporal-parts view, we think only in the sense of having temporal parts that think. But then the ontology of temporal parts has all sorts of repugnant consequences. Its advocates are willing to live with them for the sake of its theoretical benefits, such as the solution it offers to the paradox of increase. Whatever the merits of this tradeoff may be, no one can say that compound dualism offers theoretical benefits comparable to those of four-dimensionalism.

Here is a third problem for compound dualism. Suppose my body is destroyed at the end of Monday and that my soul continues to exist without a body on Tuesday. Compound dualism ought to allow for this: a substantial soul shouldn't need a body to exist. Now if my soul could survive this, *I* could survive it. (That's what compound dualists say.) But in what form should I survive? It seems that I should survive as a soul. There is nothing else there on Tuesday that I could be. But compound dualism rules out my being my soul on Tuesday, for I was not my soul on Monday, and a thing cannot come to be identical with something that was previously only a proper part of it.

Here is the problem laid out stepwise. Compound dualism implies that I could survive the destruction of my body at the end of Monday, so that

1. The thing that is I on Monday is the thing that is I on Tuesday.

In that case I should be identical with my soul on Tuesday:

2. The thing that is I on Tuesday is the thing that is my soul on Tuesday.

And we supposed that my soul survives the destruction of my body, so that

3. The thing that is my soul on Tuesday is the thing that is my soul on Monday.

From these three claims it follows by the transitivity of identity that

4. The thing that is I on Monday is the thing that is my soul on Monday,

which contradicts compound dualism. Call this the *problem of disembodied survival*. The obvious solution, for those who believe in disembodied survival, is to accept 4 and say that I was identical with my soul all along: that is, to adopt pure dualism.

Now the problem of disembodied survival is a special case of the amputation puzzle. And we have already seen that compound dualists need to find a solution to that problem anyway. (They need an account of what happens if I lose a hand, for instance.) Can they not solve the problem of disembodied survival in the same way? Well, maybe they can. But it looks harder to solve the problem of disembodied survival than to solve the amputation puzzle generally. That is, even if we can explain how it is possible for a thing to survive the loss of *some* part, it looks harder to explain how a soul-body compound could survive the loss of its body. Obviously the way of sparse ontology won't work, for that would mean denying the existence of embodied souls. The way of funny persistence conditions doesn't look very nice, either: it would mean that a person's disembodied soul is not identical with the soul she had when she was embodied. No dualist would accept that.

What about the way of constitution? Perhaps when I lose my body, my soul comes to constitute me in the way that a lump of clay constitutes a clay statue. In that case, I don't come to be my soul when my body is destroyed, contrary to 2. But what would it mean to say that my soul constitutes me? The things philosophers typically say about the constitution relation don't apply in the case of souls and people. For instance, it seems to belong to the idea of constitution that when one thing constitutes another they must be made of the same stuff or composed of the same proper parts. They have to *coincide* in some sense. The idea that disembodied souls constitute people numerically different from them therefore seems to require souls to have parts, or to be made of some sort of immaterial stuff. Most dualists reject that.

Moreover, all constitutionalists accept three principles. First, a constituting thing can outlive the thing it constitutes: squash a clay statue and you destroy it, but the lump of clay that constituted it will still exist.

Second, a constituting thing can constitute different things of the same kind at different times: if we squash a statue of Thatcher and model the clay into the shape of Pinochet, the lump will constitute first one statue and then another. Third, a constituted thing can be constituted by different things at different times: by partial replacement of its matter, a statue constituted by one lump today can come to be constituted by another lump tomorrow. Now if your disembodied soul could constitute you, the first principle implies that your soul could outlive you: the survival of your soul is not enough for *you* to survive. The second principle implies that what is now your soul might one day come to be someone else's soul. The third implies that you could have different souls at different times. Compound dualists are unlikely to accept these claims.

A fourth principle that constitutionalists generally accept is that whatever is constituted by something at one time must be constituted by something or other whenever it exists. If your soul constitutes you when you are disembodied, this implies that something must constitute you when you are embodied as well. It will presumably have to be something composed of your soul and your body: otherwise you and it would not in any sense coincide. (Remember that constitution, in the sense that is relevant here, is by definition a one-one relation: your soul and your body could not jointly constitute you.) So there would have to be *two* things now made up of your soul and your body: you and the thing that now constitutes you.[7] Only one of them would be able to survive disembodied. That is a perfectly absurd thing to say.

These objections suggest that compound dualism is more interesting than it is attractive. If I were a dualist, I would be a pure dualist.

7.7 Hylomorphism

The idea that we are each composed of an immaterial soul and a material body might call to mind the Aristotelian view that we are compounds of form and matter. The idea is something like this: a human person, or indeed any material thing, comes into being when a certain human form or configuration is imposed on some matter. That form is not a universal—it is not *the* human form that all human people share—but rather a particular state that configures a particular batch of matter. The state that configures your matter comes into being when you do, namely when your matter first takes on your particular human form; and it is located where

[7] I owe this point to David Hershenov. I say more about compound dualism in Olson 2001a, where I probably treat it a bit too harshly.

you are. You are in some sense made up, at a given time, of your human form and the matter that the form configures at that time. Or rather you are made up of those things and also various "accidental" forms, such as your mass and posture. Your accidental forms are only contingently parts or constituents of you, but your human form is an essential part: you couldn't exist without having it as a part, and it couldn't exist without being a part of you. It determines what you most fundamentally are. Because of this it is called your *substantial* form.

Aristotle called the substantial form of a living thing a soul; let us call it a *hylomorphic soul* to distinguish it from the Cartesian or Platonic soul that figures in immaterialism. A hylomorphic soul is not a substance, but rather a sort of state: the substance is what you get when a soul configures some matter. That is what distinguishes this proposal from compound dualism. Call the view that each of us is made up (at any given time) of a hylomorphic soul and some matter *hylomorphism*.

I have serious misgivings about discussing hylomorphism. I don't properly understand it. It is true that I have discussed a number of views that I understand no better: the universal bundle view and the program view, for instance. I was happy to give my opinion about those views because I don't think anyone properly understands them. But there *are* people who at least appear to have a profound understanding of hylomorphism, and they will no doubt find my remarks amateurish. Because they take hylomorphism to be an important account of our metaphysical nature, however, I feel I ought to say something.

Hylomorphism is not a version of immaterialism. It says that we are material things. In fact all versions of hylomorphism that I know of say that we are biological organisms, so hylomorphism is, strictly speaking, a version of animalism. And hylomorphism as I have stated it appears to be compatible with everything I said about animalism in chapter 2. However, some versions of hylomorphism diverge considerably from what I said there, and these differences might appear to make it more attractive than "ordinary" animalism.

Someone might claim that hylomorphism combines the virtues of animalism with those of the constitution view. It implies that we are animals, just as we appear to be, and thus avoids the thinking-animal problem. More generally, it doesn't make the troublesome claim that the same matter can make up qualitatively different things at the same time. Yet it may avoid the traditional objections to animalism having to do with our identity over time. Suppose your cerebrum is transplanted into another head. Many people want to say that you would go along with that organ. Yet the human organism appears to stay behind with an empty head. If you are an organism, it follows that *you* stay behind with an empty head in the transplant case, which many people find incredible. Hylomorphists might be able to avoid this consequence without denying that we are animals. That is, they might be able to say that the human organism goes along with its transplanted cerebrum. How? Well, your soul—the configurational state that makes you what you most fundamentally are—is a *rational* soul. It is what gives you the capacity for rational thought. And your capacity for rational thought goes along with your cerebrum in the transplant case, rather than staying behind. Your hylomorphic soul therefore goes along with your transplanted cerebrum. And where your soul goes, you go. Thus, transplanting your cerebrum transplants you. It doesn't move you from one animal to another; rather, it moves an animal from one batch of matter to another. In a similar way, hylomorphists might argue that each human animal is essentially rational, which ordinary animalism denies.

Hylomorphists might say this, though it is not clear whether their hylomorphism demands it. (One of the reasons I don't understand hylomorphism is that I can't work out what follows from it.) *Should* they say it? Should anyone say it?

I myself find it deeply implausible. Forget about personal identity for a moment and think about biological organisms. Not even the hylomorphist will suppose that there are *two* human animals located where you are before the transplant. (That would be a version of constitutionalism, or perhaps four-dimensionalism.) So the view that a human animal goes along with its transplanted cerebrum implies that the animal left behind with an empty head (which may be alive and breathing on its own—the cerebrum plays no role in the regulation of life-sustaining functions) is not the animal that was previously whole. It is a brand-new human animal. At least, it is biologically human. Hylomorphists may say that because it lacks the capacity for rational thought, it is not human in the fullest sense. But never mind what sort of animal it is; the point is that according to the hylomorphist proposal you can bring a good-sized primate into existence by surgically removing someone's cerebrum. That sounds wrong. Isn't the result of removing an animal's cerebrum simply that the animal loses an important organ? Couldn't an animal—even a human animal—lose its cerebrum and continue living in a debilitated condition, just as it would if it lost a liver? The hylomorphist proposal says no.

Or consider the empty-headed organism into which your cerebrum is implanted. What happens to *it* when the transplant is carried out? Doesn't it acquire a new organ, much as an animal without a liver might acquire one? Not according to the hylomorphist story: when your cerebrum gets put into that animal's head, the animal must cease to exist. Otherwise there would be two human animals in the same place at once—the one that lately had an empty head and the one that got transplanted—which is absurd. But implanting a cerebrum into an empty cranium doesn't seem to be a way of destroying an animal. It seems, rather, to be a way of giving an animal a new organ. (We can see that this proposal commits its adherents to something like the way of funny persistence conditions of §7.4.)

Now think of the animal that is supposed to move from one head to another. It would cease to be a living organism at all when it is removed from its head: a detached cerebrum is no more an organism than a severed arm is an organism. So the story implies that the animal ceases to be an organism while it is being transplanted and becomes a mere organ, and later becomes an organism once more. Being an organism is only a temporary and contingent property of organisms.

It seems to me that there are *two* organisms in the story and that one of them gives the other one an organ. But according to the hylomorphist proposal, there are three: one that comes into being when the cerebrum is removed, one that ceases to be when the cerebrum is placed in the new cranium, and one that moves from one cranium to another. Hylomorphists will say that there are three organisms in the story because there are three different substantial forms: one rational soul, which moves from one head to another; and two nutritive souls, one of which configures the brainless matter left over after the cerebrum's removal and one of which informs the brainless matter that receives that transplanted organ. But this explanation doesn't seem to make the proposal any more plausible.

To my mind, the divergence of hylomorphism from ordinary animalism makes it less plausible than ordinary animalism, not more. An even more radical departure from ordinary animalism is *Thomistic hylomorphism*. It says that your hylomorphic soul can continue to exist after your death, when it no longer configures any matter. Not that it comes to configure some sort of immaterial stuff: it exists in a disembodied state as *pure form*. The soul can even engage in mental activity while it is disembodied: it can think and remember and be happy or sad (though it cannot, for lack of the relevant physical organs, perceive or act bodily). Some Thomists say that *you* can exist in this disembodied state; others say that you cease to exist when your soul becomes disembodied but come back into being if your soul once again comes to configure some matter.

When I try to think about Thomistic hylomorphism, I see nothing but problems. Most obviously, I cannot see how a thing's substantial form could continue to exist without being the form *of* anything (other than itself, perhaps). Remember, a hylomorphic soul is supposed to be neither a substance nor a universal, but a particular configurational state of a substance. Your hylomorphic soul is supposed to stand to you as a dent stands to a dented car, or a knot stands to a knotted rope. The claim that a human being's form could continue to exist after the human being is burned to ashes is like the claim that a knot could continue to exist after the rope it was in is burned to ashes.

Thomists will want to say that the human soul is different from such states as dents and knots, and that this difference explains how the human soul can exist disembodied. It may be, for instance, that the human soul is not a physical or material state like a knot: you can explain what it is for a thing to be knotted in physical terms, but not what it is for a thing to be rational. But even if that is true, a nonphysical state that is not a state of anything is no less mysterious than a physical state that is not a state of anything.

Nor do I see how a state, disembodied or otherwise, could think. That is like saying that thoughts think or dreams dream. This was one of the main objections to the bundle view. It appears to be an objection to Thomistic hylomorphism as well.

Now consider the relation between yourself—the person or organism—and your soul. Suppose you could continue to exist in an immaterial state when your soul becomes disembodied. If it is hard to understand how an organism could persist without being an organism, that is nothing compared to understanding how an organism could persist without being a material thing at all (or, for that matter, a substance). Thomists may say that you would no longer be an organism if you were disembodied, but that hardly helps. The trouble is not how something could be at once immaterial and an organism, but how something that is a biological organism at one time could be entirely immaterial at another time.

And how would you relate to your disembodied soul? You couldn't *be* your soul when it is disembodied, for you were not your soul when it was embodied. Yet there is nothing else, after your matter is dispersed or destroyed, that you could be. This is the same problem of disembodied survival that afflicts compound dualism.

What if you couldn't persist in a disembodied state and would cease to exist, at least temporarily, if your soul became disembodied? That would mean that psychological continuity was not sufficient for you to persist: here would be a case in which your soul is uniquely psychologically continuous with you as you were when you existed, yet without being you. This is precisely the objection most commonly made against ordinary animalism, and which hylomorphism was supposed to avoid. Someone who says that you could be outlived by your thinking soul can hardly object to ordinary animalism's implication that you might pass away even though someone has your intact cerebrum.

More seriously, if your soul can think when it is disembodied, why can it not think when it is embodied? If it does think when it is embodied, yet it isn't you, then you are not the being that now thinks your thoughts, but are merely something that has that thinker as a part. Thomists would then face the same thinking-soul problem as compound dualists face. The obvious way to avoid the problem would be to say that we *are* souls. That would be a version of the bundle view. But it would not be hylomorphism.

Thomistic hylomorphism seems to me to combine the problems of the bundle view with those of compound dualism. Thomists have attempted to reply to these objections, but the replies I have seen do not seem to me to answer them. The reason may be that I have not understood the replies. Or it may be that the Thomists have not understood the objections. Or perhaps I have misunderstood Thomistic hylomorphism in the first place. I don't know. I will say no more about hylomorphism.

7.8 Simple Materialism

We have considered the view that we are simple immaterial things and the view that we are each composed of a simple immaterial thing and a biological organism. What about the view that we are simple *material* things? Though this thought lies far off the beaten track, two important figures have defended it.

Chisholm (1989) once argued that we are tiny physical particles. Although he didn't say that these particles must be simple, his reasoning suggests that they would have to be.[8] More precisely, he reasoned that we must be tiny particles if we are material things at all. He argued for this in much the way that I argued for immaterialism in earlier sections: If we were material things, we should be either our bodies or parts of our bodies. But there are really no such things as our bodies, for they would change their parts, and nothing can change its parts. So we cannot be our bodies. We must therefore be parts of our bodies—in particular, parts of our bodies that never gain or lose any parts themselves. Chisholm suggested that each of us is a tiny particle within the brain. Call this view *Lilliputian materialism*.

Why suppose that we are simple material things rather than immaterial ones? Chisholm would probably turn the question around: Why suppose that we are *im*material? Once we have accepted that we are simple, what do we gain by taking ourselves to be immaterial as well? What can an immaterial thing do that a material thing can't? As we noted earlier, it is no easier to understand how an immaterial thing could think than it is to understand how a material thing could think. And supposing

[8] Quinn (1997), who discusses a different Chisholmian argument for the same conclusion, says explicitly that we are simple material things.

that we are immaterial makes trouble that materialism avoids; recall the pairing problem, the remote-control argument, and the duplication problem of §7.5. Lilliputian materialism is designed to bypass both the problems of materialism—the paradox of increase, for instance—and the problems of immaterialism.

Here is an obvious objection: If we are material things, our thought arises in our brains. But a tiny physical particle hasn't got a brain, and surely a material thing needs something like a brain to think. Chisholm replies that the tiny particle that you are *has* got a brain, even though its brain isn't a part of it. Your brain needn't be a part of you for you to use it to think. "The brain," says Chisholm, "is the *organ* of consciousness, not the *subject* of consciousness" (1989: 126).

A more serious worry is this. There are many particles in the brain. Why is only one of them the subject of the mental states realized there? If a particle within the brain really could use the brain to think, why don't they all think? And if only one particle thinks, what determines which one it is? Come to that, why must the thinking particle be located within the brain at all?

The only answer I can think of to these questions is that the particles in the brain are not all equal. One of them is special: it directs the brain's activities in something like the way that a conductor directs an orchestra. That is why it thinks and no other particle does. If it were removed from the brain, the brain would stop working as it ordinarily does, and the organism would show all the signs of complete unconsciousness—at least until some other particle takes over the conductor's baton. Mysterious though the brain's workings may be, however, I take it that neuroscience has pretty well ruled this out.

Lowe has also argued that we are simple material things, or at least simple things with physical properties. His view is not that we are tiny particles, however, but that we have the size, shape, and weight that we think we have: we are six-foot, 150-pound mereological atoms (1996: 36; 2000: 15–20; 2001: 151–154). We can get bigger or smaller without gaining or losing any parts. Call this *Brobdingnagian atomism*.

This remarkable view contradicts the widely held principle that every extended thing must have proper parts—a north half and a south half, for instance—even if they cannot be separated. I hesitate to endorse this principle. But Brobdingnagian atomism also conflicts with the more compelling claim that internally heterogeneous objects must have parts. Something that is internally heterogeneous has different properties in different places: it might be red in one place, for instance, and not red in another. And nothing can be both red and not red. At most a thing might be *partly* red and partly not red. But what could it be for a thing to be partly red and partly not red, if not for it to have parts that are red and other parts that are not red? And of course, if we are as big as we appear to be, *we* are internally heterogeneous: you yourself might be partly red and partly not red. It seems, therefore, that you must have parts.

Not everyone agrees that internally heterogeneous objects must have parts. Spinoza thought that the cosmos had no parts, despite being as heterogeneous as can be. Spinoza and Lowe don't say how a thing can be red in one place and not red in another without having any proper parts. One thing they might say is that things in space have properties relative to places, just as things in time have properties relative to times. For an ordinary thing to be red, it seems, is for it to be red at some time. And many philosophers believe that a thing can be red at a time without having a temporal part located exactly at that time that is red without temporal qualification. (Four-dimensionalists disagree: see §5.2.) Analogously, Lowe might say that a thing can be red in a place without having a spatial part located exactly in that place that is red without spatial qualification. For a thing to be red would be for it to be red at a place as well as a time (or at a space-time location): here now, or in Chicago in 1975, or at every place and time where it exists. In that case, things could vary across space without having spatial parts, just as things can change over time without having temporal parts.

It is hard to know what to make of all this. If nothing else, it ought to lead us to wonder whether *anything* has parts. Take living organisms. Surely *they* have parts—vast numbers of them. (Lowe agrees. Although Brobdingnagian atomism is at least formally compatible with our being organisms, Lowe says that we are not our animal bodies, but merely coincide in some way with them.) But if the particles within your boundaries are not parts of you, and your vastly complex internal structure is compatible with your having no parts whatever, what reason could we have for supposing that organisms have parts? To put it the other way round, isn't any reason to suppose that organisms have parts equally a reason to suppose that *we* have parts—supposing we have the physical properties of organisms? It is tempting to consider this a reductio ad absurdum of Brobdingnagian atomism.

In any case, Lowe has an argument for the claim that we are simple (1991: 88–89; 2001). Although it does not imply that we are simple *material* things, it is interesting in its own right. The idea is roughly this: if I had proper parts, I should have the same parts as my body. That would make me identical with my body. But I am not identical with my body. Therefore I have no proper parts. The main premises of the argument are these (where 'part' means proper part):

1. I am not my body (though both my body and I exist).
2. I am not a part of my body.

3. I have no parts that are not parts of my body.
4. No two things can have all the same parts.

Suppose I had parts. Then those parts would have to be parts of my body as well (by 3). Moreover, they would have to be *all* my body's parts: if my parts were only some of my body's parts, that would make me a part of my body, which (by 2) I am not. So if I had any parts, they would all be parts of my body, and all of my body's parts would be parts of me. In that case, I should *be* my body (by 4), which I am not (1). So I have no parts.

The premises of this argument are all attractive, and although the conclusion doesn't strictly follow, the further premises needed to make it formally valid are relatively uncontroversial. I suppose it might provide some reason to suppose that we are simple. But it is unlikely to make many converts, for the allure of its premises is more than matched by the repugnance of its conclusion. If we are to come to believe that despite appearances we have no parts, we are going to need more than just a valid argument from attractive premises. We are going to need an argument that makes it seriously uncomfortable to believe that we have parts.

As far as I can see, Lowe's argument fails to do this. It does nothing to undermine the principal alternatives to its conclusion, for its premises amount to little more than bald denials of those alternatives. Premise 1 denies, in effect, that we are animals. (That is how Lowe understands it.) Premise 2 denies that we are spatial or temporal parts of animals. Premise 3 is inconsistent with most versions of the bundle view: if we are bundles of mental states, those states are unlikely to be parts of our bodies. (Bundlers who think the mental states composing us *are* parts of our bodies will probably deny 2.) And most advocates of the constitution view deny 4: they say that we have the same proper parts as human animals, even though we are not those animals. So Lowe's argument will not trouble anyone who accepts one of these alternative views. Nor will it help those who are undecided about what we are. Imagine someone wondering, "What am I? A simple substance? An organism? A part of an organism, or something constituted by an organism? Or maybe a bundle of perceptions?" Such an inquirer would find Lowe's argument of little help, for in order to accept its premises she would have to rule out the main alternatives to our being simple things in advance. That is, she would have to believe, on grounds independent of Lowe's argument, that we are not animals, or parts of animals, or bundles of perceptions, or things constituted by animals. The argument is presumably aimed at those who are inclined to accept its premises but who deny its conclusion. It is hard to think of anyone who fits that description.

8

Nihilism

8.1 We Do Not Exist

We have considered many sorts of things that we might be: material things and immaterial things, persisting things and momentary things, simple things and composite things. But there is one possibility that we haven't yet considered: there is no sort of thing that we are. We don't exist. Our personal pronouns refer to nothing, there being nothing there for them to refer to. Nothing thinks our thoughts. Nothing wrote these words, and nothing is now reading them. Call this view *nihilism*.

Nihilism is not the view that you and I are not people, or "selves," or that there is some other important kind that we thought we belonged to but don't. It is the view that we are *nothing*. It does not, however, say that there are no people at all: it doesn't rule out the existence of nonhuman people, such as gods or angels. Like the other answers to our question, it is a view about us and not about people generally.

Nihilism is more or less the same as what Strawson called the "no-ownership doctrine of the self," that "it is only a linguistic illusion that one ascribes one's states of consciousness [to anything] at all, that there is any proper subject of these apparent ascriptions, that states of consciousness belong to, or are states of, anything" (1959: 94). I say "more or less" because nihilism does not say that the belief that we ascribe states of consciousness to something is the result of a linguistic illusion—though this might be a plausible thing for a nihilist to say.

The view that we do not exist might seem so far detached from reality that only a madman could believe it. Or it may appear self-refuting: Mustn't anyone who denies her own existence be mistaken? We will deal with these charges presently. Let us first ask what can be said in support of nihilism.

Nihilism may appeal to those dissatisfied with the other answers to our question. Suppose we take there to be things of a certain description, but despite our best efforts we cannot discover an account of their nature that looks even approximately right. This might of course be our fault: our best efforts might not be up to the task. But another possibility is that there is no such nature to be found, for there were never any such things in the first place. The longer we seek an account of the nature of these things without success, the more tempting it will be to suspect that their existence is some sort of illusion.

Nihilism has the advantage of solving at a stroke all metaphysical problems about personal identity. It solves them by depriving them of their subject matter, in the way that atheism solves all metaphysical problems about the nature of God. It may face other problems, of course. For instance, it might seem to face our old friend the thinking-animal problem. If there are human animals, and they think our thoughts, how could we not exist? Surely the existence of a being that thinks my thoughts is sufficient for me to exist. Unless nihilists can argue that human animals cannot think, they will have to deny that there are any such things. But if there are no human organisms, there are no organisms of any other sort. And whatever rules out the existence of organisms is likely to rule out the existence of *all* ordinary things: houses, bicycles, planets, the lot. That's not a very appealing picture.

Now once someone has denied the existence of people, herself included, it may seem odd for her to worry that she must also deny the existence of trees and houses. If *we* don't exist, how can it matter whether there are trees? But some philosophers seem more willing to doubt their own existence than that of other concrete objects. In any case, nihilists can turn this apparent problem to their advantage. They can accept that there are no trees or houses. They will probably want to deny the existence of any composite objects at all—any objects with parts other than themselves. Just as denying the existence of people does away with all problems about the metaphysical nature of people, denying the existence of composite objects does away with all problems about the metaphysical nature of composite objects: the replacement puzzle, the amputation puzzle, the paradox of increase, the problem of the ship of Theseus, the sorites paradox, and so on. Nihilism is probably best seen as a corollary of a more general metaphysical program that would do away with all the ordinary furniture of the earth and the troubles that go with it.

Nihilism is not my own invention. Though not many philosophers have explicitly denied their own existence, a surprising number have held views that seem to imply it. Parmenides said that the world was thoroughly homogeneous: despite appearances to the contrary (which are admittedly rather hard to explain away), the world never differs from one time or place to another. And what things, in a thoroughly homogeneous world, could you or I be?

Spinoza thought that there was just one substance—God or Nature. It is not homogeneous, on his view, but exhibits a wide range of local variation: it has different modes or states in different places. For instance, it exhibits a certain mode of extension and a certain mode of thought here: it is locally anthropomorphic and thinking about philosophy. Many commentators take this to imply that you and I and other ordinary objects are modes, or collections of modes. That would be a version of the bundle view. But we can just as easily read Spinoza as a nihilist: it is doubtful whether any anthropomorphic state of Nature is a human being, or whether any episode of thinking thinks.

Wittgenstein said in the *Tractatus*, "There is no thinking, representing subject" (5.631; for a similar remark, see Carnap 1967: 261). That certainly seems to imply that we don't exist; if we are anything, surely we are thinking, representing subjects. We could hardly be *un*thinking things (see §6.1).

Russell once wrote,

> All the ordinary objects of daily life are apparently complex entities: such things as tables and chairs, loaves and fishes, persons and principalities and powers. . . . For my part, I do not believe in complex entities of this kind. . . . Suppose you made any statement about Piccadilly, such as: 'Piccadilly is a pleasant street'. If you analyse a statement of that sort correctly, I believe you will find that the fact corresponding to your statement does not contain any constituent corresponding to the word 'Piccadilly'. (1918: 50; see also 1921: 17–18)

Russell's view (in 1918 anyway) was that the world consists entirely of momentary property instances, such as "little patches of colour or sounds." We can collect these things into classes, such as the class of all Socrates' experiences, but classes, Russell thought, are "logical fictions" and don't really exist. Strictly speaking, then, there are many experiences, but no beings that have them. (A few pages later Russell jokes, "The point of philosophy is to start with something so simple as not to seem worth stating, and to end with something so paradoxical that no one will believe it'' [53].) And although Hume is often said to have thought that we are bundles of perceptions, his remarks are also consistent with a view like Russell's, that there are perceptions but no perceivers.

Unger is the most notable recent philosopher to have endorsed nihilism, though he has since changed his mind.[1] It appears to be a recurrent theme in Buddhist philosophy, and it appeals to undergraduates of a certain temperament. The idea that we do not exist undeniably has a certain magnetism.

Nihilism is hard to come to grips with. This chapter has given me more trouble than any other, and I am still not sure what to say about the view in the end. But I think I know what to say to begin with.

8.2 Is Nihilism Mad?

According to nihilism, there are no human people, just as there are no dragons. This may sound like an absurd denial of the obvious. We believe that there are no dragons because if there were it is likely that someone would have seen one, or some fossilized remains, or some other good evidence of dragons, and no one has. Our experience tells against the existence of dragons. But our experience doesn't tell against the existence of human people. On the contrary, it tells us that there are vast numbers of them. No sane person can walk through London and believe that it is uninhabited. Yet according to nihilism, there are no more people in London than there are dragons.

Nihilism is of course intended to be a sober metaphysical hypothesis and not an insane delusion, so it had better not be the view that people are mythical, like dragons. What is the difference, then, between the nihilist's denial that there are people and the ordinary denial that there are dragons? Well, when philosophers deny the existence of things we thought we could observe or otherwise know about, they do not deny that there appear to be such things. In fact they typically concede that those of our ordinary beliefs and statements that appear to entail the existence of such things are often in some sense correct—in contrast to the belief in the existence of dragons. But they claim that what makes these beliefs and statements correct is something not involving the existence of those things. So when the ordinary nonphilosopher, in the course of discussing the sizes

[1] Unger 1979a, 1979b; his recantation is in 1990. See also Stone 1988 and 2005; Horgan 1993; Giles 1997: chap 5; and Rosen and Dorr 2002. Though Parfit sometimes sounds like a nihilist, he says explicitly that it is not his view (1984: 341).

of European cities, asserts that there are around six million people in London, the nihilist will accept that there is something right about this claim. We can take it for ordinary purposes to be true. It describes some real, unified state of affairs.[2] Since that state of affairs does not strictly contain any people, the ordinary statement may describe it in a way that is loose or misleading or perhaps even wrong. But it isn't completely wrong. It isn't wrong in the way that it would be wrong to say that there are six million dragons in London, or that there are six million people on the moon. Something about the state of London—something having to do only with things other than people—makes it appropriate or useful or perhaps even true to describe it by saying, "There are six million people there."

It is common enough for philosophers to deny the existence of things whose existence we appear to assert in nonphilosophical contexts. Suppose I say that there is an acute shortage of food in Zimbabwe.[3] This appears to assert the existence of a shortage. But we might wonder whether there really are such things as shortages. A shortage doesn't seem to be a sort of *thing*. It is, rather, a lack or an absence of a thing; and we may doubt whether the furniture of the earth includes not only things but also absences of things. Now if there are no such entities as absences, then there is no such entity as the current shortage of food in Zimbabwe. But it ought not to follow from this metaphysical claim that food is plentiful there. There is clearly *something* going on in Zimbabwe that journalists and aid workers describe as a shortage of food: many people in Zimbabwe have less food than they need.

More seriously, some philosophers propose a sparse ontology of material objects. We saw in §3.2 how denying the existence of statues and lumps of clay can help solve the clay-modeling puzzle, and we saw in §7.4 how denying the existence of such things as undetached hand complements can help solve the paradox of increase. Yet surely there is something right in the statement that there is a large copper statue on an island in New York Harbor. How can that be if there are no statues? Well, there is a large region of space in New York Harbor, shaped roughly like a robed woman holding aloft a torch, filled with a vast number of copper atoms. They are in a solid state, and are strongly bonded to one another but not to the atoms surrounding them (apart from those they rest on). They were put there by a sculptor with the intention of creating a work of art. And so on. None of this entails—in any obvious way, at least—that there is a statue.

In each of these cases there is an appearance of inconsistency: what the intellectuals say in the seminar room appears to conflict with what the rest

[2] Here I follow van Inwagen 1990b: 100–102.

[3] I have borrowed this example from Jonathan Bennett.

of us (and for that matter the intellectuals themselves) say in the street. If I say both "There is a shortage of food in Zimbabwe" and "There are no such things as shortages", I seem to be contradicting myself. If I am to stand by both statements I shall need to explain away this appearance of conflict. Nihilists and sparse ontologists are in a similar situation: they need to say how our ordinary statements and beliefs could be true or at least somehow appropriate even though there are no people or shortages or statues. They cannot simply assert that, despite appearances, their claims are consistent with our ordinary beliefs and then stop. They must say *how* they can be consistent. At any rate, their inability to do so will be reason to doubt whether they have a coherent position. (Another example: philosophers who deny the existence of abstract objects will need to say something about such statements as "There are prime numbers between 10 and 20," which, though undoubtedly in some sense correct, appear to entail the existence of numbers, which are abstract. They will need to explain what makes this statement correct in a way that is consistent with their ontology.) We will return to this point in §8.5.

8.3 Is Nihilism Self-Refuting?

Nihilists are philosophers who deny their own existence. But no one can deny her own existence and be *right*. Anyone who denies that she herself exists is bound to be mistaken, for you have to exist in order to deny anything. We owe this point to Descartes. He imagined a powerful demon bent on deceiving him; yet even an all-powerful demon, he reasoned, could not deceive him by causing him to believe wrongly that he exists, for the simple reason that you can't deceive someone who isn't there to be deceived. If there is no such being as Descartes—never was and never will be—then there is nothing that anyone could possibly do to deceive him. Or rather, in order to deceive Descartes we should first have to bring him into being; only then could we practice our deceptive arts upon him. Because I believe that I exist, and I couldn't do so unless I did exist, it therefore follows that I exist, and nihilism is false. Nihilism looks self-refuting.

The claim that I do not exist is not self-contradictory. I might not have existed: what I say when I utter the words 'I do not exist' could easily have been true. It would have been true if my parents had never met. It may seem, though, that the claim that one does not exist could never truly be asserted in the first person. For if it is asserted, then someone or something asserts it, and it refers to that being. That being is therefore asserting that it itself does not exist, which is bound to be false. So the claim that one does not exist will be false whenever it is asserted in the first person. It is like the claim that one is not making an assertion: although it could be true, it could never truly be asserted. It is what philosophers of language call "pragmatically inconsistent": the conditions necessary for it to be asserted ensure that it is false. Contrariwise, the claim that one exists can never falsely be asserted. And the first-person belief that one exists could never falsely be held. So our quick refutation of nihilism is this: I believe that I exist, and that belief can never falsely be held; therefore it is true—I exist—and nihilism is false.

This sort of argument is often criticized. The critics concede that anyone who believes that he exists must be right, but they question whether anyone believes anything. If *I* believe that I exist, then that belief will be true; but what justifies the claim that *I* believe something? That is already to assume too much: it presupposes that there is such a thing as I. The argument that nihilism is self-refuting therefore assumes the point at issue. For the argument to give us a reason to believe that we exist, the objection goes, it would have to begin with a premise that can be established without illicitly assuming that anyone exists. So no useful argument for the claim that I exist can start with the claim that *I* think. It would have to start, rather, with the claim that there is thinking, or that there is an occurrence of the belief that I exist, or the like. But from these claims it doesn't follow, at least not in any obvious way, that I or anyone else exists. Without further argument, we cannot infer that anyone thinks, and therefore that anyone exists, from the premise that there is thinking. Even if Descartes' demon could not get me to believe falsely that I exist, he might be able to cause an instance of the thought *I exist* to occur on an occasion when it is false—that is, when it is not a thought *of* anyone or anything. Likewise, it may be that anyone who asserts that he does not exist is bound to be mistaken; but from the fact that such an assertion is made, it doesn't follow that anyone makes it. So for all I know (or perhaps I ought to say for all that is known), my belief that I exist (or the belief that is called mine) might be false. The pragmatic inconsistency of denying one's own existence does not therefore refute nihilism.

I suppose the critics are right that there is no obvious valid inference from the occurrence of thinking to there being someone or something that thinks. Nihilism is not self-refuting, or at least not obviously so. There is no quick and easy way to defeat it. To argue that we exist, we need something more substantial. We need a metaphysical argument. Can we find one?

8.4 Unity and Simplicity

Let us suppose that human thinking goes on. This is something that even Descartes' critics grant; they simply doubt whether this thinking has to be done by anything. But *can* there be thinking without anything doing it? Is it possible for there to be mental states and activities—beliefs, wishes, dreams, and so on—and yet nothing that is a subject of those states or events? If not, then the existence of human thought entails that nihilism is false. (If it *is* possible, on the other hand, it would not follow that nihilism is true, though it might cast some doubt on our existence.)

One argument for the claim that thought requires a thinker is that mental states and events "owe their identity as particulars to the identity of the person whose states they are" (Strawson 1959: 97). Here is one thing this might mean. Suppose there is a particular pain *P1* and a particular pain *P2* simultaneous with *P1* and qualitatively just like it. *P1* and *P2* are either the same pain or two different pains. But what could make it the case that they were two and not one, or vice versa? The only possible answer, the argument says, is that they are one if they have the same subject and two if they have different subjects (Carruthers 1986: 57–58). No being could have two qualitatively indistinguishable pains at once, and two beings could never share a single pain. So the number of pains is determined at least in part by the number of suffering beings. It follows that there could not be a pain that was not the pain of some sentient being. And what goes for pains goes for mental states and events generally. Thus, all thinking requires a thinker, and nihilism is false.

I have two worries about this argument. First, I see nothing to prevent a single sentient being—one that is mentally disunified—from having two indistinguishable pains at once (Olson 2003b). If this is possible, then the claim that every mental state must have a subject would not answer the question of what determines whether particular mental states are identical or distinct, and the claim would therefore get no support from the argument.[4] Second, it is not clear whether the question of what makes *P1* and *P2* two (if they are two) and not one must have any interesting answer. Why must something *make* them two—apart from the bare fact that they are two?

Another argument begins with the claim that the very idea of a state that was not a state *of* anything is incoherent. There couldn't be a dent without a dented object. There couldn't be a knot that wasn't a knot in a rope or a string or the like. Think of the Cheshire cat in *Alice in Wonderland*, which disappears and leaves behind its grin—no head, no lips, just the grin. This is a metaphysical joke: you can't have a grin without anything grinning. For the same reason, there could not be a pain or a dream that was not a state of some suffering or dreaming being. (Roald Dahl's story

[4] Someone might appeal to the psychological individuation principle (§6.3) to argue that this sort of disunity is impossible. But if we accept that principle, we needn't bother with Strawson's argument, for it implies all by itself that nihilism is false—assuming, anyway, that there are mental states.

about a giant who catches dreams and keeps them in jars until he can put them into the heads of sleeping children is another joke.)

Sensible though this sounds, however, there is a weakness in it. You could deny that thoughts require thinkers without endorsing an *Alice in Wonderland* metaphysic by supposing that many unthinking things combine or cooperate to produce thought. Thinking might be like putting on a play. Although someone could put on a play all by herself, it is more often a joint production: many actors, directors, stage hands, and others each do something less than performing the play, and those lesser activities together make it the case that the play is performed. To take another example, the cables of a suspension bridge cooperate to hold up the deck of the bridge, for although no single cable supports the bridge by itself, they hold it up jointly or collectively. This shows that things can "cooperate" to get something done without intending to do so.

It seems possible for many people to put on a play together without thereby composing anything that performs the play individually. The fact that a dozen people cooperate to put on a play does not entail the existence of a disconnected concrete object made up of those dozen people. At any rate, it would be a contentious metaphysical claim to suppose that it does. Though there may be reasons for believing in the existence of something the twelve people compose, the fact that they put on a play together does not appear to be one of them.

It seems, then, that at least some tasks can be performed without any one thing performing them, if several objects, by individually doing other things, cooperate to perform the task jointly. This is not the *Alice in Wonderland* view that things can get done or that properties can be exemplified all by themselves. For all the *Alice in Wonderland* argument says, then, thinking might be a cooperative activity like putting on a play. Perhaps many unthinking things—atoms, say—could each do something less than thinking in such a way that these lesser contributions add up to an act of thinking, but without making up any subject of the thinking they jointly produce. In that case, there might be thought without a thinker.

But *is* thinking like putting on a play or holding up a bridge? Could it be a mere cooperative activity—something that many things can cooperate to bring about without anything doing it individually? Some say no. Van Inwagen, for instance, says that things working together to produce thinking are "forced, by the very nature of the task set them," to produce thinking *by* composing something that thinks individually (1990b: 118). This is not the case, he says, for putting on a play or holding up a bridge. If he is right, it is impossible for things to cooperate to produce thought without there being a subject of that thought. There could not be thought without a thinker. Nihilism is incompatible with the existence of thinking, and therefore false. But van Inwagen doesn't say why thinking could not be a mere cooperative activity. He simply finds it obvious. Can we do any better? Can we say what it is about thinking that requires things that do it jointly to compose (or at least be parts of) something that does it individually?

Suppose that an act or state of thinking—a mental event or state—really could be produced jointly by a lot of nonthinkers. Then we might expect that act of thinking to be made up of parts: as many parts as there are unthinking beings cooperating to produce it. The reason why many people can put on a play jointly is that this task can be parceled out into smaller subtasks that individuals can perform singly: uttering certain words, making certain gestures, and so on. It is the job of the play's producer to assign these tasks to individual people. Likewise, the task of holding up a bridge can be broken down into subtasks that individual cables can perform: each cable has to exert enough upward force so that the sum of those forces equals the weight of the bridge. So if atoms, say, produced thought collectively, we should expect every such act or state of thought to be divisible into a vast number of atom-sized "subthoughts"—acts or states that are not themselves thoughts—each of which is produced individually by a single atom. Of course, we have only the vaguest idea of what these atomic roles would be—that is, what each atom would have to do for the sum of the atoms' activities to amount to an act of thinking. But that, the nihilist will say, is only because we know so much less about how thought is produced than we do about how plays are performed or bridges held up, and not because it is impossible for atoms to produce thought collectively.

Someone might suggest that atoms could jointly produce a simple, monolithic act of thought, not composed of parts distributed over those atoms. Thought might be something "new" or "emergent" that is in no way reducible to anything nonpsychological.[5] Given how little we know about the metaphysics of thinking, it is hard to rule this out with any confidence. That said, I shouldn't expect any nihilist to accept it. Nihilism is a paradigmatically "reductionist" claim: it says that we can account for thinking beings—or the appearance of there being thinking beings—in terms of smaller and simpler things. By contrast, the idea that acts of thought, despite being carried out jointly by a lot of unthinking atoms, are in fact simple, is strongly antireductionist. It says that we cannot account for acts of thought in terms of smaller and simpler things. There may be no formal inconsistency in saying that we can account for thinking beings, but not acts of thought, in terms of smaller and simpler things; but it would be a strange combination of views. In any case, it would be

[5] I owe this suggestion to Dean Zimmerman.

important news if the only way of defending nihilism were to accept that acts of thought must be simple.

Let us suppose, then, that an act of thought produced collectively by atoms that don't think individually would have to be made up of nonthoughts, each produced individually by a single atom. But *are* acts of thought made up of nonthoughts? You might think not. For one thing, it is hard to imagine what the parts of an act of thinking could be. Some acts of thinking may have other acts of thinking as parts: for instance, thinking that it's cold and windy might be made up of thinking that it's cold and thinking that it's windy. But what could be the parts of an act of thinking that it's cold? The very idea of a part of that thought sounds like a muddle—like the idea of the back side of a rainbow. If acts of thinking do not have parts, and if they would have to have parts for nonthinkers to produce them jointly, then nonthinkers cannot cooperate to produce thought without there being a subject of that thought. Thought without a thinker could only be an *Alice in Wonderland* phenomenon like a grin without a cat.

Even if there were such things as subthoughts, some argue that it would remain a mystery how they could come together to compose a whole thought unless they were all states of one subject.[6] If Blott thinks that it's cold, and Clott thinks that it's windy, the parts of the compound thought that it's cold and windy will exist, but they won't make up that compound thought unless Blott *is* Clott. Things can be parts of a single act of thinking only if they are unified in the right way; their mere existence doesn't suffice for them to compose a thought. And the only way for parts of thoughts to be unified in such a way as to make up a whole thought, it seems, is for them to be states of the same being—in which case the thought has got a subject after all. For there to be an act of thought without a thinking subject, that act would have to be decomposable into subthoughts performed by nonthinkers; but those subthoughts would compose a genuine thought only if they were states of some one thinking being. So again there cannot be thought without a thinker.

There are two different arguments here. Both start from the premise that a thought with no subject, produced cooperatively by many unthinking things, would have to be made up of subthoughts—parts that aren't themselves thoughts. The first argument goes on to say that acts of thought

[6] We find this argument in Kant 1929: A351–352. See also Brentano 1987: 290–297; and Hasker 1999: 123–135. Kant rejects it, but only after conceding that it is "no mere sophistical play, contrived by a dogmatist to impart to his assertions a superficial plausibility, but an inference which appears to withstand even the keenest scrutiny and the most scrupulously exact investigation."

are not composed of subthoughts and therefore cannot be produced cooperatively. The only way to avoid the *Alice in Wonderland* view that thoughts simply occur, like clouds, is to say that they must have a subject. Call this the *simplicity-of-thought argument*. The second says that even if acts of thought did have such parts, they could compose a whole thought only by being states of a single being—that is, only by having the same subject. Again, thought requires a subject. Call this the *unity-of-thought argument*.

These arguments would entail that every act of thought must have a thinker, ruling out nihilism. But they would also entail something more, namely that thinking beings must be mereologically simple. If they entail that we exist, they also entail that we have no parts. Suppose a thinking thing—something that thinks in the strictest sense, not merely something that thinks by virtue of having a part that thinks—were composed of unthinking parts. Then our two arguments suggest that its thoughts would be composed of subthoughts distributed over its parts (or at least some of its parts). Now as we stated them, the arguments said only that a thought *with no subject* produced cooperatively by many unthinking things would have to be composed of subthoughts. But the idea behind this premise was that any task that many beings could carry out jointly must be decomposable into subtasks, like roles in a play. And this seems to be so whether or not those beings thereby compose something that performs the task individually. Even if it were impossible for a dozen people to put on a play together without thereby composing a disconnected object that performs the play individually, mustn't the performance be composed of parts, each of which can be carried out by an individual person? So it seems that any act of thinking produced by the cooperative activities of many atoms, whether or not those atoms thereby compose a subject of that thinking, must be made up of subthoughts performed individually by atoms.

And both arguments say that no act of thought *could* be composed of subthoughts performed individually by nonthinkers. According to the simplicity argument, there are no subthoughts at all. It follows that thought could be produced only by a simple thinker. According to the unity argument, subthoughts would have to be states of the same thing and not of different things, else they wouldn't make up a thought. Suppose there are many unthinking atoms, each in a different state; and suppose those states are intrinsically suited to compose a certain sort of thought: they would compose a thought if they were suitably unified. Still, they can't compose a thought because they are all states of different objects. They can no more add up to a thought than Blott's thought that it's cold and Clott's thought that it's windy can add up to the thought that it's cold and windy (assuming that Blott isn't Clott).

It may be that if certain atoms compose something, then their individual states *are* states of the same thing, namely the thing they compose. So how does the unity argument imply that every thought must have a simple thinker, and never a composite one? Well, suppose for the sake of argument that Blott, who thinks that it's cold and not that it's windy, and Clott, who thinks that it's windy and not that it's cold, compose some larger, disconnected object. That clearly would not suffice for an occurrence of the thought that it's cold and windy. Perhaps the thing Blott and Clott compose would believe that it's cold and also believe that it's windy, but it would not believe that it's cold *and* windy. So the mere fact that states of different individuals that are intrinsically suited to compose a thought are all states of something or other does not suffice for them to compose a thought. What does suffice? It seems that states could compose a thought only if they are all states of the same *simple* being. You and I, who obviously think, must therefore be simple.

Because the simplicity and unity arguments have such drastic implications, we ought to be on our guard. And grounds for doubt are not hard to find. Start with the main premise of the simplicity argument: that no act or state of thought could be composed of nonthoughts. Though this has some attraction, it is hardly compelling, and I shouldn't know how to begin to argue for it. I admit that I have no idea what the parts of a thought might be, except in the special case where they are themselves thoughts. But that is because the nature of thought is obscure to me, and not because I can see by the clear light of reason that acts of thought must be mereologically simple.

What about the main premise of the unity argument, that states or activities of different objects could never add up to a whole thought? To my mind, it is nothing more than an intriguing speculation. You may well ask: How *could* states of different things add up to a whole thought? What *does* it take for different states or activities to compose a state or act of thought? That is, how do states or activities that are intrinsically suited to compose a mental activity have to relate to one another (and to their surroundings, if that is relevant) in order for them to compose a mental state or activity? We might call this the *mental composition question*. It is analogous to asking how atoms of the sort that are intrinsically suited to compose an organism—atoms of carbon, oxygen, hydrogen, phosphorus, and so on, in the right proportions—have to relate to one another and to their surroundings in order for them to compose an organism. If mental states and events can have parts, then the mental composition question must presumably have an answer. The unity-of-thought argument answers it by saying that states intrinsically suited to compose a thought actually do compose a thought if and only if they are states of the same simple object.

I have no alternative answer to the mental composition question. (If I had to guess, I would say that states compose a thought by virtue of their causal relations to one another and to their surroundings, along the lines of §6.3. But that is little more than a vague gesture.) If accepting that states of different objects could never compose a thought would help us to answer the mental composition question, that would be a reason to accept that principle. But it isn't clear whether it does help. For all I know, states intrinsically suited to compose a thought might be states of a single object—even a mereologically simple object—without composing a thought. Why couldn't a being—even a simple being, if a simple being could think at all—believe that it's cold and believe that it's windy at the same time without believing that it's cold and windy? That is, why couldn't a simple being have a disunified mental life? Being states of a simple object doesn't appear to suffice for appropriate states to add up to a thought. And if it's not sufficient, why suppose that it's necessary? If we had an account of what sufficed for states of a simple object to make up a thought, I should expect it to suffice also for states of different parts of a compound object to make up a thought. And if unthinking things can cooperate to produce thought, it is not obvious what could prevent them from doing so without composing any subject of that thought.

These arguments for the claim that thought requires a thinker are disappointing. Thinking may not seem like the sort of thing that could be carried out jointly by many nonthinkers without having a subject, but, for all I have been able to show, this is little more than a hunch. So I have failed to find any good argument for our existence. But it hardly follows that this that we don't exist, or that the belief in our own existence is unwarranted. You can't argue for everything. There are some things, surely, that it is reasonable to believe without an argument. And that we exist might be as good a candidate as any for being one of them.

8.5 Paraphrase: The Mentalistic Strategy

Let us return now to the topic of §8.2. Nihilism entails that the true story of the world—the story that is strictly true and not misleading—is not a story about people, for according to nihilism there are no people. If nihilism is true, it ought to be possible, in principle at least, to tell that story. That is, it ought to be possible to state all the facts without mentioning or otherwise implying the existence of people. Yet even though none of these facts involve people, some of them must make certain ordinary statements that appear to be about people in some way right, and others just plain wrong. Sensible nihilists will agree that in most contexts it would be a mistake to say that London is uninhabited. There is *something* right about the claim that there are many people in London. We can take it for ordinary purposes to be true. Even if nihilism is true, there is some state of affairs—one not involving people—that this ordinary statement describes, albeit in an unperspicuous and misleading way, and which makes that statement true—or if not true, at least somehow right. The nihilist's "impersonal" story of the world must include this state of affairs.

If this is correct, then every ordinary statement that appears to be about people will be true, or at least somehow right, if and only if a certain state of affairs not involving people obtains. And it ought to be possible to describe that impersonal state of affairs in a way that is strictly true and perspicuous and not misleading—in a way that does not even appear to entail the existence of people. That is, it should be possible, in principle if not in practice, to *paraphrase* any ordinary statement about people into a statement that nihilists can accept without qualification. The paraphrase ought to capture the truth behind the original statement. It is unlikely to be strictly synonymous with the original—it can't be if the paraphrase is true and the original is false—but it must be close enough to capture what is right or wrong about the original. (This is a difference between the nihilistic paraphrase strategy and the project of "logical construction" mentioned in §6.1: a logical construction of person talk out of vocabulary of some other sort would count as a nihilistic paraphrase, but a nihilistic paraphrase needn't count as a logical construction.) Of course, nihilists are not obliged to *use* these paraphrases, which are likely to be forbiddingly complex. Once nihilists have satisfied themselves and their critics that such ordinary sayings as 'Martina has three brothers' can be made correct in ordinary circumstances by facts about nonpeople and are thus in a sense compatible with nihilism, they can continue to use them like anyone else.

Earlier I said that ordinary statements about food shortages could be true even if, strictly speaking, there are no such entities as shortages: they might be made true by facts about the distribution of people and food. For instance, when the papers say that there is a shortage of food in Zimbabwe, this might be true if and only if many people in Zimbabwe have less food than they need. This paraphrase does not appear to imply the existence of shortages. (More elaborate examples can be found in Lewis and Lewis 1970 and in van Inwagen 1990b: §11.) Nihilists will want to do for ourselves, so to speak, what we seem to be able to do for shortages. But what might stand to ourselves as people and food stand to food shortages?

Two thoughts come to mind. The first is a "mentalistic strategy." Maybe there could be particular mental states and events (human ones) even if nihilism is true and they are not the states *of* anything. The truth behind the statement that I am now hungry would then have something to do with the existence of a certain hunger sensation. The second thought, an "atomistic strategy," will be the subject of the next section.

Now we cannot simply paraphrase 'I am now hungry' as 'there is now a hunger sensation', for the mere existence of a hunger sensation cannot make it right to say that *I* am hungry, but at most that someone or something is. Likewise, we cannot paraphrase 'I am not now hungry' as 'there is not now a hunger sensation' (Williams 1978: 97). Nor does the existence of a hunger sensation and a thirst sensation make it right to say that someone is both hungry and thirsty, but at most that someone is hungry and someone is thirsty. Plainly the nihilist needs some device for collecting together those mental states and events that we correctly but loosely describe as having the same subject. She needs to say that the ordinary statement 'someone is hungry and thirsty' is correct if and only if there is a hunger sensation and a thirst sensation and those sensations relate to one another in a certain way, a way that it is somehow apt, even if false or misleading, to describe as their being states of the same person. But this has to be a relation that mental states can stand in without being states of the same being.

At this point, we might return to the idea that mental states come in bundles (§6.3).Perhaps when mental states are related in a certain way—in the way non-nihilists say they are related when they are the mental states of a thinking being—they compose a bundle. We might be able to characterize this relation in causal terms: the mental states that non-nihilists ascribe to a single subject, but not those they ascribe to different subjects, are disposed to interact in certain characteristic ways that often lead to action. This will of course help the nihilist only if these bundles are never themselves subjects of the mental states that compose them, for if the bundles think, then something thinks our thoughts, and so we exist, contrary to nihilism. The idea must be, rather, that ordinary statements that appear to ascribe mental properties to people are made right or wrong by facts about bundles of subjectless mental states. Then the statement that I am hungry would be correct if and only if a certain bundle—*this* one, the one producing this utterance—includes a hunger sensation.

Bundles would help in other cases too. The ordinary statement that there are six million people in London would seem to be right if and only if there are six million bundles of thoughts of the appropriate human sort there. (I say "of the appropriate human sort" to exclude nonhuman bundles: feline and angelic bundles, for instance. When we speak of the number of people in London, we are not taking a stand on the number of cats or angels there.) It is wrong to say that there are people on the moon because that barren world contains no such bundles. Bundles of thoughts would be convenient for the nihilist because they would be good substitutes, so to speak, for thinking beings.

One difficulty for the mentalistic strategy is statements ascribing nonmental properties to people: that Brita is riding a bicycle, say. The truth behind this statement may have something to do with a certain bundle of mental states, but it clearly involves more. It may be tempting to say that this something more has to do with a certain human body or organism. Yet nihilists will not want to accept the existence of organisms, for they would be thinkers.

But the real problem for the mentalistic strategy is that if there are no people, there are unlikely to be any bundles of thoughts either. If bundled thoughts—mental states that relate to one another in a way that gives the appearance of their being states of a single thinking being—compose bundles, then we should expect the physical particles that now appear to compose *you* to compose something as well. Why should bundled thoughts compose something, whereas physical particles arranged in human form compose nothing? Why should there be things made up of mental states but no things made up of quarks and electrons? And if "your" particles—those particles now arranged in human form and resting on your chair—compose something, the thing they compose will be a good candidate for being you: something that thinks your thoughts and performs your actions. And if anything thinks your thoughts and performs your actions, surely you do, in which case you exist, and nihilism is false.

It looks, then, as if anyone who denies that we exist will want to deny that any things ever compose anything. Nothing is ever a part of anything. There are no composite objects. Everything is mereologically simple. And presumably this is no accident: there *couldn't* be composite objects. Let us call this claim *compositional nihilism* to distinguish it from nihilism about ourselves. If it is true, then statements apparently about ourselves will have to be made correct or incorrect by facts about mereological simples.

Compositional nihilism is an interesting thesis raising worries of its own. One is that no one knows for certain whether there *are* any simples. Perhaps all particles, even the smallest known to science, are composed of yet smaller parts. That would be incompatible with compositional nihilism. Whatever is not simple is by definition composite; so if there were neither simples nor composites, there would not be anything at all, and we know that *that* isn't true. If nihilism about ourselves entails compositional nihilism, then nihilism too is committed to there being simples.

A more serious difficulty is that mental states and events might themselves be composite. This would not be at all surprising if each particular mental state or event were a physical state or event in the brain—that is, if some sort of token-identity theory were true. Any physical event that was a candidate for being a mental event would be vastly complex, involving the activities of hundreds of millions of cells. If it makes sense to speak of the parts of states or events, we should expect states and events of this sort to have parts. In that case, compositional nihilism entails that there are no mental states or events; at best, there could be simple nonmental states and events that it is somehow apt to describe as if they composed thoughts. The nihilist could not then simply replace talk of bundles of thoughts with talk of bundled thoughts.

The nonexistence of mental goings-on would be troublesome for another reason too. Recall Descartes' argument for his own existence: I think I exist, and I couldn't think anything unless I existed; therefore I must exist. Descartes' critics say that it is assuming too much to suppose that *I* think; I am entitled to say only that thinking is going on. It looks now as if even that weaker claim assumes too much. If I think, then I exist. If I *didn't* exist, I should not be thinking. Thus, insofar as my existence is doubtful, so is the claim that I think. In the same way, it now seems that if I didn't exist, there would be no acts or states of thinking either. Thus, insofar as my existence is doubtful, so is the existence of thinking.

But is it really coherent to doubt the existence of thinking? Even if there could be an occurrence of the thought *I think* on an occasion when it is false because no one thinks it, not even an omnipotent deceiver could cause an occurrence of the thought *thinking is going on* to occur on an occasion when it is false because there is no thinking. The thought *thinking is going on* could never be false. And there are clearly occurrences of the thought *thinking is going on*. It is occurring right here. At any rate, it *appears* that thinking is going on; isn't this appearance itself an instance of thinking?

It seems that nihilists will have to account for the appearance of thinking in nonmental terms. This is a challenge that eliminative materialists also face. They too deny that there is any thinking, though not on metaphysical grounds but on the grounds that "folk psychology"—the theory according to which we can explain people's actions in terms of their mental properties—has been shown empirically to be false. Even if this is so, the challenge goes, there still *appear* to be mental goings-on, and this appearance itself looks like something mental. Unless nihilists and eliminative materialists can deny that the appearance of there being mental states is itself mental, their views will be self-refuting. We will consider a suggestion for doing this in the next section.

8.6 Paraphrase: The Atomistic Strategy

Though nihilists deny that we exist, they will nonetheless want to say that there is something right about many ordinary statements that appear to imply the existence of people, such as the statement that more people live in London than in Berlin. We considered an attempt to state this something right in terms of bundles of mental states, but abandoned it on the grounds that if mental states compose bundles, there are likely to be things that compose human thinkers as well: whatever prevents your atoms (if we may so speak) from composing a thinking being is likely to prevent your mental states from composing bundles. To be safe, nihilists will probably want to deny that any things ever compose anything: they will want to be compositional nihilists. But compositional nihilism threatens to imply not only that there are no thinking beings, but that there are no states or acts of thought either. Is there a way of telling the whole story of the world without implying the existence of either thinkers or thinking?

Perhaps we could tell it in terms of simple particles. Some simple particles—quarks and electrons, according to current physics—have certain properties and relate to one another and to other simple particles in such a way that they *would* compose a person if they composed anything. They are the ones that non-nihilists take to compose people, and the ones that would compose people if nihilism were false. They are the particles that collectively produce a certain sort of thought—the sort that (to lapse once more into person talk) distinguishes people from nonpeople. At any rate, it is appropriate for ordinary purposes to describe their activities (or some of them) as making up thought. We might abbreviate all this by saying that such particles are "arranged personwise." The proposal, then, is to replace talk of people with talk of simple particles arranged personwise. This would be an *atomistic strategy* for paraphrasing person-talk, as opposed to the mentalistic strategy we began with.[7]

The general idea is something like this. We replace quantification over people by quantification over particles arranged personwise: for instance, if an ordinary statement says 'Someone...', we replace it with 'Some particles arranged personwise...'. Thus, we can paraphrase the ordinary statement that someone is in the boat as 'there are particles arranged personwise enclosed within or resting on the particles arranged boatwise'. The statement that there are two people in the boat becomes 'there are particles arranged personwise, and some other particles arranged personwise, different from the first (let us ignore conjoined twins, who share particles), and they are all enclosed within the particles arranged boatwise'. I leave it as an exercise for the reader to paraphrase the ordinary statement that there are six million people in London in this way. In similar fashion, we replace singular reference to particular people with plural reference to particular particles: we replace 'Socrates', for instance, with

[7] Rosen and Dorr (2002) propose this strategy. Merricks (2001b: 2–8) adopts it for inanimate objects, but not for us.

'the Socrates-particles': those particles that, according to non-nihilists, compose Socrates at the appropriate time. It will not be easy to say, in nihilistic terms, what makes a particle a Socrates-particle, but this might be a mere technical detail rather than a principled obstacle in the way of the atomistic strategy. (This would mean that our personal pronouns and proper names do refer to something, despite our initial characterization of nihilism as the view that they refer to nothing. They don't refer in the singular to people, but rather in the plural to many particles.) Finally, we replace the predicates attached to these expressions—terms like 'is hungry' and 'is taller than'—with *plural collective predicates* true of particles.

A collective predicate is one that applies (or fails to apply) to a number of things jointly, rather than to each individually; examples are 'surrounded the house', 'are putting on a play', 'outnumber', and 'are arranged personwise'. To say that Tom, Dick, and Harry are eating lunch is just to say that Tom is eating lunch, and Dick is eating lunch, and Harry is eating lunch; 'are eating lunch' is a plural *distributive* predicate, not a collective one. But to say that Tom, Dick, and Harry surrounded the house is not to say that Tom surrounded the house, and so did Dick, and so did Harry. They eat lunch individually, but they surround the house jointly: each individually does something less than surrounding the house, and these activities add up to their surrounding the house collectively. (Whether a predicate is collective or distributive can be ambiguous. To say, for instance, that Tom, Dick, and Harry are carrying a piano is ordinarily to say that they are carrying a piano together, but it could mean that each is carrying a piano by himself.)

Now consider the statement that someone is hungry. We cannot paraphrase this as 'some particles are hungry', because 'are hungry' is a distributive and not a collective predicate. That is, to say that x, y, and z are hungry is to say that x is hungry, y is hungry, and z is hungry: 'are hungry' is like 'are eating lunch' and not like 'surrounded the house'. Because no particle is hungry, it follows that if there are only particles and nothing composed of particles, then nothing is hungry. Nihilists might try to argue that despite appearances the ordinary predicate 'are hungry' *is* a collective predicate, not a distributive one. But there may be no need for them to say this, for we might be able to invent a collective "hunger" predicate that applies jointly to a lot of particles just in the case that it is correct for ordinary purposes to describe them as composing a being that is hungry. The predicate might be 'are collectively hungry'—though it is important to keep in mind that being collectively hungry is not a way of being hungry. So what makes it right for ordinary purposes to say that someone (or something) is hungry would be that some particles are collectively hungry. What does that mean? Well, maybe particles are collectively hungry if and only if they are of such a nature and relate to one another and to other particles in such a way that they would compose something hungry (in the ordinary sense of the word) if they composed anything.

None of this appears to require the existence of either thinking beings or composite objects. In particular, it doesn't appear to require the existence of mental states or events. What about the *appearance* that there are mental states? Isn't that itself a mental state? The atomistic strategy suggests that it is correct in ordinary circumstances to say that thinking appears to someone to go on if and only if there are particles arranged in such a way that they would compose someone to whom it appeared that thinking was going on if they composed anything.

If the atomistic strategy can be made to work, it would have an important implication: despite appearances, nihilism is not committed to the possibility of thought without a thinker. In §8.4 we considered arguments to the effect that particular mental states could not be produced cooperatively by many unthinking beings, or that they would have to be individuated by their subjects, and hence could not exist unless they were states of some thinking being. But now it looks as if those arguments are powerless against nihilism, for even if they succeed on their own terms, they are perfectly compatible with it. Nihilists can agree that there can't be thoughts without thinkers: they will simply deny that there are thoughts. And they will be able to account for what is right about talk that appears to be about thoughts in terms of simple particles alone.

The statement that someone is hungry is easy to paraphrase. Or at least it is easy given that there could be such a thing as the made-up predicate 'are collectively hungry', true of particles if and only if it is correct for ordinary purposes to describe them as composing something hungry—and given that we could understand that predicate. Other cases, however, will be more challenging. Take statements about identity over time. Suppose we say that Mina is taller than she was a year ago. It is no good paraphrasing this as 'there are certain particles arranged personwise now (let us ignore the problem of how to specify which ones), and there were certain particles arranged personwise a year ago, and the first particles are now arranged in such a way that their collective lengthwise extent is greater than the lengthwise extent the other particles had a year ago'. This can at most make it correct to say that Mina is now taller than *someone* was a year ago. Not just any particles that were arranged personwise a year ago are relevant to statements about Mina's height then, but only those that, according to those who reject nihilism, then composed Mina. The nihilist will need to find a time-spanning relation holding among particles that stands in, as it were, for the identity of a person over time—something vaguely analogous to the personal temporal counterpart relation mentioned in §5.8.

Or consider the modal statement that anyone in Fargo might have been in Hong Kong. We cannot paraphrase this as 'Any particles arranged personwise in Fargo might have been arranged personwise in Hong Kong', for that is at once too strong and too weak. It is too strong because, as non-nihilists would say, an inhabitant of Fargo could have been in Hong Kong without being composed of the very particles that actually compose him. It is too weak because the particles non-nihilists say compose an inhabitant of Fargo could be arranged personwise in Hong Kong without making it correct to say that that very person is in Hong Kong. As non-nihilists say, anyone's particles might have composed someone else in Hong Kong.

For another challenge, try paraphrasing statements with complex quantificational structure, such as 'Some people are taller than all their friends' or 'Anyone who is taller than all his friends is envied by his neighbors' in terms of simple particles. (Difficulties of this sort affect even the "shortage" example of §8.2. Although we can paraphrase 'There is a shortage of food in Zimbabwe' easily enough as 'Many people in Zimbabwe have less food than they need', paraphrasing 'Food shortages are more frequent than they used to be' is far more difficult.)

For all I know, someone with enough patience and ingenuity could come up with atomistic paraphrases of statements like these. The paraphrases might be cumbersome, but I can see no insuperable obstacle in the way of producing them.[8] The interesting question about the atomic-paraphrase project is whether the psychological collective predicates we have imagined actually mean anything.

If atomistic paraphrase is possible, it would answer the charge that nihilism is an absurd denial of the obvious. We should not suppose, however, that this would make nihilism plausible. Atomistic paraphrase stands to nihilism as temporal counterpart theory stands to the stage view. One could defend the stage view against the charge that it contradicts the

[8] Compare Argle's increasingly contrived attempts to paraphrase statements about holes in terms of material objects in Lewis and Lewis 1970. It is noteworthy that van Inwagen, who denies the existence of all composite material objects save organisms, claims that it is impossible to paraphrase statements about such things as artifacts in terms that mention only simple particles. His proposed paraphrases appeal to events he calls "histories of maintenance" (1990b: §13)—though I suspect that nihilists will be no happier with histories of maintenance than they will be with bundles of thoughts. Merricks argues that the atomistic strategy must fail because the truth of statements about conscious beings does not supervene on facts about particles (2001b: chaps. 4–5; see also Olson 2002a and Dorr 2003). A discussion of his complex and important argument would require a chapter (at least) of its own, however. Elder (2004: esp. chap. 3) objects to atomistic paraphrases on grounds that are not very clear to me.

things we say about our persistence over time by showing how to paraphrase our ordinary talk into statements that mention only momentary stages. Even so, the mere existence of such paraphrases hardly makes the stage view easy to believe. And nihilism is considerably harder to accept than the stage view.

8.7 What It Would Mean If We Did Not Exist

Let us turn now to a different sort of question. What would it mean if we did not exist? What practical consequences would it have? How would it affect our lives if we came to believe it and acted accordingly? How bad would it be if it were true? It might not matter much, practically speaking, whether we are organisms or temporal parts of organisms or bundles of thoughts or what have you. That question is primarily of theoretical interest. But it might be of more than merely theoretical interest whether we exist at all. Here are two thoughts about what the practical consequences of nihilism might be.

One is that it would be unbearably depressing. To be a nihilist is to believe that all the people you thought you had ever loved or respected or known have never existed. Compare nihilism with solipsism. A solipsist is someone who believes that there are no people other than herself: what appear to be other people are either unthinking brutes (organisms with no mental properties) or mere persistent hallucinations on her part. Most of us will find this an utterly appalling prospect. If nothing else, it would be impossible for a solipsist to love or admire anyone other than herself: you cannot sustain a feeling of love toward someone if you believe that there has never been any such person. At any rate, a solipsist could not love or admire anyone else except by believing something incompatible with solipsism. A *consistent* solipsist could not love anyone but herself. The nihilist goes the solipsist one better and says that she herself does not exist either. So a consistent nihilist could not even love herself. That seems to make nihilism even worse than solipsism. Or maybe not quite as bad: it might be better for me not to exist than to be the only thinking being in the universe. Either way, we can only hope that nihilism isn't true.

You might wonder how nihilism could be depressing if it implies that there is no one to be depressed. Well, I might want something to be the case even if no one would be in any way unhappy if it were not: for instance, I might find it a good thing that the universe contains sentient life. And although it may be that if nihilism were true we couldn't be depressed, it could make us depressed if we falsely believed it to be true. The question is not whether we ought to be depressed if nihilism were true, but whether we ought to find the prospect that nihilism is true depressing.

The second thought is that our not existing might have its bright side. Perhaps accepting it would make us less selfish. At any rate it would mean that self-interest was not a rational motive for action. How could it be, if there is no "self" to have any interests? If there are no such beings as myself or others, there can be no reason to put my interests above those of others. Nihilism might imply that all interests are of equal value. We might find that liberating.

If either of these thoughts is right, nihilism would have enormous practical consequences. Just how a nihilist ought to think or act may be hard to say, but few of us could accept nihilism and carry on living as before—or at least not without doing something that presupposes that nihilism is false.

But *is* any of it right? Take the complaint that nihilism would be as depressing as solipsism, because it would mean that none of the people we care about ever existed. Someone might object to this comparison. Sensible nihilists, as we have seen, will accept that there are particles arranged personwise other than their own. Solipsists will disagree: they believe that the only particles arranged personwise, and the only thoughts, are their own. (At least that's what I suppose a solipsist would believe. I have never had the misfortune to meet a real solipsist. But that is what I should believe if I were a solipsist.) The difference between solipsism and nihilism is not just the difference between there being one person and there being none. Nihilism does not merely take solipsism and subtract something. It has something that solipsism lacks, namely particles other than one's own that collectively think and are collectively conscious.

This may leave us wondering whether nihilism would deprive us of anything valuable at all. My particles—the ones producing these words—can still collectively love or admire other particles arranged personwise, and those other particles can collectively relate to my particles in the same way. Nihilism is consistent with the occurrence of births and deaths, memories and dreams, conversations, relationships, and everything else that we care about—or at least with activities at the level of particles that it is appropriate for ordinary purposes to describe as births, deaths, relationships, and so on. Once our beliefs and statements are reformulated in terms compatible with nihilism, we might find that everything we thought was true of people is true (as it were) of particles arranged personwise. All that is missing are thinking subjects. And why should anyone but a metaphysician care whether there are thinking subjects? Nothing of any practical importance is lost. Ordinary life can go on just as before.

Let us have an example. Imagine that one of my strongest desires is to be married. As it happens, I believe that I *am* married. I believe therefore that I have what I want. But should I have what I want if nihilism were true? It may seem not. The desire to be married is the desire to be married *to* someone, and nihilism implies that there is no one for me to be married to. If nihilism would frustrate one of my strongest desires, it would matter a great deal to me whether it were true.

On the other hand, nihilism allows that my particles are "collectively married" to certain other particles. Would that give me what I want? Well, what would it be for particles to be collectively married to other particles? The collective-marriage relation is not the familiar relation of marriage that beings enter into pairwise: a particle cannot be married to another particle. The atomistic paraphrase strategy of the previous section suggests something like this: for the *x*s to be collectively married to the *y*s is for the *x*s and the *y*s to be of such a nature and to relate to one another and to their surroundings in such a way that, if the *x*s composed something and the *y*s composed something, the *x*s would compose something that was married (in the ordinary sense) to something the *y*s composed. If that is anywhere near right, then the truth behind the belief that I am married, according to nihilism, is roughly this: the world's particles are arranged in such a way that, if nihilism were false, my particles would compose a person and certain other particles would compose a person and the first person would be married to the second.

Suppose the particles really are arranged in that way. That may not appear to satisfy my desire to be married. What I want, surely, in wanting to be married is that *I* be *married*, not that certain particles be "collectively married" to certain other particles. And according to nihilism, no one is married. It is merely the case that *if* I existed, and a certain other person existed, but everything at the level of particles were equal, *then* I should be married. And that purely hypothetical state of affairs can hardly satisfy my desire to be married—any more than the fact that if I inherited a million dollars then I should be rich does anything to satisfy my desire to be rich. So it seems that if nihilism is true I don't have what I want in wanting to be married. I could have it only if certain particles arranged personwise composed something—that is, only if nihilism were false.

This is not right as it stands, however. The fact that my particles are collectively married to other particles is not the purely hypothetical fact that if I existed and a certain other person existed and all else were equal, then I should be married. It is, rather, that the world's particles are in fact arranged in such a way that, if nihilism were false but other things were equal, my particles would compose a person and certain other particles would compose a person to whom the first person was married. That is not a purely hypothetical state of affairs. It implies that certain particles actually are arranged in a special way, a way that we ordinarily describe—in a misleading way if nihilism is true, but nonetheless aptly—by saying that two people are married. The impediment that nihilism would put in the way of my being married is not like the usual impediments—poverty, egotism, slovenly habits, that sort of thing. What nihilism offers as a substitute for my being married is not merely the hypothetical fact that if something incompatible with nihilism were the case then I should be married, but rather a categorical state of affairs having to do with particles.

We might still wonder how facts about things that could not possibly be married could satisfy my desire to be married. What do I care about particles if they never compose anything I could be married to? Well (the idea goes), my desire to be married is an attitude whose content I express in the words 'that I be married'. And nihilism appears to allow that it is correct to say, in contexts that have nothing to do with metaphysical speculation, that I am married: it is correct if there are particles arranged in the right way. Moreover, my desire to be married is an ordinary desire, not one freighted with metaphysical content. So it ought to suffice to satisfy it that it be correct to say, in ordinary contexts, that I am married. And so it is. If that is right, then the way the particles are arranged gives me what I want in wanting to be married.

This reasoning is based on two claims. First,

1. It is correct to say, in ordinary circumstances, that Olson is married if and only if the particles are arranged in such a way that, if the Olson particles composed something and certain other particles composed something, the Olson particles would compose something that was married to something the other particles composed.

(The "Olson particles" are those that would be collectively denoted by the name 'Olson' at the relevant time if nihilism were true. As before, let us set aside the considerable problem of specifying which ones they are.) This, or something like it, is what would make the ordinary statement that Olson is married correct if nihilism were true. Second,

2. Olson's desire to be married is satisfied if it is correct to say, in ordinary circumstances, that Olson is married.

It follows that

3. Olson's desire to be married is satisfied if the particles are arranged in such a way that, if the Olson particles composed something and certain other particles composed something, the Olson particles would compose something that was married to something the other particles composed.

In other words, the way the particles are arranged suffices to satisfy my desire to be married.

The premises of this argument are plausible. If 1 were false, it would mean that nearly everything I said about paraphrase in the previous section is wrong. There might perhaps be a way of paraphrasing talk of people in nihilistic terms that is radically different from the atomistic strategy. Failing that, however, nihilism would imply that all statements that appear to entail the existence of people are not only strictly false but cannot even be taken to be true for ordinary purposes. The statement that there are six million people in London would be no better than the statement that there are six million dragons there. That would reduce nihilism to absurdity. A similar argument would presumably show any view according to which there are fewer concrete objects than we might have thought to be an absurd denial of the obvious: for instance, the sparse ontology of §§3.2 and 7.4.

If 2 were false, it would apparently be because my desire to be married demands not merely that it be correct for ordinary purposes to say that I am married, but that it be strictly true, which is incompatible with nihilism. My desire to be married would have a content that goes beyond that of the ordinary statement that Olson is married—it would have metaphysical content, or at least metaphysical implications. That might be surprising.

If 1 and 2 are true, then 3 follows, and my desire to be married can be satisfied even if nihilism is true. In that case, it is hard to see how nihilism could deprive us of anything that we ordinarily desire. Perhaps there is nothing especially depressing about nihilism after all. And if so, the thought that nihilism would make us less selfish is likely to be mistaken as well.

What makes me suspicious of all this is that one could argue in the same way that there is nothing depressing about solipsism. Solipsism is not meant to be an absurd denial of the obvious, any more than nihilism is. Solipsists can accept that statements appearing to entail the existence of other people can be in some sense right: there ought to be *something* right, even for a solipsist, in the claim that that there are six million people in London and none on the moon. What makes it right will have to do with unthinking brutes or sense impressions or the like. Thus, solipsists can accept a variant of 1 that replaces the bit about particles with something about unthinking brutes or sense impressions. In other words, they can play the paraphrase game as well as the nihilist can. If I were a solipsist, I could maintain that it is correct to say, in ordinary circumstances, that I am married if and only if an unthinking brute relates to me in a certain way. (What this way is might be hard to say, but no harder than saying what facts about particles could make it correct to say that I am married.) And

I could say that my desire to be married is satisfied if and only if it is correct to say, in ordinary circumstances, that I am married. It would follow that my desire to be married does not require the existence of anyone other than myself and would be in no way frustrated by the truth of solipsism. This suggests that solipsism would not deprive me of anything I desire and, more generally, that it would have few if any practical consequences. Becoming a solipsist would be a purely intellectual affair and need not have any effect on the rest of one's life.

Surely that is wrong. Solipsism is a paradigm case of a depressing philosophical claim. What makes it depressing? Well, it implies that, strictly speaking, I am not married and have no children or friends. It implies that no one other than myself will ever read this book. And so on. Those are all bad things, or at any rate things that I want very much not to be the case. And it would be little consolation to me that certain facts about unthinking brutes or about my sense impressions make it correct for certain purposes to say that I am married and have friends. That is nothing more than the well-founded appearance of my being married and having friends, and although it may be better than nothing, it falls dismally short of giving me what I want in wanting to be married and have friends. If this means that those desires have metaphysical content, then so be it.

What about nihilism, then? Would it be as depressing as solipsism? Would it frustrate those of our desires that have to do with people? That depends on the content of those desires. It depends on whether the desire to be married (for instance) can be satisfied by particles' being arranged in certain ways without their composing people. It depends, that is, on whether our desires involving people demand that there really be people, or whether it is enough that it merely be correct for ordinary purposes to say that there are. I am inclined to say that nihilism does not give me what I want, and that the comparison with solipsism is apt. That certain particles are "collectively married" to my particles doesn't seem to be enough: I want those particles to compose beings that really are married to each other. At least that's what I think I want. The way the particles are arranged seems to me to be of little value, if any, unless they compose thinking, sentient beings.

For this reason, nihilism seems to me a hard philosophy to live by. It is not merely counterintuitive, in that it seems on reflection to be false. It is hard in the sense that it would take some doing to get oneself to believe it, to accept its consequences, and to change one's behavior and one's practical attitudes accordingly. It is hard to live by for the same reason as solipsism is hard to live by. At least anyone who thinks that nihilism leaves everything else as it is and has no practical consequences will need to explain what makes it different in this regard from solipsism.

Here is one final thought about nihilism's practical implications. Nihilism might be not just hard to live by, but literally impossible to live by. It might be psychologically impossible to believe, or at least impossible to accept consistently without going mad.

A number of philosophical claims are impossible to live by. We might call them *pathological* views. Consider, for instance, the view that there is no free will. I mean the view that we can never do otherwise than we in fact do: whenever it appears that one has a choice between two incompatible courses of action, *A* and *B*, it is never the case that it is possible for one to do *A* and also possible for one to do *B*. What would it mean for us if we really believed this and acted accordingly? It seems that we should have to stop deliberating (van Inwagen 1983: 154–156). I don't mean that we could not deliberate if we actually had no free will, but that we could not deliberate if we consistently *believed* that we didn't. You cannot deliberate about whether to do something unless you believe that it is possible for you to do it, and also possible for you not to do it. If you were in a room with two doors, and you knew that one of them was locked and impassable, you could not deliberate about which door to leave by. You might be able to deliberate about which door to *try*; but to deliberate about which door to try is not to deliberate about which door to leave by, and in any case you could do it only if you believed that it was possible for you to try either door first. If you were convinced that there was never more than one option open to you, even if you didn't know which it was, and if you had no beliefs inconsistent with this, you could not deliberate about what to do. How someone who never deliberated would behave is hard to know, but it would clearly be a pathological condition.

How might nihilism be pathological? Well, it threatens to imply that there could never be any reasons for action. Why do we act? What reason have we for doing anything? Ordinarily we act for the good of someone or something. We don't always succeed in benefiting anyone, but that is our aim. Let us understand the word 'good' or 'benefit' broadly: to make someone happier than she would otherwise be, or to satisfy a desire or preference of hers, or to act in her interests, or to prevent a violation of her rights is to do her good or to benefit her. But if there *are* no people or other sentient beings, there are no beings that our actions could benefit. Think of solipsism again. According to solipsism, the only reason for me to act is for my own benefit. At any rate, I am the only one who can benefit from any action. What could be the point of acting for someone else's benefit if there *is* no one else and never could be? For a solipsist to act in the interests of others would be like an atheist acting to propitiate the gods. But if nihilism is true, then *I* don't exist either. There is no one at all. In that case, there is no reason to act for anyone's benefit. A nihilist, it seems, would have to conclude that there is no point in doing anything.

Now it is not quite true that the only possible reason for acting is to benefit someone. Suppose I could do something that would prevent the existence of beings who would have utterly miserable lives. That would be a reason for acting that did not aim at benefiting anyone. (It couldn't benefit those who would thereby be spared a miserable life, for if I act there will be no such beings. It might, of course, benefit those who would have to care for these wretched beings, but it needn't.) This sort of thing could not be a reason for acting if nihilism is true, however. If nihilism is true, I cannot prevent the existence of beings who would have utterly miserable lives, for there will be no such beings no matter what I do: I could no more prevent the existence of certain miserable beings than I can prevent the existence of objects that move faster than light. The only reasons a consistent nihilist could have for acting would be reasons that did not even require the possibility that anyone or anything *could* be benefited or harmed. And it is not clear whether there could be such reasons.

I don't think anyone could consistently believe that there is never any reason for doing anything. At any rate, someone who did believe it, and acted accordingly, would be in a state similar to that of someone who never deliberated. So maybe there really is something mad about nihilism. It is not mad because it denies obvious facts, such as the fact that London is populous. There is nothing mad about denying the existence of ordinary objects other than ourselves, provided that one does it for good philosophical reasons and that one can account for the difference between those claims apparently concerning such objects that can be taken to be correct for ordinary purposes and those that cannot. So I have argued, anyway. But denying that *we* exist might be mad, in that we could not consistently do it and remain sane. Our every action seems to presuppose that nihilism is false.

I am not confident that this is right. Perhaps there could be reasons for acting that don't require it to be possible for anyone or anything to be harmed or benefited as a result. There might be a point, for instance, in acting to promote pleasure and prevent suffering, even if there could never be any subjects of pleasure or suffering.[9] Now I argued in §8.5 that nihilism might rule out the existence of states of pleasure or suffering just as it rules out the existence of pleased or suffering beings. But nihilism might allow that particles are arranged in ways that would make it correct for ordinary purposes to say that someone or something is pleased or

[9] Parfit (1984) argues for something like this, though whether his "impersonal utilitarianism" is compatible with nihilism is anyone's guess.

suffering, and there might be a reason for preferring particles to be arranged in some of those ways rather than others. Perhaps the fact that particles can be "collectively benefited" can provide reasons for acting. Some arrangements of particles might be better than or preferable to others even if there are never any sentient beings or mental states. The challenge, for those who take this line, will be to say how the nihilist's position differs from that of the solipsist: how the facts about particles (or whatever) that, according to nihilism, make it correct for ordinary purposes to say that someone is benefited provide reasons for acting, but not those facts about unthinking brutes (or whatever) that, according to solipsism, make it correct for ordinary purposes to say that other people are benefited.

What if nihilism really is pathological? That would put its advocates in an embarrassing position: if they really believed their nihilism, they would have no reason to advocate it. Or rather, they would *believe* that they had no reason to advocate it, unless they were unaware of its implication that there is no reason to do anything. Anyone who advocated nihilism would be either insincere or inconsistent.

Although this might give non-nihilists some satisfaction, however, it would not be a reason to suppose that nihilism is false. That we could not consistently deny our existence without going mad is no evidence for the claim that we do exist—any more than the impossibility of denying consistently that we have free will without going mad is evidence for our actually having it. Why should the truth be believable? For all we know, the true account of what we are might be pathological. That would be a truly absurd situation. It is one thing to accept humbly that our metaphysical nature might remain forever beyond our intellectual grasp. It would be a nasty surprise indeed if we could work out our metaphysical nature all right, but the knowledge of it would inevitably result in madness.

9

What Now?

9.1 Some Results

That completes my survey of accounts of what we are. I have tried to discuss the most interesting and important ones. There are almost certainly other views that I ought to have considered, and views that I dismissed too quickly. I hope I have at least made a good start. What have we learned? Let me try to summarize our main conclusions up to now.

We began with animalism. If there is a human animal located where you are, and it thinks just as you do, it is hard to see how you could be anything other than that animal, or how you could ever know that you are. This "thinking-animal problem" is not only an argument for animalism, but also a challenge for any other account of what we are: How can we know we are not the animals that think our thoughts? The most common objection to animalism is that it conflicts with popular claims about personal identity: that our identity over time has something to do with psychology, that we have certain mental properties essentially, and that facts about how mental states relate to one another determine how many of us there are at any one time (the psychological individuation principle). Animalists must reject these claims. They are not alone in this, however: the psychological individuation principle appears to conflict with almost any account of what we are.

The constitution view says that we are material things constituted by organisms. It is an instance of constitutionalism, the general claim that qualitatively different material objects can coincide exactly. Constitutionalism purports to solve many hard metaphysical problems, such as the clay-modeling puzzle and the paradox of increase. And if constitutionalism in general is true, it is likely that we are nonanimals constituted by animals. Constitutionalists will want to avoid the thinking-animal problem by denying that the animals constituting us are just like us mentally; but it will be hard for them to explain why this should be so. The view also appears to rule out any good account of when constitution occurs or of what determines our boundaries.

The view that we are brains gets its support from the idea that only brains think in the strictest sense. That would solve the thinking-animal problem: we could know that we are not animals because we obviously think in the strictest sense, and animals don't. And anyone who says that we are *not* brains faces the problem of how we could know that we are not our thinking brains. But the idea that only brains really think turned out to rest on the assumption that all the parts of a genuine thinker must be somehow directly involved in its thinking, and that principle collapsed under scrutiny.

The view that we are temporal parts of animals is based on the general ontology of temporal parts. It offers to solve the metaphysical puzzles about lumps and statues and the like that constitutionalism purports to solve, but without claiming that physically identical objects can differ in other respects (though this requires a counterpart-theoretic account of modal predication). It also offers a nifty solution to several problems of personal identity. However, it has the startling implication that there are a vast number of thinking beings now sitting in your chair, most of which have very different pasts and futures from those we ascribe to you. Worse, it implies that in the strictest sense we ourselves don't think at all; only our momentary stages do. We could avoid this by saying that we ourselves are stages—the stage view—but that is desperately implausible.

According to the bundle view, we are made up of mental states and events. This appears to be the only account of what we are that is compatible with the psychological individuation principle. But a bundle of mental states doesn't seem to be the sort of thing that could think. Nor does the bundle view suggest any solution to the thinking-animal problem.

The paradox of increase provides what may be the best argument for our being immaterial substances. The easiest solution to the paradox is to deny that anything can change its parts; the only things we could be that don't change their parts, yet have anything like human histories, are immaterial substances. This would also solve the thinking-animal problem by ruling out the existence of animals. Immaterialism faces grave problems, however, about the apparent dependence of the mental on the physical.

Then there is nihilism, the view that we do not exist. It would solve all the problems about our metaphysical nature in one fell swoop. If nihilism is to be a serious claim and not a mad denial of the obvious, however, it must allow that statements apparently about people can be somehow right; so it must be possible to paraphrase those that are right into claims that capture their rightness without implying the existence of people. This will not be an easy task. Like solipsism, nihilism seems a depressing view. And it threatens to deprive us of any possible reason for acting.

These seven views (eight if you count the stage view) have been the main focus of my attention. I also discussed, more briefly, a number of "minor views." There is the view that we are temporal parts of brains and the view that we are material things that brains constitute when they are in the right states. The indeterminate-size view says that it is indeterminate whether we are brains, human organisms, or beings of some intermediate size. According to homunculism, nothing thinks all of your thoughts: each sort of mental activity is carried out by a different part of the brain. There is the view that we are unthinking bundles of thoughts, the view that we are bundles of psychological universals, and the view that we are something like computer programs. We might be "masses of matter," which either exist only as long as they are in human form (the momentary-mass view) or endure as long as the particles composing them exist, but are human and able to think for only a moment (the persisting-mass view). There is compound dualism, the view that each of us is composed of an immaterial substance and an organism. Hylomorphism says that each of us is somehow a compound of a particular form and a parcel of matter. Finally there is the view that we are simple material things: either particles in the brain (Lilliputian materialism), or things coinciding with an entire human organism (Brobdingnagian atomism). Although there is something to be said for each of these, those that are not simply variants of the principal views are hard to take seriously.

9.2 Some Opinions

I will say no more about the minor views. What about the seven principal views? We have seen that each has its virtues but also faces worrying objections. And it is hard to get philosophers to agree about how these virtues and vices stack up. Some, for instance, are so impressed with the way the temporal-parts view handles metaphysical puzzles that they are happy to accept its unwelcome implications; others find these implications so repugnant that they will do almost anything to avoid them. Disagreements about such fundamental matters are notoriously hard to resolve.

Rather than leave it at that, though, I will let my hair down and say what I myself am inclined to think. Many of my opinions about the relative merits of the various views have been evident in previous chapters, despite my attempt to be evenhanded. But I can say more. This section is sheer autobiography, and I don't expect it to persuade anyone. My attempts at persuasion are in the earlier chapters.

As I see it, the brain view and the bundle view are out. I suppose it is just about conceivable that the brain view might be true. It is certainly better than saying that my brain does my thinking for me. I reject it because there is no reason to believe it. There *are* reasons to accept the bundle view, but it is founded on the idea that bundles of thoughts think, which I see as a conceptual mistake.

Immaterialism is more promising. There are arguments for it that, though inconclusive, are not grounded in confusion in the way that the attraction of the brain view is grounded in confusion. It faces more than its share of problems, however. It is shrouded in mystery and impenetrable to reason, yet fascinating—a bit like theism.

Many advocates of the constitution view see it as purely angelic, and regard all objections to it as based on misunderstanding. I have made it plain enough that I disagree. Though the constitution view is part of a package that would do much useful work, it strikes me as deeply implausible and, above all, unprincipled. There are too many questions about how constitution is supposed to work that have no answers, yet seem to demand answers. It is, like immaterialism, impenetrable to reason. That leaves nihilism, the temporal-parts view, and animalism. I judge these to be the finalists in the contest.

As I have said, I am unsure what to make of nihilism. It would solve many problems, particularly if it is combined with compositional nihilism. (Composite objects attract metaphysical problems like ripe fruit attracts flies.) But I am suspicious of the idea that it solves all problems about composite objects without incurring any of its own. I don't know whether it is possible to tell an adequate story of the world in terms of mereological simples. I also suspect that nihilism may have grave implications for ethics, practical reason, and the value of our lives. Because it is unclear to me what follows from nihilism, however, I have been unable to turn these suspicions into conclusive arguments. This is an area that needs more work. Nihilism remains, as they say, a live option.

The consequences of the temporal-parts view are better understood, and to my mind they're not very nice. I don't like being forced to accept counterpart theory, which seems to me to make important questions about what it is possible for us to do into matters for arbitrary decision. I find it hard to accept that there are millions of beings sitting here and writing these words, most of which diverge radically in the past and future from what I take to be my own trajectory through space-time. Most of all, I don't like the claim that all things have all their properties without temporal qualification—an essential feature of four-dimensionalism as we know it. This is what implies that persisting things have properties temporarily only in the sense of timelessly having temporal parts located at different times that have those properties timelessly. It seems to me more or less incredible that I don't think or act in the strictest sense, but something other than me does; and to say that I do think and act in the strictest sense but exist for only a moment, as the stage view has it, is hardly better. That goes against my deepest instincts. I suppose I might be persuaded to put my instincts aside, but only by means of an argument for four-dimensionalism more forceful than any so far proposed.

And animalism? I cannot hide the fact that I have argued for animalism in the past. But it was not my intention to promote it here. Although on most days I still find animalism the best account of what we are, that preference rests on my aversion to the temporal-parts view and nihilism; and I don't expect to convince anyone that those views are false, apart from those who share my aversion to begin with.

There is more to say, however. So far I have discussed only the best-known objections to animalism, to do with its implications about personal identity (§§2.8–2.9). I argued that they are less troubling than they might appear. And indeed, they might seem rather slight compared with the problems facing the other accounts of what we are. But I also said that there are more serious objections to animalism, and I promised to return to them later. Now is the time.

9.3 Animalism and the Thinking-Parts Problem

Recall the thinking-brain problem (§4.2). Doesn't my brain think my thoughts? And if it does, how do I know that I'm not it? Now we dispensed with one version of this problem, according to which a human animal can think only in the sense of having a brain that thinks. That would mean that according to animalism I don't think in the strictest sense, which is absurd. I answered this objection by arguing that there is no reason to suppose that *only* brains think in the strictest sense and that larger things think only in the sense of having thinking brains as parts. But even if brains are not the only true thinkers, it doesn't follow that they don't think at all. Perhaps *both* brains and whole organisms think in the strictest sense. In that case, we should expect every part of an organism that includes a brain to think: heads, upper halves, left-hand complements, and so on. That would be trouble enough for animalism. It would not imply that we are *not* animals, but it would make it hard to see how we could ever know that we *are* animals. If you think you're an animal, then your head, which thinks just as you do, ought to think, mistakenly but on the same grounds, that it is an animal. So for all you know, you might be your head. Why suppose, then, that you are an animal, rather than a head or a brain or some other thinking part of an animal?

Call this the *thinking-parts problem*. It is structurally analogous to the thinking-animal problem: both consist in the apparent existence of beings other than ourselves that think our thoughts. Animalists need to solve the thinking-parts problem. At any rate, they are committed to its having a solution compatible with animalism. Otherwise—if there is no way of knowing that we are animals rather than brains or heads or the like—there will be no reason to accept animalism. I find the thinking-parts problem considerably more troubling than the familiar objections to animalism. It seems far more serious than animalism's unintuitive consequences in brain-transplant cases, for instance. How bad is it?

Well, it is no worse for animalism than it is for many other accounts of what we are. The same problem arises for any view according to which we are animal-sized things: for the constitution view and the temporal-parts view, for instance. They too presuppose that we are able to know that we are not brains or heads; and their advocates have no resources for solving this problem that are not available to animalists as well. So the thinking-parts problem is no reason to prefer any other view to animalism. (Or at least none except nihilism and immaterialism, which allow solutions to the thinking-parts problem that are unavailable to anyone else: for instance, adopting compositional nihilism.)

Even so, the thinking-parts problem threatens to show that animalism is no *better* than its rivals. Thus, although it may give us no reason to prefer any other account of what we are to animalism, it may leave no reason to prefer animalism either. The main reason to suppose that we are animals is the apparent fact that human animals think our thoughts. If this really is a fact, then it is hard to see how we could have any reason to suppose that we are anything other than animals. In other words, animalism has the virtue of avoiding the thinking-animal problem. But if brains and heads also think our thoughts, it is hard to see how we could have any reason to think that we are animals either. The thinking-parts problem threatens to imply that if anything thinks our thoughts and performs our actions, many beings of different sizes do so: organisms, heads, brains, and many other such things.

That would be a mess. Which of these beings should *we* be? Well, if the question of what we are is the question of what beings think our thoughts, the answer would be that many beings of different sorts do. If the question is what our personal pronouns and proper names denote, the answer may be that it is indeterminate: they refer ambiguously to brains, heads, human organisms, and many beings of intermediate sizes. Either way, it would apparently be indeterminate whether we are animals, brains, or something in between. This is the indeterminate-size view mentioned in §4.2.

No one is going to find the indeterminate-size view appealing. But maybe it needn't come to that. Perhaps animalists can solve the thinking-parts problem. How? Well, we saw that the thinking-parts problem is structurally analogous to the thinking-animal problem; so the possible solutions to the thinking-parts problem ought to parallel the possible solutions to the thinking-animal problem. Let us set aside the possibility of solving the thinking-animal problem by accepting animalism, for the analogous solution to the thinking-parts problem is to accept the indeterminate-size view, which is what we wanted to avoid. There are three other possibilities.[1] One is to deny that human animals think: a *psychological solution* (§2.5). Another is to accept that human animals think our thoughts and argue that we are nonetheless able to know that we are not those animals: an *epistemic solution* (§§2.6–2.7). The third is to deny the existence of human animals: a *metaphysical solution* (§2.4). Whatever merits these proposed solutions may have, it is easy enough to transform them into solutions to the thinking-parts problem. And if anything, the solutions to the thinking-parts problem look rather better than the corresponding solutions to the thinking-animal problem.

A psychological solution to the thinking-parts problem would say that brains, heads, and other spatial parts of human organisms cannot think, or at least not in the way that you and I can. We considered some possible reasons for this in §4.2: brains cannot think because they are not organisms, or because thinking is a maximal property and brains are parts of larger thinking beings, or because the concept we use the word 'thinking' to express simply does not apply to brains. Those proposals were not very satisfying. Still, the view that our brains think and act in just the way that

[1] Or maybe four: inspired by Geach (1997: 310), someone might propose that the animal and its brain are the *same* thinker, even though they are different material things. Animal and brain are not numerically identical, but neither are they numerically distinct. The proposal is that there is no such thing as numerical identity without qualification, but only a lot of "sortal-relative" identity-like relations. I find this more or less unintelligible. Consider the one thinker that your animal body and your brain are supposed to be. How big is it? No answer to this question appears to be possible. But surely a material object has to have *some* size.

we do *sounds* wrong, even if it is hard to say why it is wrong. Maybe I just haven't been clever enough to see it. So there may be a good psychological solution to the thinking-parts problem. It certainly looks more promising than a psychological solution to the thinking-animal problem: whatever it is that prevents brains and heads from thinking is unlikely to prevent human animals from thinking—unless it is impossible for a material thing of any sort to think.

What about epistemic solutions? Could we somehow know that we are thinking animals rather than thinking heads or brains? Someone might suggest that the meaning of the word 'person' prevents it from applying to undetached heads, brains, and other proper parts of human animals, despite their eminent psychological qualifications. Why this should be—what it is about the word 'person' that explains this surprising gap in its extension—will not be easy to say. In any case, the suggestion would go on to assert that our personal pronouns and first-person thoughts refer only to people. This would be something we could know a priori, just in virtue of being competent speakers of English. It would follow that our personal pronouns do not refer to brains and the like, and that we could know this. And because we are whatever our personal pronouns refer to, we could conclude that we are not brains or heads or other parts of human animals.

This is the personal-pronoun revisionism of §2.7, applied to the thinking-parts problem. As a solution to the thinking-animal problem, personal-pronoun revisionism seems rather desperate: it takes some doing to believe that human animals, despite being psychologically indistinguishable from ourselves, somehow don't count as "people." But the idea that undetached brains don't count as people, even if they really are just as clever as we are, sounds a bit more hopeful. Such things are certainly very different from what we *thought* people were like. It sounds wrong to say that brains are people, just as it sounds wrong to say that they think and act. So an epistemic solution to the thinking-parts problem may have more promise than an epistemic solution to the thinking-animal problem.

Then there is the metaphysical solution: there are no brains or heads or upper halves. (Cases in which a human animal has lost so many parts that it has itself become a brain or what have you, if that is possible, would be an exception: the proposal is that there are no *undetached* brains, heads, and so on.) Of course, my head isn't empty: the proposal is that there are particles "arranged cerebrally" there, but they don't compose anything. Although it is no doubt in some sense correct to say in ordinary circumstances that human beings have brains, what makes it correct are facts about particles or the like that do not entail the existence of brains. This is the sparse ontology once more. And if there are no brains or heads, we needn't worry about the possibility that *we* might be brains or heads.

The claim that there are no such things as undetached heads may not be very appealing. Even so, a metaphysical solution to the thinking-parts problem is surely better than a metaphysical solution to the thinking-animal problem. There is something at least a little bit peculiar about undetached brains and heads—not to mention upper halves and left-hand complements. Their boundaries are to some extent arbitrarily drawn. Aristotle denied their existence, or at least denied that they were substances. Unless *every* matter-filled region of space, no matter how arbitrary and gerrymandered, contains a material object, we can understand why someone might doubt whether there have to be such things as undetached heads. If there were no human organisms, by contrast, just about everything we ever believed about the ontology of material things would be wrong. Organisms look like paradigm cases of material things. To deny their existence is to deny the reality of all ordinary objects.

So although the thinking-parts problem is a serious objection to animalism, it is at least as bad for its main rivals (apart from nihilism, anyway). And a solution is not beyond hope. Moreover, it looks less threatening to animalism than the thinking-animal problem looks to its rivals.

9.4 Animalism and the Clay-Modeling Puzzle

Even if the thinking-parts problem is no worse for animalism than it is for any other popular account of what we are, however, there are other metaphysical problems that threaten to afflict animalism in particular. The clay-modeling puzzle, for one, looks like a problem for animalism but not for its main rivals. A lump of clay modeled into the shape of Thatcher seems able to survive being squashed, but not the clay statue of her; yet the lump appears to *be* the statue. The most popular ways of reconciling these claims appeal to constitution or temporal parts. Constitutionalists accept that the lump but not the statue can survive squashing by saying that they are numerically different and have different persistence conditions, despite coinciding materially: the lump constitutes the statue (§3.2). Most four-dimensionalists say that the statue and the lump are numerically different because one is a proper temporal part of the other, and explain why we appear to attribute different persistence conditions to the two objects in terms of counterpart theory (§§5.3–5.4).

Now animalists *could* say the same thing. They could say that statue-shaped lumps of clay constitute statues and accept constitutionalism, or say that statues are temporal parts of lumps and accept four-dimensionalism. At least these views are formally consistent with animalism. But animalism does not sit easily with either view.

Constitutionalism suggests that human animals coincide materially with beings that would appear to be mentally just like we are. Animalists will not want to accept that, as it raises the problem of how we could ever know that we are the animals.

Suppose, for instance, that something stands to a human animal as a lump of clay stands to a clay statue—something that would outlive the animal if it were squashed. If clay statues have to be constituted by something, shouldn't human animals have to be constituted by something too? Now suppose that you are an animal and that a lump of something constitutes you. The lump would be physically indistinguishable from you for as long as it constitutes you. It would have the same brain and nervous system as you have—it would be neurologically identical to you—and the same surroundings. It would show the same behavioral evidence of intelligence and conscious awareness as you do. This suggests that for a while at least, the lump would *be* conscious and intelligent—indeed, it would be mentally just like you. What grounds could you ever have, in that case, for supposing that you are the animal and not the lump?

Or again: if the right sort of lump of clay in the right circumstances constitutes something that is essentially statue-shaped, we might expect the right sort of human organism in the right circumstances to constitute something that is essentially able to think. No human animal is itself essentially able to think. But our animal bodies would seem to be of the right sort and in the right circumstances to constitute essential thinkers. So constitutionalism suggests that each human animal coincides with an essential thinker. Again, how could you ever know which thinker you are?

Now it doesn't strictly follow from constitutionalism that human animals coincide with lumps or with essential thinkers. Someone might say that there is a lump of clay constituting a clay statue of Thatcher but no lump of anything constituting Thatcher herself. Or maybe lumps of clay sometimes constitute essential statues but human organisms never constitute essential thinkers. But either proposal would be surprising. More to the point, they seem arbitrary and unprincipled—rather like holding that statues of women are constituted by lumps but that statues of men are not. We should have no idea *why* the two cases—the case of statues and the case of organisms—are so different; and we should expect there to be a reason why. For all we know, perhaps, it could be true; but it is hard to see how we could ever know that it was.

So combining animalism with constitutionalism raises problems that animalists will want to avoid. They will want to deny that animals constitute or are constituted by anything. Animalists are ill advised to accept constitutionalism. And we saw in §§5.4 and 5.6 why animalism fits badly with the ontology of temporal parts: if four-dimensionalism is true, the best candidates for being people, and so the best candidates for being us, would seem not to be animals but proper temporal parts of animals: parts composed of thinking person-stages and including no unthinking embryonic stages. A four-dimensionalist *could* be an animalist without inconsistency, but it is unsurprising that almost no one holds this combination of views.

Animalists will not want to solve the clay-modeling puzzle by adopting constitutionalism or four-dimensionalism. They will not want to solve the paradox of increase, the amputation puzzle, or the replacement puzzle in that way either. Nor can they simply accept the paradoxical conclusion that it is impossible for anything to gain or lose parts, for that is incompatible with our being animals. What *can* they say, then?

There is always the way of funny persistence conditions (§7.4), but it's not very attractive. There remains the way of sparse ontology. It says, in the case of the paradox of increase, that when an object acquires a new part, there is then nothing composed of the object's original parts. If you assimilate an atom, there is no such thing, immediately afterward, as "all of you but that atom": you are now composed of your old atoms together with the new one, and the atoms that composed you a moment ago now compose nothing. In the case of the amputation paradox, the solution is that you have no part that you could survive being pared down to: you could survive the loss of your left hand, but there is no such thing, now, as "all of you but your left hand," your left-hand complement. The way of sparse ontology also implies that there is no such thing as your undetached head or brain—supposing, anyway, that you could be pared down to a head or a brain. This has an important implication: solving the amputation paradox by the way of sparse ontology would solve the thinking-parts problem as well. That is because the entities that would generate the thinking-parts problem also figure in the amputation paradox.

Adopting a sparse ontology of material objects can solve the paradox of increase, the amputation paradox, and the thinking-parts problem. We can use the same strategy to solve the clay-modeling and replacement puzzles as well: we can deny that there are any such things as clay statues or lumps of clay. There may be tiny particles arranged by sculptors in a statuesque fashion, but they don't compose anything.

I am inclined to think that this is what animalists ought to do: they should solve their metaphysical worries by denying the existence of the entities that would generate them. (Some animalists have done it: see Hoffman and Rosenkrantz 1997; Merricks 2001b; van Inwagen 1990b.) Anyone who likes animalism but dislikes the sparse ontology will have to solve the problems we have been considering—both the puzzles about the ontology of material objects and the thinking-parts problem—in some other way, and no other way looks very nice.

This might come as something of a shock. No one wants to be told that there are no such things as lumps or statues, or undetached brains or heads. It goes against what we learned at our mother's knee. This outcome is especially surprising because animalism seemed at first to be so sensible. That our being animals conflicts with things we are inclined to say about brain transplants may be something we could live with. But now animalists are asking us to give up some of the most ordinary beliefs in the world. What appeared to be a pleasant landscape turns out to have a coal pit running through it.

Let me say three things in defense of the sparse ontology. First, it doesn't imply that we are mistaken to think that we have heads, or that there are many Greek statues in the British Museum. At least it doesn't imply that these beliefs are mistaken in the way that it would be mistaken to think that we have tails, or that there are many Martian statues in the British Museum. As we saw in our discussion of nihilism, the sparse ontology allows that such beliefs can be taken for all ordinary purposes to be true. We can say, or try to say, what is right about these ordinary beliefs in terms of objects the sparse ontology recognizes, such as simple particles and people: even if there are, strictly speaking, no heads or statues, some of our particles are arranged in such a way that they would compose undetached heads if they composed anything, and many particles in the British Museum were arranged more or less as they are now by Greek sculptors. Because our mothers were trying to teach us anatomy and not metaphysics, they were perfectly correct to tell us that we have heads, and we were perfectly correct, as far as our juvenile purposes were concerned, to believe them. So the conflict between the sparse ontology and our ordinary beliefs is less jolting than may appear. (Some sparse ontologists even deny that there is any conflict at all: see van Inwagen 1990b: §10.)

Second, the other ways of solving the puzzles are not clearly any better. They may even be worse. If you don't like the sparse ontology, consider the alternatives. Think about the ontology of temporal parts, constitutionalism, funny persistence conditions, and the doctrine of mereological constancy. Now think about the indeterminate-size view, personal-pronoun revisionism, and the other possible responses to the thinking-parts problem. If the sparse ontology is false, one of each of these groups of repugnant views must be true.

Third, the sparse ontology follows from what most of us will take to be the best approach to another important metaphysical problem: when composition takes place. So it is not only animalists who have reason to accept the sparse ontology. I will develop this thought in the next section.

9.5 Theories of Composition

Suppose that animalists really are best advised to solve the thinking-parts problem, the clay-modeling puzzle, the amputation puzzle, and the rest by denying the existence of undetached heads and brains, lumps and statues, and the other troublesome entities. This proposal may appear not only implausible, but unprincipled as well. If there are so many fewer composite objects than we thought, why suppose that there are any at all? In particular, why suppose that there are any human animals? The proposal is this: there are particles arranged in ever so many ways—undetached-human-headwise, brainwise, clay-lumpwise, statuewise, anthropomorphically, and so on. When particles are arranged anthropomorphically, they compose something. (And not just something; they compose an organism, a thing that persists as a living thing for many years despite wholesale material turnover. They don't compose a mere mass of matter.) But no particles arranged in any of those other ways compose anything. In those cases, there are only particles. In other words, the troublesome objects are all unreal, but *we human animals* are an exception. That may sound like mere wishful thinking. *Why* should particles arranged anthropomorphically compose something, but not particles arranged headwise or statuewise or lumpwise? What accounts for the difference? No one ought to accept this fairy-tale ontology unless there is some principled reason why it must be so.

This worry has to do with a general question about composition: When does it occur? Under what conditions do smaller things (let us restrict ourselves to concrete material things) make up or compose something bigger? If we have some things, the *x*s, what is necessary, and what is sufficient, for there to exist something composed of the *x*s—something that has all the *x*s as parts, and all the parts of which share a part with one or more of the *x*s? What must those things be like, and how must they relate to one another and to their surroundings, for them to compose something? This is what van Inwagen has called the *special composition question*.[2] Call an answer to this question a *theory of composition*. The worry is whether any principled theory of composition is consistent with both animalism and the sparse ontology we have been considering.

We have already encountered the view that there are *no* circumstances in which smaller material things compose something bigger: there are no composite material things at all, but only simples. In other words, things compose

[2] "Special" because van Inwagen distinguishes it from a "general" composition question that does not concern us here. The earliest statement of the special composition question that I know of is Hestevold 1981; see also van Inwagen 1987 and 1990b: 21–32.

something if and only if there is only one of those things (by definition everything composes itself). This is compositional nihilism. It would rule out our being composite objects of any sort. Since animals are composite,[3] it is incompatible with our being animals. Come to that, it is incompatible with almost any account of what we are apart from nihilism and immaterialism.

Another theory of composition is that things *always* compose something, no matter what they are like in themselves or how they are arranged or situated: composition is universal or unrestricted or automatic. This is *compositional universalism*. It is of course incompatible with the sparse ontology. It is also highly counterintuitive. It implies that there are vastly more material objects than we would ordinarily have thought. Virtually all material things, on this view, have completely arbitrary boundaries: they are mere "ontological junk." The proportion of material objects that are dogs or bicycles or planets or anything else of interest would be about the same as the proportion of regions of the earth's surface exactly occupied by continents.

What's wrong with this surplus of objects? Well, for one thing it implies that every dog or bicycle—or person, if we are even partly material things—will almost exactly overlap with a vast number of other beings that differ from it only by a few particles. That will probably make it indeterminate which of the many candidates *you* are—that is, which one we refer to when we say 'you' or use your name. This is the problem of the many of §5.6. Universalism also gives us many objects that differ from ourselves in more disturbing ways. It implies that there is, for instance, an object now made up of your upper half and my lower half—a being that we should expect to be psychologically indistinguishable from you. In fact universalism appears to imply that virtually all the beings that now think your thoughts are pieces of ontological junk. For all you know, it seems, you could be one of them.

There are things that universalists can say to assuage these worries. They can say that it doesn't matter if it is indeterminate which of the many good candidates for being you is you because for all practical purposes we can't tell them apart anyway. So everything we ordinarily want to say about you comes out true on any assumption about which one you are. And they can say that in ordinary contexts we ignore the monstrous and arbitrary objects. Our names, pronouns, general terms (such as 'dog' and 'man'), and quantifiers simply pass them by as if they weren't there. There is endless room for debate about the extent to which stories like these make

[3] I suppose someone might say that animals are mereologically simple. That may have been Aristotle's view, and Lowe's Brobdingnagian atomism (§7.8) is close to it. Combining this with compositional nihilism might enable animalists to dispense with the troublesome entities. It's a pretty wild idea, though.

universalism easier to believe. But it takes a pretty tough-minded philosopher to feel comfortable with it. (We will consider another disputable consequence of universalism in the next section.)

In any case, animalists who accept the sparse ontology must reject both compositional nihilism and universalism, and many others will too. They will say that some objects compose bigger things and others don't, depending on what those objects are like and how they relate to one another and (perhaps) to their surroundings. There are *some* composite objects, so to speak, but not just any: a few special matter-filled regions of space contain (exactly contain) material objects, but most don't. They will plead for an *intermediate* theory of composition. Sensible though that may sound, however, it raises our worry once more: if some things compose bigger things and others don't, then which do, which don't, and why? In particular, why suppose that any good theory of composition will be consistent with both the existence of human animals and the nonexistence of undetached heads, clay statues, and the rest of the troublesome lot?

We should expect an intermediate theory to say that things compose something just when they are somehow *unified*: when they relate to one another, and to nothing else, in some special causal or spatiotemporal way. Things not unified in this way will be those that would compose arbitrary or gerrymandered objects if they composed anything. The particles that we take to make up a live cat look like good candidates for being unified: a cat is the very opposite of an arbitrary object. The particles that are now located within the North Sea are considerably less likely candidates, and those located within either the North Sea or the further half of the Andromeda Galaxy are less likely still—though even they are a good deal more unified than most.

What sort of unity might be necessary and sufficient for things to compose something? It is surprisingly hard to say. I don't know of any answer that has much plausibility on the face of it. I certainly don't know of any that entails both the existence of most of the familiar furniture of the earth—dogs, bicycles, stones, that sort of thing—and the nonexistence of most of what I have called ontological junk. To my knowledge, only two intermediate answers to the special composition question have ever seriously been proposed.[4] Both count as "sparse."

[4] Or maybe three. Hestevold (1981) suggests (though never actually states) that things compose something just when there is no material thing between them. More precisely, things compose something if and only if any two of them are either directly joined by a straight line that does not pass through any third thing, or indirectly joined via a series of things, each of which is directly joined to the next by a straight line that does not pass through any third thing. So the atoms of my house compose something, but the bricks of my house don't, because they are separated by mortar. This answer seems to have all the disadvantages of universalism and then some, and I will say no more about it.

One is van Inwagen's view that things compose something if and only if their activities constitute a biological life—a self-organizing event that maintains the internal structure of an organism (van Inwagen 1990b; see also §2.2 above). This has the startling implication that there are no nonliving composite objects. The only material things are simples—presumably elementary particles—and things with lives. What sorts of things have lives? Well, organisms do. Whether anything other than a living organism has a life depends on whether an organism can coincide materially with a nonorganism (a point I will return to presently). If not, then the proposal is that the only composite objects are biological organisms.

It is plausible enough to say that things compose something if their activities constitute a life. A life provides just the sort of unity that leads us to suppose that the particles caught up in it compose something bigger. But why should things compose something *only* if their activities constitute a life? Why could there not be nonliving composite objects? Van Inwagen's argument is roughly that nothing other than a biological life provides the right sort of unity: taking any other unity relation to be necessary and sufficient for composition—any sort of physical bonding, for instance—leads either to repugnant consequences or to grave logical difficulties.

Call the view that things (or at least material things) compose something if and only if their activities constitute a life *biological minimalism*. This is not the place for a full-scale evaluation of minimalism. Whatever its merits, though, it is a principled theory of composition. And it has a most convenient consequence for the animalist: it entails the existence of human animals and rules out the existence of nearly all the entities that would cause trouble for animalism. Undetached heads, proper temporal parts of human animals, statues, and lumps, for instance, do not have lives. Neither are they simples. Biological minimalism therefore implies that there are no such things. Thus, the way of sparse ontology not only enables animalists to solve their metaphysical problems, but it also follows from one of the few principled theories of composition on offer.

Now there is one sort of troublesome entity whose existence biological minimalism does not explicitly rule out: things coinciding materially with human animals. Minimalism is formally consistent with constitutionalism. It says that things compose something just when they are caught up in a life, but it doesn't say that such things compose only *one* thing, namely an organism. For all it says, particles caught up in a life might compose both a human organism and a human nonorganism. That would be trouble again: an awkward surplus of thinkers.

But as we saw in §3.6, no one will want to combine biological minimalism with constitutionalism. Minimalism provides its own solution to the metaphysical puzzles that constitutionalism was invented to deal with:

the clay-modeling puzzle, the replacement puzzle, the paradox of increase, and so on. If you've already accepted minimalism, there is no point in adopting constitutionalism as well. That would be paying twice for the same thing. The two views are also fundamentally opposed in spirit. Constitutionalism is a rich ontology; minimalism is an austere one. No one is going to suppose that almost none of those particles we think of as composing something actually compose anything, but those few that do compose something compose more than one thing. No one will say that the furniture of the earth consists of nothing but simple particles, organisms, and things coinciding with organisms. That would be like recommending a diet of bread, water, and chocolate fudge cake.

So animalists can solve all their metaphysical worries at a stroke by adopting biological minimalism.[5] That may seem a high price to pay, but it does the job. And it may not be such a great sacrifice in the end, compared with the other theories of composition.

Hoffman and Rosenkrantz have proposed a second intermediate theory of composition. They agree with van Inwagen that there are living organisms, though they disagree about what it is for things to compose a living organism: they propose an account in terms of what they call "functional unity" rather than in terms of lives. The important difference is that on their account there are also nonliving composite objects, which they call "mereological compounds." Things compose a mereological compound, they say, just when they are physically bonded in a certain rigid way. The precise definitions of functional unity and rigid bonding are not important for present purposes (see 1997: 80–90 and 128–134). Their theory of composition is roughly this:

> Things compose something if and only if they are either functionally united or rigidly bonded.[6]

[5] Or at least all the metaphysical worries we have considered. I don't mean to imply that there are no others. There are always more worries. Most notably, perhaps, there are serious worries to do with "metaphysical vagueness" (see Sider 2001b: 120–139, 148–150; van Inwagen 1990b: §§18–19). A discussion of these matters is beyond the scope of this book. In any case, they are not unique to animalism.

[6] More precisely, things compose something if and only if they are either functionally united or they *and all their parts* are rigidly bonded. It seems that two organisms firmly glued together would be rigidly bonded, yet no one but a universalist, and certainly not Hoffman and Rosenkrantz, would want to say that they would compose something. Another caveat: for technical reasons that we needn't go into, Hoffman and Rosenkrantz do not actually attempt to give a theory of composition, and the view stated here is extrapolated from their discussion of other matters. I believe that it accurately reflects their intent, however.

Call it *biological disjunctivism.*

Disjunctivism implies that organisms have virtually no parts except tiny particles. That is because the particles that would make up a brain or a head or an arm or the like are neither functionally united nor rigidly bonded. They are not functionally united because of their relation to a larger set of particles—those composing the whole organism—that are functionally united. They are not rigidly bonded because some of them are in a liquid state: it belongs to the nature of an organism that few, if any, of its particles are rigidly bonded. According to disjunctivism, then, such particles compose neither organisms nor mereological compounds. That is, they compose nothing at all. This makes disjunctivism a sparse ontology of material objects, even if it is less sparse than minimalism. Like minimalism, then, disjunctivism implies the existence of human animals and the nonexistence of the parts of human animals that would generate the thinking-parts problem. It also solves the paradox of increase and the amputation paradox, or at any rate the versions of those problems that threaten to imply that organisms cannot change their parts, by the way of sparse ontology.

Now disjunctivism does not by itself imply that the particles making up a human animal compose only one thing. For all it says, functionally united particles might compose both an organism and something else: an essential thinker or the like. But I doubt whether anyone will find this combination of views any more appealing than combining constitutionalism with minimalism.

I won't try to judge whether disjunctivism is more attractive than biological minimalism, less attractive, or about as bad. The important point is that it would solve the metaphysical worries facing animalism just as minimalism would.

9.6 Composition and What We Are

We have seen that animalists can solve the most serious problems facing their view by denying the existence of the troublesome entities that generate them. That may not be the only solution, but it is the simplest and, in my view, the best. We have also seen that it is not merely ad hoc, but follows from either of two principled theories of composition: minimalism and disjunctivism. So animalism leads very naturally to a certain sort of theory of composition.

It seems, moreover, that the reverse also holds: these two theories of composition lead almost inevitably to animalism. Biological minimalism rules out the existence of most of the things we could be apart from animals. No one who believes that the only material things are elementary particles and organisms will want to say that you and I are *not* organisms. Biological disjunctivists will also say that we are animals, for similar reasons. Someone could, without formal contradiction, combine disjunctivism with immaterialism, or the constitution view, or even nihilism, but that would have no appeal.

Minimalism and disjunctivism are not the only possible intermediate theories of composition—that is, the only ones apart from universalism and compositional nihilism. But it is no accident that they are the only ones that anyone has actually endorsed. Any other theory of composition that I can think of is considerably less plausible than either of them. It looks, then, as if anyone who rejects universalism and compositional nihilism ought to say that we are animals. In other words, animalism will be the best account of what we are if some but not all material things compose something bigger. There may perhaps be a good intermediate theory that does not lead almost inevitably to animalism, but rather supports some other view of what we are or leaves it entirely open; but it appears that none has ever been proposed.

Here, then, is a bold conjecture: there is an intimate connection between the question of what we are and the question of when composition takes place or what material objects there are. Each theory of composition implies an account of what we are, or at least a narrow range of accounts. Compositional nihilism leads to nihilism about ourselves (or perhaps to immaterialism). Universalism leads to some version of the temporal-parts view. And anyone who accepts an intermediate theory of composition will find it hard to avoid animalism. Let us explore this thought.

It is easy to see the link between compositional nihilism and nihilism about ourselves. Compositional nihilism entails that the only things we could be are mereological simples, as that is all there is on that view. That is of course compatible with our being simple immaterial substances or even simple material things. But I doubt whether anyone tough-minded enough to endorse compositional nihilism will be drawn to either of those views. In any case, compositional nihilism implies that we are simple things if we exist at all.

How does universalism lead to the temporal-parts view? Nearly all universalists accept four-dimensionalism. They think that elementary particles are composed of temporal parts—particle-stages—and that any particle-stages whatever compose something. That makes it natural to suppose that we are composed of particle-stages, which is a version of the temporal-parts view. I will explain.

Suppose, for *reductio*, that universalism is true and you are not composed of particle-stages but rather of particles. And suppose for a moment that no particles ever compose more than one thing at once: suppose that constitutionalism is false. (I will return to this assumption presently.) Now consider the particles that currently compose you. Call them the *P*s. The *P*s did not compose you a month ago. Most of them were not even parts of you then, but were widely dispersed over the earth's surface. But all the *P*s existed then. (If you have doubts about whether elementary particles really persist, think of atoms.) And according to universalism they composed something then, for they compose something at every time when they exist. Call the thing the *P*s composed then *M* (for 'mass of matter').

Where is *M* now? Does it still exist? It would seem to. If the *P*s compose something whenever they exist, no matter how they are arranged, we should expect them always to compose the *same* thing. If the arrangement of the *P*s makes no difference to whether they compose something, how could it make a difference to *which* thing they compose (van Inwagen 1990b: 77)? In other words, *M* would seem to be what I earlier called a persisting mass (§7.3): something composed of particles that exists, composed of the same particles, whenever those particles exist. In that case, *M* is now located exactly where you are, and is now composed of the very particles that now compose you. Given that those particles cannot compose two things at once, it follows that you *are M*. But you are not *M*. You are not a persisting mass. You were not composed of the *P*s a month ago. You were never widely dispersed. Our original assumption, that universalism is true and you are composed of particles, must therefore be false.

What if *M* doesn't exist now? What if the thing your current particles composed a month ago no longer exists? Well, why doesn't it? What caused its demise? Presumably it was that its parts, the *P*s, got rearranged in some way. What way? The *P*s have been in constant motion relative to each other for the last month. At what point during this period did *M* cease to exist? Which particular rearrangement of the *P*s brought about *M*'s demise? The most plausible answer is that *M* ceased to exist as soon as the *P*s got rearranged at all. It would be hard to believe that *M* managed to survive all the rearrangements the *P*s have undergone during the past month, only to perish the moment those particles came to be arranged in human form. If a thing cannot survive its particles' coming to be arranged in human form, surely it cannot survive its particles' being rearranged in any way at all. And if a thing cannot survive any rearrangement of its particles, then an object whose particles are in constant motion can exist for only a moment. But *your* particles are in constant motion. It follows that you exist for only a moment: you are what I earlier called a momentary mass. But surely you are no more a momentary mass than you are a persisting mass. Once again, the assumption that you are composed of particles, given universalism, must be false.

So you could not be composed of particles if universalism is true. What could you be composed of, then? The most obvious answer is that you are composed of particle-stages. None of the *P*s are parts of you; rather, your parts include certain temporal parts of the *P*s. (Though it may not be easy to say which ones. Animalists can say it is those caught up in your biological life, but nonanimalists will deny this.) And if you are composed of temporal parts of particles, then you yourself have temporal parts.

This is the sort of reasoning that leads universalists to the temporal-parts view. It is not a watertight proof, for it is consistent with universalism that we are composed neither of particles nor of particle-stages. We might be composed of mental states. Or we might be simple. One could even say that *M* survived all the rearrangements of the past month but perished when the *P*s came to be arranged in human form—another version of the way of funny persistence conditions (Rea 1998). But these are eccentric views.

The most obvious weakness in this argument, you might think, is the assumption that constitutionalism is false. Why not say that *M* still exists now and simply coincides materially with you? More generally, perhaps any particles whatever compose a persisting mass (or a momentary mass; it doesn't matter), but none of us is a mass; rather, each of us is constituted, at any moment, by a mass. In that case, *M* would stand to you roughly as a lump of clay stands to the clay statue made from it, except that you come to be constituted by a different mass every fraction of a second, whereas a statue coincides with the same lump for a longer period.

I won't repeat my earlier arguments against constitutionalism. Even if constitutionalism is completely unobjectionable, there is no point in bringing it in now, to block the inference from universalism to the temporal-parts view. The proposal we are considering is to answer the special composition question by accepting universalism, and to make this compatible with our being composed of particles rather than particle-stages—different particles at different times—by asserting that we coincide materially with masses. But this only raises a new question about composition: Under what circumstances do particles compose something other than a mass? Call this the *new composition question*. (It is a close relative of the question of when constitution occurs of §3.5.) We should expect it to have an answer if the special composition question has an answer.

Constitutionalists will not want to give a "universalist" answer to the new composition question. They will not say that any particles whatever, no matter how they are arranged or what they are like in themselves, compose something other than a mass. It is bad enough to have to say that the particles now composing you composed anything at all a month ago when they were randomly scattered; it is far worse to say that they composed *two* things then: not only a persisting mass, but also something other than a mass, something that stood to the mass then as clay statues stand to lumps of clay. If universalism is a bloated ontology of material objects, this is double bloating. Nor can constitutionalists give a "nihilistic" answer to the new composition question: they cannot say that particles never compose something other than a mass. They will want to give an intermediate answer: they will say that whether particles compose something other than a mass depends on what they are like and how they are arranged and situated. But then what is the point of answering the special composition question with 'always'? Whatever intermediate answer constitutionalists can give to the new composition question will do just as well as an answer to the special composition question. If we could say how things have to be arranged and situated for them to compose something other than a mass, why not say that that is what it takes for things to compose anything at all? What is gained by adding a capacious ontology of masses to a moderate ontology of ordinary material things? As far as I can see, nothing at all.

So the combination of universalism and constitutionalism is unappealing. Universalists are under considerable pressure to accept the temporal-parts view, and it is unsurprising that nearly all succumb to it.

If this is right, then there really is a link between when composition occurs and what we are. Universalism leads by a devious but fairly secure path to the temporal-parts view. Compositional nihilists are almost certain to accept nihilism or perhaps immaterialism. And we have seen that the only other serious theories of composition on offer, minimalism and disjunctivism, lead almost inevitably to animalism. None of these inferences is irresistible. A determined metaphysician could devise an account that combined universalism with animalism, say, or compositional nihilism with the constitution view, or biological minimalism with immaterialism. But I doubt whether there would be any point in such an exercise. So it appears that a theory of composition would tell us what we are. At any rate, what we say about composition will constrain severely what we are able to say, or what it would be sensible to say, about our metaphysical nature. The way to find out what we are—one way, at least—is to find out when composition occurs.

9.7 Brutal Composition

Earlier I expressed the opinion that the three best accounts of our metaphysical nature are nihilism, the temporal-parts view, and animalism. And I have argued that each of these accounts follows naturally, if not quite inevitably, from one of the available theories of composition: compositional nihilism leads to nihilism about ourselves, universalism leads to the temporal-parts view, and intermediate theories lead to animalism. The dependence also runs the other way: nihilism about ourselves leads to compositional nihilism, the temporal-parts view presupposes universalism, and animalism is plausible only on an intermediate theory of composition. If that is right, then we can just about answer the question of what we are by giving a theory of composition, and we can just about work out when composition occurs on the basis of what we are.

This picture may be too neat, however, for I haven't considered the possibility that there is *no* true theory of composition—that is, that the special composition question has no answer. Or rather that it has no systematic or principled or intellectually satisfying answer: no complete and nontrivial answer that we could know or write down. It may be that certain conditions are necessary for things to compose something: perhaps objects that exert no causal influence over one another cannot compose anything, for instance. Certain conditions may also be sufficient: perhaps things whose activities make up a biological life always compose something. Even so, there may be no complete, finite set of conditions, each of which is necessary and all of which are jointly sufficient for things to compose something.

Markosian (1998) has called this *brutal composition*—the idea being that whether things compose something is a brute fact, not explainable in terms of any general principle. Its attraction is plain enough. It seems to most of us that some things compose bigger objects and others don't, ruling out the two "extreme" theories of composition, compositional nihilism and universalism. Yet neither biological minimalism nor biological disjunctivism sounds right either: most of us are inclined to believe that there are many visible parts of organisms. The fact that no plausible answer to the special composition question compatible with these two convictions has ever been proposed might suggest that the question has no answer.

Although brutal composition is a response to the special composition question, it does not actually answer that question. It doesn't tell us when composition occurs. It claims, rather, that we cannot say when composition occurs. So the possibility that composition might be brute challenges the idea that we could find out what we are by finding out when composition occurs.

Well, how does brutalism relate to the question of what we are? It might seem to support animalism. Brutalists will almost certainly accept the existence of human animals. Human animals are paradigm cases of composite objects: anyone who denies that particles arranged anthropomorphically compose human organisms might as well accept compositional nihilism. And if there are such things as animals, it is hard to deny that *we* are animals. Animalism and brutal composition also share the same air of humble plausibility—especially when compared to the alternatives, which in both cases are rather wild.

They may even seem an ideal match. Animalism would be threatened by the existence of such troublesome entities as thinking parts of animals and material things coinciding materially with animals. I suggested ridding ourselves of these entities by accepting a sparse ontology of material things, such as biological minimalism. Could we not dispense with them at a lower cost by going brutalist?

I think the answer is no. As far as I can see, brutalism is no help in defending animalism against the objections we have considered in this chapter. It is hard to combine brutalism with animalism. In fact it is hard to combine it with any attractive account of what we are. At any rate, the considerations that make brutalism attractive make it hard to say what we are.

Brutalism would help the animalist if the troublesome entities were all arbitrary objects: pieces of ontological junk, things that only friends of universalism would believe in. And some are: undetached hand complements, for instance. But not all. Consider undetached heads: they belong to the nursery-school ontology that we learned as children. And undetached brains belong to the anatomy-textbook ontology that we learned later on. The conviction that there have got to be such things, and not merely particles arranged capitally or cerebrally, is just the sort of thing that leads philosophers to reject minimalism and disjunctivism and retreat to brutalism. If there are *any* composite objects other than organisms, one is tempted to say, there are surely heads. If there are no heads, we may as well accept minimalism. So brutalists are likely to accept the existence of undetached heads and brains, even if they deny the existence of arbitrary parts of human organisms. This will prevent them from giving a metaphysical solution to the thinking-parts problem—that is, from saying that we know we are not heads or brains because there are no such things. And I have not seen any other satisfactory solution to the thinking-parts problem. Certainly brutal composition suggests none.

For the same reason, brutalists cannot solve the amputation paradox or the paradox of increase by the way of sparse ontology. If there are such things as undetached heads, and if you were pared down to a head and kept alive by life-support machinery, how would you then relate to your head? Brutalists could of course turn to funny persistence conditions, but that would diminish their view's attraction considerably. They are more likely to be constitutionalists. Suppose they accept that there are undetached heads, that you could survive being pared down to a head, and that you are not already an undetached head. If they also reject the ontology of temporal parts and funny persistence conditions, they will have to say that you and your undetached head would come to coincide materially if the rest of you were cut away. The clay-modeling puzzle will also push brutalists toward constitutionalism. Because they want to give an account of what material objects there are that comes close to what we are ordinarily inclined to say, they will want to accept the existence of statues and lumps. So they will be unable to solve the clay-modeling puzzle by denying the existence of statues and lumps of clay or by saying that there is a lump there but no statue. Nor will they want to solve it by turning to temporal parts, for they reject universalism. Funny persistence conditions aside, constitutionalism looks once again like the only alternative. The trouble with brutalism is that the very ontological generosity that makes it attractive gives us many of the material things that make it hard to say what we are.

Brutalists might try to solve this problem by persisting in their brutalism. Suppose they adopt constitutionalism and say that we are things constituted by animals. They might go on to say that things constituted by human animals can think but that neither human animals themselves, nor brains, nor any other proper parts of human animals can think. Why can't they? What is it about animals or undetached brains that prevents them from thinking? Brutalists might reply that nothing does: their inability to think is simply a brute fact, not consisting in or explainable in terms of other facts. They can't think, and that's all there is to it. The question of what it takes for something to be able to think has no principled answer. Or at least we shouldn't assume that it does, and thus our inability to answer it need not trouble us. One might go brutalist in response to other questions that this proposal raises as well, such as when constitution occurs and what determines our boundaries. I complained earlier that many questions about how constitution is supposed to work have no answers, yet seem to demand answers. One might simply reject this demand.

This is not the place to discuss the merits of brutalism as a general philosophical strategy. But the brutalism about thinking that I have suggested here has little of the attraction of brutal composition. The brutalist about composition wants to say that there are such things as organisms, undetached heads, lumps of clay, and clay statues, and no such things as hand complements and disconnected objects composed of the upper half of one human being and the lower half of another. That sounds good. The only worry is that it might be unprincipled: we can't think of any reason *why* there should be heads but no hand complements. (Someone might say that hand complements would be arbitrary objects, whereas heads are not; but then the question is what this arbitrariness comes to.) Brutalism denies that there must be any such reason why. The brutalist about thinking, however, claims that human animals cannot think but that material objects physically indistinguishable from them can. That isn't plausible on the face of it. Quite the opposite. To say further that there is no explanation for this astonishing state of affairs only makes matters worse. Perhaps we could be warranted in believing that there are such things as undetached heads but no such things as undetached hand complements, even if we have no principled reason for it. But we are surely not warranted, without a principled reason, in denying that human animals ever think.

So whereas accepting one of the proposed theories of composition would more or less settle the question of what we are, accepting brutal composition would not. It would tell us next to nothing about what we are. Those versions of brutal composition that look more attractive than minimalism actually make the question of what we are very hard to answer. They give us too many sorts of things that we could be. Despite its initial attraction, then, brutal composition is not so appealing when all is said and done.

If brutalism is false, it seems that we really can find out what we are by finding out when composition occurs. Alternatively, we can find out when composition occurs by finding out what we are. Or we can try to work out both together. I won't speculate about which procedure is the best one. In any case, the connection between the two questions ought to make progress on both easier.

References

Anscombe, G. E. M. 1981. The first person. In *Metaphysics and the Philosophy of Mind: Collected Philosophical Papers*, Vol. 2. Minneapolis: University of Minnesota Press. (Reprinted in D. Rosenthal, ed., *The Nature of Mind*, New York: Oxford University Press, 1991.)

Ayer, A. J. 1946. *Language, Truth, and Logic*, 2nd ed. London: Gollancz.

Ayers, M. 1991. *Locke*, Vol. 2. London: Routledge.

Baker, L. R. 1997. Why constitution is not identity. *Journal of Philosophy* 94: 599–621.

——. 2000. *Persons and Bodies: A Constitution View*. Cambridge: Cambridge University Press.

——. 2001. Materialism with a human face. In Corcoran 2001.

——. 2002. On making things up: Constitution and its critics. *Philosophical Topics* 30: 31–52.

Bennett, K. 2004. Spatio-temporal coincidence and the grounding problem. *Philosophical Studies* 118: 339–371.

Blackburn, S. 1997. Has Kant refuted Parfit? In J. Dancy, ed., *Reading Parfit*. Oxford: Blackwell.

Brentano, F. 1987. *On the Existence of God*. Dordrecht: Nijhoff. (Original work published in 1928.)

Burke, M. 1992. Copper statues and pieces of copper. *Analysis* 52: 12–17.

——. 1994. Dion and Theon: An essentialist solution to an ancient puzzle. *Journal of Philosophy* 91: 129–139.

——. 1996. Tibbles the cat: A modern sophisma. *Philosophical Studies* 84: 63–74.

——. 2003. Is my head a person? In K. Petrus, ed., *On Human Persons*. Frankfurt: Ontos, 107–126.

Butler, J. 1975. Of personal identity. In Perry 1975a. (Original work published in 1736.)

Campbell, K. 1990. *Abstract Particulars*. Oxford: Blackwell.

Campbell, S. 2006. The conception of a person as a series of mental events. *Philosophy and Phenomenological Research* 73: 339–358.

Carnap, R. 1967. *The Logical Structure of the World.* Berkeley: University of California Press. (Original work published in 1928.)

Carruthers, P. 1986. *Introducing Persons.* London: Routledge.

Carter, W. R. 1989. How to change your mind. *Canadian Journal of Philosophy* 19: 1–14.

Chisholm, R. 1976. *Person and Object.* La Salle, IL: Open Court. (Partly reprinted in Rea 1997a.)

——. 1981. *The First Person.* Brighton: Harvester.

——. 1989. Is there a mind-body problem? In *On Metaphysics.* Minneapolis: University of Minnesota Press. (Partly reprinted in P. van Inwagen and D. Zimmerman, eds., *Metaphysics: The Big Questions.* Malden, MA: Blackwell, 1998. Original work published in 1979.)

Clark, A., and D. Chalmers. 1998. The extended mind. *Analysis* 58: 7–19.

Corcoran, K., ed. 2001. *Soul, Body, and Survival: Essays on the Metaphysics of Human Persons.* Ithaca, NY: Cornell University Press.

Dennett, D. 1978. Where am I? In *Brainstorms.* Cambridge, MA: MIT Press. (Reprinted in D. Hofstadter and D. Dennett, eds., *The Mind's I*, Toronto: Bantam, 1981.)

——. 1981. True believers: The intentional strategy and why it works. In A. F. Heath, ed., *Scientific Explanation.* Oxford: Clarendon. (Reprinted in W. Lycan, ed., *Mind and Cognition*, Oxford: Blackwell, 1990.)

——. 1991. *Consciousness Explained.* Boston: Little, Brown.

Doepke, F. 1982. Spatially coinciding objects. *Ratio* 24: 45–60. (Reprinted in Rea 1997a.)

——. 1996. *The Kinds of Things: A Theory of Personal Identity Based on Transcendental Argument.* LaSalle, IL: Open Court.

Dorr, C. 2003. Merricks on the existence of human organisms. *Philosophy and Phenomenological Research* 67: 711–718.

Elder, C. 2004. *Real Natures and Familiar Objects.* Cambridge, MA: MIT Press.

Foster, J. 1991. *The Immaterial Self: A Defence of the Cartesian Dualist Conception of the Mind.* London: Routledge.

——. 2001. A brief defense of the Cartesian view. In Corcoran 2001.

Furth, M. 1988. *Substance, Form, and Psyche: An Aristotelian Metaphysics.* Cambridge: Cambridge University Press.

Garrett, B. 1998. *Personal Identity and Self-Consciousness.* London: Routledge.

Geach, P. T. 1997. Selections from *Reference and Generality.* In Rea 1997a. (Original work published in 1980.)

Gibbard, A. 1975. Contingent identity. *Journal of Philosophical Logic* 4: 187–221. (Reprinted in Rea 1997a.)

Giles, J. 1997. *No Self to Be Found: The Search for Personal Identity.* Lanham, MD: University Press of America.

Grice, H. P. 1941. Personal identity. *Mind* 50: 330–350. (Reprinted in Perry 1975a.)

Hasker, W. 1999. *The Emergent Self.* Ithaca, NY: Cornell University Press.

——. 2001. Persons as emergent substances. In Corcoran 2001.

Haslanger, S. 2003. Persistence through time. In M. Loux and D. Zimmerman, eds., *The Oxford Handbook of Metaphysics.* Oxford: Oxford University Press.

Hawley, K. 2001. *How Things Persist.* Oxford: Clarendon.

Heller, M. 1984. Temporal parts of four-dimensional objects. *Philosophical Studies* 46: 323–334. (Reprinted in Rea 1997a.)

——. 1990. *The Ontology of Physical Objects*. Cambridge University Press.

Hershenov, D. 2005. Do dead bodies pose a problem for biological approaches to personal identity? *Mind* 114: 31–59.

Hestevold, H. S. 1981. Conjoining. *Philosophy and Phenomenological Research* 41: 371–385.

Hoffman, J., and G. Rosenkrantz. 1997. *Substance: Its Nature and Existence*. London: Routledge.

Horgan, T. 1993. On what there isn't. *Philosophy and Phenomenological Research* 53: 693–700.

Hudson, H. 2001. *A Materialist Metaphysics of the Human Person*. Ithaca, NY: Cornell University Press.

Hume, D. 1978. *A Treatise of Human Nature*. Oxford: Oxford University Press. (Original work published in 1739. Partly reprinted in Perry 1975a.)

Johnston, M. 1987. Human beings. *Journal of Philosophy* 84: 59–83.

Kant, I. 1929. *Critique of Pure Reason*. Translated by N. K. Smith. New York: St. Martin's.

Kim, J. 2001. Lonely souls: Causality and substance dualism. In Corcoran 2001.

Levey, S. 1997. Coincidence and principles of composition. *Analysis* 57: 1–10.

Lewis, D. 1968. Counterpart theory and quantified modal logic. *Journal of Philosophy* 65: 113–126. (Reprinted, with postscripts, in his *Philosophical Papers*, Vol. 1, New York: Oxford University Press, 1983.)

——. 1971. Counterparts of persons and their bodies. *Journal of Philosophy* 68: 203–211. (Reprinted in his *Philosophical Papers*, Vol. 1, New York: Oxford University Press, 1983.)

——. 1976. Survival and identity. In A. Rorty, ed., *The Identities of Persons*. Berkeley: University of California Press. (Reprinted in his *Philosophical Papers*, Vol. 1, New York: Oxford University Press, 1983.)

——. 1983. Postscripts to "Survival and identity." In Lewis, *Philosophical Papers*, Vol. 1. New York: Oxford University Press

——. 1986. *On the Plurality of Worlds*. Oxford: Blackwell.

——. 1993. Many, but almost one. In K. Campbell, J. Bacon, and L. Reinhardt, eds., *Ontology, Causality, and Mind*. Cambridge: Cambridge University Press. (Reprinted in Lewis, *Papers in Metaphysics and Epistemology*, Cambridge: Cambridge University Press, 1999.)

——. 2002. Tensing the copula. *Mind* 111: 1–13.

Lewis, D., and S. Lewis. 1970. Holes. *Australasian Journal of Philosophy* 48: 206–212. (Reprinted in D. Lewis, *Philosophical Papers*, Vol. 1, New York: Oxford University Press, 1983.)

Locke, J. 1975. *An Essay Concerning Human Understanding*, ed. P. Nidditch. Oxford: Clarendon. (2nd ed. published in 1694. Partly reprinted in Perry 1975a.)

Lowe, E. J. 1991. Substance and selfhood. *Philosophy* 66: 81–99.

——. 1996. *Subjects of Experience*. Cambridge: Cambridge University Press.

——. 2000. *An Introduction to the Philosophy of Mind*. Cambridge: Cambridge University Press.

——. Identity, composition, and the simplicity of the self. In Corcoran 2001.
——. 2002. *A Survey of Metaphysics*. Oxford: Oxford University Press.
Markosian, N. 1998. Brutal composition. *Philosophical Studies* 92: 211–249.
Matthews, G. 1982. Accidental unities. In M. Schofield and M. Nussbaum, eds., *Language and Logos*. Cambridge: Cambridge University Press.
McDowell, J. 1997. Reductionism and the first person. In J. Dancy, ed., *Reading Parfit*. Oxford: Blackwell.
McMahan, J. 2002. *The Ethics of Killing*. Oxford: Oxford University Press.
Mellor, D. H. 1998. *Real Time II*. London: Routledge.
Merricks, T. 1998. There are no criteria of identity over time. *Noûs* 32: 106–124.
——. 2001a. How to live forever without saving your soul: Physicalism and immortality. In K. Corcoran, ed., *Soul, Body, and Survival*. Ithaca, NY: Cornell University Press.
——. 2001b. *Objects and Persons*. Oxford: Oxford University Press.
Nagel. T. 1986. *The View from Nowhere*. New York: Oxford University Press.
Noonan, H. 1989. *Personal Identity*. London: Routledge.
——. 1998. Animalism versus Lockeanism: A current controversy. *Philosophical Quarterly* 48: 302–318.
——. Forthcoming. Persons, animals and human beings. In J. Campbell and M. O'Rourke, eds., *Time and Identity*. Cambridge, MA: MIT Press.
Nozick, R. 1981. *Philosophical Explanations*. Cambridge: Harvard University Press.
O'Leary-Hawthorne, J., and J. A. Cover. 1998. A world of universals. *Philosophical Studies* 91: 205–219.
Olson, E. 1996. Composition and coincidence. *Pacific Philosophical Quarterly* 77: 374–403.
——. 1997a. *The Human Animal*. New York: Oxford University Press.
——. 1997b. Relativism and persistence. *Philosophical Studies* 88: 141–162.
——. 2001a. A compound of two substances. In Corcoran 2001.
——. 2001b. Material coincidence and the indiscernibility problem. *Philosophical Quarterly* 51: 337–355.
——. 2002a. The ontology of material objects. *Philosophical Books* 43: 292–299.
——. 2002b. Thinking animals and the reference of 'I'. *Philosophical Topics* 30: 189–208.
——. 2002c. What does functionalism tell us about personal identity? *Noûs* 36: 682–698.
——. 2003a. An argument for animalism. In R. Martin and J. Barresi, eds., *Personal Identity*. Malden, MA: Blackwell.
——. 2003b. Was Jekyll Hyde? *Philosophy and Phenomenological Research* 66: 328–348.
——. 2004. Animalism and the corpse problem. *Australasian Journal of Philosophy* 82: 265–274.
——. 2006a. Is there a bodily criterion of personal identity? In F. MacBride, ed., *Identity and Modality*. Oxford: Oxford University Press.
——. 2006b. The paradox of increase. *Monist* 89.
——. 2006c. Temporal parts and timeless parthood. *Noûs* 40: 737–751.
Parfit, D. 1976. Lewis, Perry, and what matters. In A. Rorty, ed., *The Identities of Persons*. Berkeley: University of California Press.
——. 1984. *Reasons and Persons*. Oxford: Oxford University Press.

Perry, J. 1972. Can the self divide? *Journal of Philosophy* 69: 463–488. (Reprinted in J. Perry, *Identity, Personal Identity, and the Self*, Indianapolis: Hackett, 2002.)

——, ed. 1975a. *Personal Identity*. Berkeley: University of California Press.

——. 1975b. Personal identity, memory, and the problem of circularity. In Perry 1975a. (Reprinted in J. Perry, *Identity, Personal Identity, and the Self*, Indianapolis: Hackett, 2002.)

——. 1975c. The problem of personal identity. In Perry 1975a: 3–32.

Persson, I. 1999. Our identity and the separability of persons and organisms. *Dialogue* 38: 519–533.

Pike, N. 1967. Hume's bundle theory of the self: A limited defense. *American Philosophical Quarterly* 4: 159–165.

Puccetti, R. 1973. Brain Bisection and Personal Identity. *British Journal for the Philosophy of Science* 24: 339–355.

Quine, W. V. O. 1960. *Word and Object*. Cambridge, MA: MIT Press.

Quinn, P. 1997. Tiny selves: Chisholm on the simplicity of the soul. In L. E. Hahn, ed., *The Philosophy of Roderick M. Chisholm*. Chicago: Open Court.

Quinton, A. 1962. The soul. *Journal of Philosophy* 59: 393–403. (Reprinted in Perry 1975a.)

——. 1973. *The Nature of Things*. London: Routledge and Kegan Paul.

Rea, M., ed. 1997a. *Material Constitution*. Lanham, MD: Rowman and Littlefield.

——. 1997b. Supervenience and co-location. *American Philosophical Quarterly* 34: 367–375.

——. 1998. In defense of mereological universalism. *Philosophy and Phenomenological Research* 58: 347–360.

——. 2000. Constitution and kind membership. *Philosophical Studies* 97: 169–193.

Reid, T. 1940. *Essays on the Intellectual Powers of Man*. Edited by A. D. Woozley. Charlottesville, VA: Lincoln-Rembrandt. (Original work published in 1785.)

——. 1975. Of identity. In Perry 1975a.

Robinson, H. 1989. A dualist account of embodiment. In J. Smithies and J. Beloff, eds., *The Case for Dualism*. Charlottesville: University Press of Virginia.

Rosen, G., and C. Dorr. 2002. Composition as a fiction. In R. Gale, ed., *The Blackwell Guide to Metaphysics*. Oxford: Blackwell, 151–174.

Rovane, C. 1998. *The Bounds of Agency*. Princeton, NJ: Princeton University Press.

Russell, B. 1918. The philosophy of logical atomism. In R. Marsh, ed., *Logic and Knowledge* (London: Allen & Unwin, 1956), and in D. Pears, ed., *The Philosophy of Logical Atomism* (La Salle, IL: Open Court, 1985); page numbers from the latter.

——. 1921. *The Analysis of Mind*. London: Allen & Unwin.

Schechtman, M. 1997. The brain/body problem. *Philosophical Psychology* 10: 149–164.

Shoemaker, S. 1977. Immortality and dualism. In S. C. Brown, ed., *Reason and Religion*. Ithaca, NY: Cornell University Press. (Reprinted in Shoemaker, *Identity, Cause, and Mind*, expanded ed., Oxford: Clarendon, 2003.)

——. 1979. Identity, properties, and causality. *Midwest Studies in Philosophy* 4: 321–342. (Reprinted in Shoemaker, *Identity, Cause, and Mind*, expanded ed., Oxford: Clarendon, 2005.)

——. 1984. Personal identity: A materialist's account. In Shoemaker and Swinburne, *Personal Identity*. Oxford: Blackwell.

——. 1995. Personal identity. In R. Audi, ed., *The Cambridge Dictionary of Philosophy*. Cambridge University Press.

——. 1997. Self and substance. *Philosophical Perspectives 11: Mind, Causation, and World*: 283–319. (Reprinted in Shoemaker, *Identity, Cause, and Mind*, expanded ed., Oxford: Clarendon, 2003.)

——. 1999. Self, body, and coincidence. *Proceedings of the Aristotelian Society*, supp. vol. 73: 287–306.

——. 2004. Functionalism and personal identity—A reply. *Noûs* 38: 525–533.

Sider, T. 1996. All the world's a stage. *Australasian Journal of Philosophy* 74: 433–453.

——. 2001a. Criteria of personal identity and the limits of conceptual analysis. In J. Tomberlin, ed., *Philosophical Perspectives* 15. Cambridge, MA: Blackwell.

——. 2001b. *Four-Dimensionalism*. Oxford: Clarendon.

Snowdon, P. 1990. Persons, animals, and ourselves. In C. Gill, ed., *The Person and the Human Mind*. Oxford: Clarendon.

——. 2003. Objections to animalism. In K. Petrus, ed., *On Human Persons*. Frankfurt: Ontos Verlag.

Sosa, E. 1987. Subjects among other things. In J. Tomberlin, ed., *Philosophical Perspectives* I. Atascadero, CA: Ridgeview. (Reprinted in Rea 1997a.)

Stalnaker, R. 1986. Counterparts and identity. *Midwest Studies in Philosophy* 11: 121–140.

Stone, J. 1988. Parfit and the Buddha: Why there are no people. *Philosophy and Phenomenological Research* 48: 519–532.

——. 2005. Why there are still no people. *Philosophy and Phenomenological Research* 70: 174–192.

Strawson, P. F. 1959. *Individuals*. London: Routledge.

Swinburne, R. 1984. Personal identity: The dualist theory. In Shoemaker and Swinburne, *Personal Identity*. Oxford: Blackwell.

——. 1997. *The Evolution of the Soul*, rev. ed. Oxford: Clarendon.

Taylor, R. 1963. *Metaphysics*. Englewood Cliffs, NJ: Prentice Hall.

Thomson, J. J. 1983. Parthood and identity across time. *Journal of Philosophy* 80: 201–220. (Reprinted in Rea 1997a.)

——. 1997. People and their bodies. In J. Dancy, ed., *Reading Parfit*. Oxford: Blackwell.

——. 1998. The statue and the clay. *Noûs* 32: 149–173.

Tye, M. 2003. *Consciousness and Persons: Unity and Identity*. Cambridge, MA: MIT Press.

Unger, P. 1979a. I do not exist. In G. F. MacDonald, ed., *Perception and Identity*. London: Macmillan. (Reprinted in Rea 1997a.)

——. 1979b. Why there are no people. In P. French et al., eds., *Midwest Studies in Philosophy* 4. Minneapolis: University of Minnesota Press, 141–156.

——. 1980. The problem of the many. In P. French et al., eds., *Midwest Studies in Philosophy* 5. Minneapolis: University of Minnesota Press, 411–467.

——. 1990. *Identity, Consciousness, and Value*. New York: Oxford University Press.

——. 2006. *All the Power in the World*. New York: Oxford University Press.

van Inwagen, P. 1978. The possibility of resurrection. *International Journal for the Philosophy of Religion* 9: 114–121.

——. 1980. Philosophers and the words 'human body'. In van Inwagen, ed., *Time and Cause*. Dordrecht: Reidel.

——. 1981. The doctrine of arbitrary undetached parts. *Pacific Philosophical Quarterly* 62: 123–137. (Reprinted in Rea 1997a and in van Inwagen 2001.)

——. 1983. *An Essay on Free Will*. Oxford: Clarendon.

——. 1987. When are objects parts? In J. Tomberlin, ed., *Philosophical Perspectives 1: Metaphysics*. Atascadero, CA: Ridgeview, 21–48.

——. 1990a. Four dimensional objects. *Noûs* 24: 245–255. (Reprinted in van Inwagen 2001.)

——. 1990b. *Material Beings*. Ithaca, NY: Cornell University Press.

——. 1994. Composition as identity. In J. Tomberlin, ed., *Philosophical Perspectives 8: Logic and Language*. Malden, MA: Blackwell, 207–220. (Reprinted in van Inwagen 2001.)

——. 1997. Materialism and the psychological-continuity view of personal identity. In J. Tomberlin, ed., *Philosophical Perspectives 11: Mind, Causation, and World*. Malden, MA: Blackwell. (Reprinted in van Inwagen 2001.)

——. 2001. *Ontology, Identity, and Modality*. Cambridge: Cambridge University Press.

——. 2002a. *Metaphysics*, 2nd ed. Boulder, CO: Westview.

——. 2002b. What do we refer to when we say 'I'? In R. Gale, ed., *The Blackwell Guide to Metaphysics*. Oxford: Blackwell.

Wiggins, D. 1968. On being in the same place at the same time. *Philosophical Review* 70: 90–95. (Reprinted in Rea 1997a.)

——. 1980. *Sameness and Substance*. Oxford: Blackwell.

Williams, B. 1978. *Descartes: The Project of Pure Enquiry*. London: Penguin.

Wilson, J. 1999. *Biological Individuality*. Cambridge: Cambridge University Press.

Wittgenstein, L. 1922. *Tractatus Logico-Philosophicus*. London: Routledge.

Yablo, S. 1987. Identity, essence, and indiscernibility. *Journal of Philosophy* 84: 293–314.

Zimmerman, D. 1998. Distinct discernibles and the bundle theory. In P. van Inwagen and D. Zimmerman, eds., *Metaphysics: The Big Questions*. Oxford: Blackwell, 58–66.

——. 1999. The compatibility of materialism and survival: The "falling elevator" model. *Faith and Philosophy* 16: 194–212.

——. 2002. The constitution of persons by bodies. *Philosophical Topics* 30: 295–338.

——. 2003. Material people. In M. Loux and D. Zimmerman, eds., *The Oxford Handbook of Metaphysics*. Oxford: Oxford University Press.

Index